THE
GEORGIAN
PRINCESSES

JOHN VAN DER KISTE

SUTTON PUBLISHING

This book was first published in 2000 by
Sutton Publishing Limited · Phoenix Mill
Thrupp · Stroud · Gloucestershire · GL5 2BU

This paperback edition first published in 2002 by
Sutton Publishing Limited

John Van der Kiste has asserted the moral right to be identified
as the author of this work

ISBN 0 7509 3051 9

Typeset in 10.5/12.5pt Plantin.
Typesetting and origination by
Sutton Publishing Limited.
Printed and bound in Great Britain by
J.H. Haynes & Co. Ltd, Sparkford.

Contents

Sources and Acknowledgements   vii
Genealogical Tables   ix
Introduction   xii

1 'I should eclipse all my sisters'
    Sophia, Electress of Hanover   1
2 'Surrounded by people without pity or justice'
    Princess Sophia Dorothea of Celle; Sophia Charlotte
    and Sophia Dorothea, Queens of Prussia   33
3 'Her will was the sole spring'
    Princess Caroline of Brandenburg-Ansbach, later
    Queen Caroline, and her daughters   66
4 'Easy, civil, and not disconcerted'
    Augusta, Princess of Wales; Queen Charlotte   95
5 'Without hope and open to every fear'
    The Daughters of George III and Queen Charlotte;
    Caroline, Princess of Wales   120
6 'How good and noble she really is'
    Princess Charlotte of Wales   146
7 'An injured wife – a depraved woman'
    Queen Caroline   170
8 'So well has she conducted herself'
    Queen Adelaide   191

Notes   222
Bibliography   227
Index   231

Sources and Acknowledgements

Excluding those who died in infancy, most of the Princesses have claimed the attentions of earlier biographers to some extent. Not surprisingly the most wayward and notorious of them all – King George IV's wife Caroline, the self-proclaimed 'injured Queen of England' – has inspired several studies since her death; while almost as many can be found about their daughter Charlotte. Others have been less fortunate; no individual biography of Queen Adelaide has been published since 1946, nor of King George II's Queen Caroline since 1939 – notwithstanding the present author's joint study of the King and Queen published in 1997. One would search in vain for a life of the latter's daughter-in-law Augusta, Princess of Wales, her sister-in-law Sophia Dorothea, Queen of Prussia, and most of the daughters of King George III and Queen Charlotte. Of the daughters of King George II, only the eldest, Anne, Princess Royal, has been thus honoured, yet had to wait till 1995 for a full biography.

Nevertheless several collective biographies have covered some of the above. From the nineteenth century Dr Doran's *Lives of the Queens of England of the House of Hanover* and Percy Fitzgerald's *The Royal Dukes and Princesses of the Family of George III*, both in two volumes, spring to mind, while in the twentieth century Dorothy Margaret Stuart's *Daughters of George III*, supplemented to some extent by Morris Marples's *Six Royal Sisters*, remains invaluable some sixty years after its first appearance. The present work aims to take this process a stage further in surveying as a whole these royal lives which between them spanned the era from the Civil War in the first half of the seventeenth century to the first twenty years of Victorian England. Acknowledgements to specific sources are in the Notes; a full list of books consulted can be found in the Bibliography.

I wish to acknowledge the gracious permission of Her Majesty The Queen to publish certain material of which she owns the copyright.

This book is respectfully dedicated to the memory of my father, Wing-Commander Guy Van der Kiste, who sadly passed away in September 1999 shortly before it was completed, and with particular thanks to my mother Kate, who nevertheless was a tower of strength as ever in reading through the draft. In addition I would like to thank the staff at Kensington & Chelsea Public Libraries for much-appreciated access to their collection; my friends Karen Roth, Sue Woolmans, Robin Piguet, Robert Hopkins and Dale Headington, for their constant help, interest and encouragement over several months; and to editors, Jaqueline Mitchell and Helen Gray, who made the book possible through overseeing it from initial planning stages to completion.

John Van der Kiste

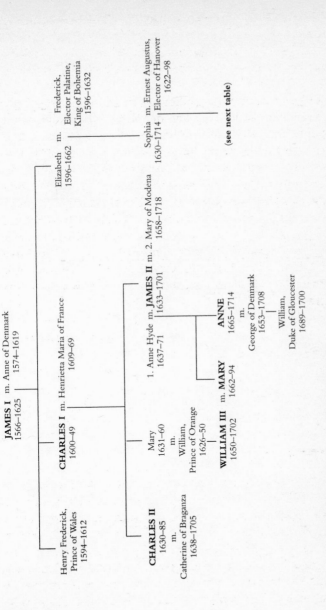

JAMES I m. Anne of Denmark
1566–1625   1574–1619

Henry Frederick,
Prince of Wales
1594–1612

CHARLES I m. Henrietta Maria of France
1600–49   1609–69

Elizabeth m. Frederick,
1596–1662   Elector Palatine,
King of Bohemia
1596–1632

Sophia m. Ernest Augustus,
1630–1714   Elector of Hanover
1622–98

(see next table)

CHARLES II
1630–85
m.
Catherine of Braganza
1638–1705

1. Anne Hyde m. JAMES II m. 2. Mary of Modena
1637–71   1633–1701   1658–1718

Mary
1631–60
m.
William,
Prince of Orange
1626–50

WILLIAM III m. MARY
1650–1702   1662–94

ANNE
1665–1714
m.
George of Denmark
1653–1708

William,
Duke of Gloucester
1689–1700

1. THE PROTESTANT SUCCESSION
AND THE HOUSE OF HANOVER

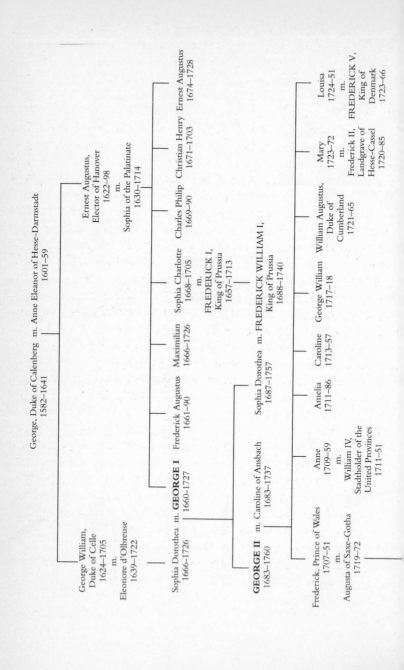

George, Duke of Calenberg m. Anne Eleanor of Hesse-Darmstadt
1582–1641   1601–59

George William,   Ernest Augustus,
Duke of Celle   Elector of Hanover
1624–1705   1622–98
m.   m.
Eleonore d'Olbreuse   Sophia of the Palatinate
1639–1722   1630–1714

Sophia Dorothea m. **GEORGE I**   Frederick Augustus   Maximilian   Sophia Charlotte   Charles Philip   Christian Henry   Ernest Augustus
1666–1726   1660–1727   1661–90   1666–1726   1668–1705   1669–90   1671–1703   1674–1728
                                                                    m.
                                                                    FREDERICK I,
                                                                    King of Prussia
                                                                    1657–1713

                 Sophia Dorothea m. FREDERICK WILLIAM I,
                 1687–1757   King of Prussia
                                    1688–1740

GEORGE II m. Caroline of Ansbach
1683–1760   1683–1737

Frederick, Prince of Wales   Anne   Amelia   Caroline   George William   William Augustus,   Mary   Louisa
1707–51   1709–59   1711–86   1713–57   1717–18   Duke of   1723–72   1724–51
m.   m.   Cumberland   m.   m.
Augusta of Saxe-Gotha   William IV,   1721–65   Frederick II,   FREDERICK V,
1719–72   Stadtholder of the   Landgrave of   King of
                             United Provinces   Hesse-Cassel   Denmark
                             1711–51   1720–85   1723–66

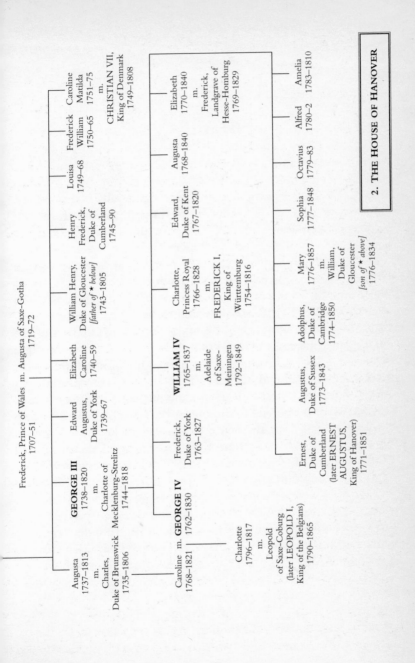

Frederick, Prince of Wales m. Augusta of Saxe-Gotha
1707–51   1719–72

Augusta
1737–1813
m.
Charles,
Duke of Brunswick
1735–1806

GEORGE III
1738–1820
m.
Charlotte of
Mecklenburg-Strelitz
1744–1818

Edward
Augustus,
Duke of York
1739–67

Elizabeth
Caroline
1740–59

William Henry,
Duke of Gloucester
[father of ★ below]
1743–1805

Henry
Frederick,
Duke of
Cumberland
1745–90

Louisa
1749–68

Frederick
William
1750–65

Caroline
Matilda
1751–75
m.
CHRISTIAN VII,
King of Denmark
1749–1808

Caroline m. **GEORGE IV**
1768–1821   1762–1830

Frederick,
Duke of York
1763–1827

WILLIAM IV
1765–1837
m.
Adelaide
of Saxe-
Meiningen
1792–1849

Charlotte,
Princess Royal
1766–1828
m.
FREDERICK I,
King of
Württemburg
1754–1816

Edward,
Duke of Kent
1767–1820

Augusta
1768–1840

Elizabeth
1770–1840
m.
Frederick,
Landgrave of
Hesse-Homburg
1769–1829

Charlotte
1796–1817
m.
Leopold
of Saxe-Coburg
(later LEOPOLD I,
King of the Belgians)
1790–1865

Ernest,
Duke of
Cumberland
(later ERNEST
AUGUSTUS,
King of Hanover)
1771–1851

Augustus,
Duke of Sussex
1773–1843

Adolphus,
Duke of
Cambridge
1774–1850

Mary
1776–1857
m.
William,
Duke of Gloucester
[son of ★ above]
1776–1834

Sophia
1777–1848

Octavius
1779–83

Alfred
1780–2

Elizabeth
1770–1840
m.
Frederick,
Landgrave of
Hesse-Homburg
1769–1829

Amelia
1783–1810

2. THE HOUSE OF HANOVER

Introduction

In the seventeenth, eighteenth and nineteenth centuries there was little choice available for a princess of the royal blood in Europe. The lives of their brothers were generally preordained – a throne for the eldest, 'education' through foreign travel and perhaps token attendance at university, followed by military or naval service and a dukedom. Theirs were also generally carved out according to equally narrow choices – marriage to a foreign prince who might be heir to a kingdom, empire, duchy or electorate for some, or tedious spinsterhood and perhaps life in a nunnery for the others. Those who married crowned heads of the future were not always the most fortunate. The first of the Georgian Princesses of this book, born Sophia, Princess of the Palatinate, was the youngest daughter of the ill-fated Frederick, King of Bohemia and his wife Elizabeth, known to posterity as the Winter King and Queen in view of their brief reign which ended with Frederick's defeat in battle in 1620. The two daughters who took the veil might have considered themselves more fortunate than their mother, destined to eke out a widowhood of thirty years in circumstances which were certainly not affluent by royal standards.

Yet Sophia, who lost her father when she was two years old, made a marriage which was not in itself dazzling. Nonetheless, thanks to the vicissitudes of her relations in a turbulent age, she was destined to become the mother of the Hanoverian dynasty in Great Britain, and had she lived six weeks longer she would have become Queen Regnant, at the remarkable age of eighty-three.

A well-read, intelligent woman, she was to impart considerable charm and intellect to most of the Princesses of the dynasty. The majority of them were well-educated and taught to make the most of their talents. Those who lacked cleverness were noted for their grace, their attractive looks and charm, while some – notably Caroline of Brandenburg-Ansbach, the future Queen Consort of King George II – had both. In the opinion of her first biographer, W.H. Wilkins, it was a misfortune that her mother-in-law Sophia Dorothea spent over half her life a captive in Ahlden Castle, as her 'grace, beauty and incomparable charm might have lent lustre to the Court of St James's', and her 'innate refinement' would have helped to tone down 'some of the grossness' of the early Hanoverian era.

The six daughters of King George III needed only a little careful flattery for the brushes of Thomas Gainsborough, that archetypal painter of contemporary court elegance, to portray them as what he called 'a ravishing constellation of youthful beauty'. Like some of the previous generation's spinster Princesses, they might in middle age bemoan their fate as 'old cats', telling their eldest brother in a moment of self-pity that they wondered why he did not choose to 'put us in a sack and drowning us in The Thames'. Only a few years earlier the poet James Bland Burges wrote that he found it hard to believe there was 'a more unhappy family in England than that of our good King'. Such a gloomy view should be measured against the more reasoned verdict of one of the King's most recent biographers, John Brooke, who states that their existence of walking, needlework, reading, card parties, visits to the theatre and concerts, was typical of the life of upper-class ladies of the time. Jane Austen's heroines, he notes, who spent all their time in the country relieved only by the occasional visit to London and Bath, would have been envious.

To some extent they accepted their fate as part of 'the nunnery' with apparent docility. Unlike Jane Austen's characters they had no chance of meeting a Mr Darcy to sweep them off their feet, propose, and lead them to the altar. They lavished their devotion on their brothers, and their father's courtiers – the only other men in their lives. There were whispers of clandestine affairs and secret marriages with good-looking gentlemen at court, at least one illegitimate child, and even far-fetched assertions in one case of incest with a brother.

The licence and liberty to indulge in furtive relationships – when they could escape from the watchful eye of an ailing and possessive mother – made them consider how much worse it might have been if they had been able to 'escape' from home. Anne, Princess Royal, eldest daughter of King George II, could not wait to fly the family nest. By the age of twenty-five, she was faced with a stark choice between perpetual spinsterhood and a 'piece of deformity in Holland', the sadly misshapen Prince William of Orange. Nevertheless she would rather marry him than 'die an ancient maid immured in her royal convent at St James's'. In her later years she might have envied her sister Amelia, who remained indifferent to the scoldings of her parents as she indulged in one shameless flirtation after another with gentlemen at court. In the last generation of Georgian Princesses there was the short and turbulent life of Charlotte of Wales, who found herself tricked by her father into betrothal to another Prince William of Orange. Only a courageous display of self-assertiveness, and support from her elders, made her father agree to breaking the engagement and sanctioning her marriage to a prince from Saxe-Gotha, a happy matrimonial union destined to end all too quickly in death in childbirth.

Marriage into other European royal houses could indeed be hazardous, and for at least one Georgian Princess the result was tragic. The hapless Caroline Matilda was barely out of the schoolroom before she was betrothed to her cousin Christian, soon to become King of Denmark. This 'Queen of tears' died a captive in 1775 at twenty-three, having seen her physician, who became her lover, executed for treason. By comparison the fate of Caroline of Brunswick, the 'happy merry soul' married to and rapidly estranged from her cousin the Prince of Wales, was a less sorry one. While her undignified odyssey around Europe did her cause little good in the eyes of those who might otherwise have supported her against the flagrant infidelities of her husband, at least she could console herself with the reflection that she had some life of her own.

The other Georgian Princesses were less notorious. Several, particularly those destined to live out their lives as spinsters, found self-fulfilment in working to alleviate the lot of those less privileged than themselves. King George II's reclusive daughter Caroline gave away most of her money to charities, particularly those which ameliorated the conditions of former prisoners; while in her last years the blind Sophia, daughter of King George III, whiled away the hours by tearing up the pages of old books as she was told that pillows filled thus were comfortable for the sick.

Though some of the Princesses were more intellectual or artistic than others, all of them knew their place in one sense at least; and that was never to interfere in politics. It was a charge often levelled at Queen Adelaide, consort of King William IV, who had the misfortune to reign during the height of the political agitation which led to the passing of the Great Reform Bill. While the Queen never strove to take an active role in politics, regarding it as her duty to merge her views in her husband's and support his role as a constitutional monarch, she was abused for exerting a reactionary influence on her good-natured but supposedly stupid and weak-willed husband, and attacked in the press by vitriolic journalists who scoffed at her German birth and upbringing, saying that 'a foreigner is not a very competent judge of English liberties'. However, such condemnations were rare, and generally followed by apologies from the newspapers involved. The Queen surely concurred with the views of her sister-in-law Elizabeth, Landgravine of Hesse-Homburg. 'Politics I know nothing of,' she wrote in 1833, after political agitation and riots in Frankfurt, 'and they are so disagreeable that I never ask any questions, for I always hated them and more than ever now, for all appears melancholy.'

Mindful of the self-willed character of her young niece Queen Victoria, as a respected member of the elder royal generation, Dowager Queen Adelaide could compliment her in 1841 on 'the good grace with which she had changed her Government', after being obliged to receive the resignation of her political mentor Lord Melbourne as Prime Minister and reluctantly appoint Sir Robert Peel in his place. The irony of such constitutional good practice would surely have been appreciated by Queen Victoria's great-great-great-great-grandmother Sophia, Electress of Hanover, who could recall to the end of her days that she was a young woman of eighteen when the monarchies of Europe were shocked to learn that her uncle King Charles had gone to the scaffold in his defence of the Divine Right of Kings.

The first of the Georgian Princesses in the present context was in fact a Stuart Princess, Sophia, Princess of the Palatinate, destined to become the mother of the Hanoverian dynasty in Great Britain. By this same reckoning the last was Mary, Duchess of Gloucester, the longest-lived and last surviving daughter of King George III. During the 227 years (1630 to 1857) which elapsed between the birth of the first and death of the last, there were four Queens Consort – the former Caroline of Ansbach, Charlotte of Mecklenburg-Strelitz, Caroline of Brunswick, and Adelaide of Saxe-Meiningen – as well as the ill-fated Sophia Dorothea of Celle, who but for the divorce court would have preceded them. To these may be added two Queens Consort of Prussia (Sophia Charlotte and Sophia Dorothea), a Queen Consort of Denmark (Caroline Matilda), and in addition a Princess of Wales (Augusta) who was denied a consort's crown by the early death of her husband.

The reform of the calendar, introduced by the Pope in 1582, was adopted in Hanover by the Elector in 1700, when he decreed that eleven days should be subtracted from the month of February. As from 1 March that year the Electorate used the New Style (NS) calendar, already in use in most European countries. England retained the Old Style (OS) calendar until September 1752, when eleven days were removed to bring the country into line with the rest of Europe. OS dates are given for Hanoverian events prior to 1700 and English events to 1752, and NS dates for other events, or both in a few cases where confusion might arise.

ONE
'I should eclipse all my sisters'

SOPHIA, ELECTRESS OF HANOVER

'I was born, they tell me, October 14, 1630,' Princess Sophia of the Palatinate, as she was at birth, noted in her memoirs, 'and being the twelfth child of the King my father, and of the Queen my mother, I can well believe that my birth caused them but little satisfaction. They were even puzzled to find a name and godparents for me, as all the kings and princes of consideration had already performed this office for the children that came before me.'[1] This problem was solved by her parents writing names on slips of paper and casting lots to make a choice, from which they settled on two ladies named Sophia as godmothers, the Countess of Hohenlohe and Princess Sophia Hedwig of Nassau Dietz.

It was an inauspicious start for the life of a princess born in exile of parents who were royal yet comparatively poor. Her father was Frederick V, formerly King of Bohemia and Elector Palatine of the Rhine, and her mother, his wife Elizabeth, daughter of King James I of England and VI of Scotland. Frederick had been called to the throne in 1619 by a country in rebellion against its Catholic Habsburg ruler, but he was defeated within a year at the battle of the White Mountain, deposed, and in recognition of his fleeting reign known thereafter as the 'Winter King'. He, his Queen and children found refuge in the Dutch republic, and it was at the Wassenaer Court Palace, The Hague, that Sophia was born.

Nobody could have predicted that this Princess, born in such humble circumstances, would become mother of the next royal dynasty of England, and only narrowly fail to become Queen Regnant of England herself. Like her siblings she was brought up at a separate establishment for the first few years. As soon as they could be parted from her, when they were aged about three months, Queen Elizabeth sent all her babies to the Prinsenhof, Leiden, a nursery presided over by Frederick's former governor, Monsieur von Pless, and his wife Anne, assisted by tutors and sub-governesses.

Frederick was a devoted father, and to the end of their days the elder children always recalled his affection for them and his keen interest in the progress of their education. A thirteenth child, Gustavus Adolphus, was born in January 1632, but by Christmas the surviving ten youngsters were fatherless when Frederick died suddenly of a fever, leaving a last wish that his widow should devote herself to the re-establishment of their family in the Holy Roman Empire.

All the children were expected to learn the living languages of French, German, English and Dutch, as well as Latin and Greek, theology, history, mathematics and law. Sophia disliked her masters and lessons, except for the daily hour given over to dancing. Nevertheless she was as bright as her brothers and sisters, learning 'everything they seemed so unaccountably anxious for me to know as quickly as possible in order to have done with learning the sooner'.[2] Ample provision was made for walks and rests between lessons, as well as long sessions of prayer and Bible reading. At an early age she could recite the Heidelberg Catechism by heart, though she admitted she did not understand a word.

Queen Elizabeth's preoccupation with European diplomacy, as well as her keen interest in artistic and intellectual pursuits, made Sophia feel starved of affection in her formative years. In later life she looked back on her years at Leiden as tantamount to banishment, and felt that her mother had cared more for her dogs and monkeys than her children. As the youngest sister she was shy and lacked self-confidence, thinking herself too thin, pale and ugly, and destined to die young. An English visitor to the court tactlessly remarked to their mother one day on the good health and appearance of the fair-haired, angelic Gustavus Adolphus, comparing him with the plain, thin, less robust-looking Sophia, in her hearing, adding even more foolishly that she hoped the little girl did not understand English. Ironically the poor boy did not live to see his tenth birthday, while she remained sprightly into her early eighties. However, she was devoted to and fiercely protective of him, and she grieved almost as much as their mother when his years of suffering came to an end.

On his death Prinsenhof was closed down. During adolescence her brothers went to study at university or joined the armies of a foreign ruler, while she and her four sisters formed part of their mother's court. What she lacked in confidence and prettiness she made up for with spirit and intelligence, appreciating that shrewdness and tact would go a long way for a princess without worldly goods. When the family decided to stage a performance of Corneille's *Medea*, they felt that she was too young to be able to learn any of the parts. Without telling anyone, and after begging them to assign her one role, she memorized the whole play and performed her part, coached in her gestures by a professional actress.

Though in the estimation of all her daughters she remained a distant, even unfeeling mother to the last, Queen Elizabeth soon recognized the positive qualities of the youngest. When Sophia became of a marriageable age, she suggested a match between her and her cousin Charles Stuart, proclaimed King of the Scots after the execution of his father King Charles I and Cromwell's declaration of an English republic in 1649. Sophia was the only one younger than Charles, though Queen Elizabeth briefly considered the next youngest daughter, Henrietta, as a possible Queen Consort of England instead. Seven years earlier Mary, Princess Royal of England, had come to the European mainland to be betrothed to Prince William of Orange, and Sophia 'heard the English milords say to each other that, when grown up, I should eclipse all my sisters. This remark gave me a liking for the whole English nation.'[3] During a visit to The Hague Charles paid her some attention as a potential bride, but spoilt his case when he expressed more interest in financial help from Lord Craven, whose fortune had long supported the family in exile, and tactlessly told her that she was 'handsomer' than his mistress, Lucy Walter.

After this sobering experience she decided to leave The Hague and settle in Heidelberg at the court of her eldest brother Charles Louis, now Elector Palatine. He was an outspoken ruler who had caused some consternation among the family as well as incurring the undying wrath of his uncle in England King Charles I for praising the Puritans as 'the children of truth and innocency', despite the fact that his brother Rupert, nicknamed 'Robert le Diable' for his bravery on the battlefield, had a reputation as one of the most loyal and dashing royalist commanders in the English Civil War. Their mother did not welcome Sophia's departure but knew there was nothing she could do to prevent it, especially as the recently married Elector was now head of the family. Her main objection, that this would spoil any chance of an English marriage – for which Queen Elizabeth had not given up hope, even though Sophia had firmly ruled Charles out – came to nothing as it was pointed out that any necessary negotiations could be carried out from Heidelberg just as well. However, Sophia knew she would probably have a better chance of finding a prospective husband at her brother's court, and without her mother around, she would have more choice in the matter.

Though Sophia had always got on well with her brother, she soon found that Heidelberg was not the happy home she had hoped for. An industrious young woman who relished mental and physical activity, she took a keen interest in his rebuilding and refurbishing the electoral palaces and gardens, meeting men from the university for intellectual discussions, and visitors who came to the court to see plays and dances, as well as the chance to accompany the Elector and Electress Charlotte on official and private journeys within the Empire. When left to her own devices she was never at a loss for anything to do, as she could keep herself amused with reading, needlework, singing lessons, or long walks which she preferred to riding and playing cards. However, she soon found that family visits gave rise to unpleasantness and quarrels.

The Elector's marriage was not turning out well, and he fell in love with one of his wife's maids of honour, Louise von Degenfeld. Charlotte had a suspicious nature and an uncertain temper which made Sophia treat her with caution. She tried to get on well with Charlotte but found they had nothing in common. Charlotte, a fine horsewoman, loved gambling, fine clothes, and talking about herself. Sophia shared none of these interests, found her sister-in-law's self-absorption a bore, and was aghast when she admitted in a soul-baring mood that she had never wanted to marry Charles Louis and had only done so at her mother's bidding; she would sooner have had her pick of several admiring young princes rather than 'this jealous old man' (who was only ten years older than she). When Charles Louis eventually tired of his bitter, mercurial wife and asked for a divorce in order to marry Louise morganatically, an idea which he was persuaded to abandon, Charlotte was furious, and made spiteful insinuations about an incestuous relationship between her husband and Sophia.

The latter knew that the only way out from this was either joining a convent, as two of her elder sisters had done, or marrying in order to obtain her own independent establishment. Too lively to consider life in a nunnery, she applied herself carefully to the prospect of matrimony. At first pride prevented her from considering marriage with a bridegroom who was not a ruling prince, but at length she allowed negotiations to take place for betrothal to Adolphus John of Zweibrücken, Regent for the German duchy on behalf of his brother, King Charles X of Sweden. The Regent took it for granted that Sophia would accept him as a husband, but he and King Charles were too slow in drawing up the marriage contract, and soon there was a more suitable prospective suitor at Heidelberg.

Late in 1656 George William, Duke of Brunswick-Lüneburg, accompanied by his younger brother Ernest Augustus, came to ask the Elector, as head of the family, for his youngest sister's hand in marriage. Three years earlier they had visited Heidelberg, and Sophia had enjoyed playing duets with Ernest Augustus, while admiring his skill at dancing and his handsome looks, though marriage had not entered her mind. His inheritance, however, was far from dazzling, as his only likely prospects were to be the next Prince-Bishop of Osnabrück, a non-hereditary position. His elder brother George William, the prospective bridegroom, had been ruling Prince of the Duchy of Calenberg-Göttingen since 1648. The Duchy had been unofficially called Hanover since 1636, when the previous Duke had demolished the old Calenberg Schloss and moved his capital to Hanover. Sophia and her brother agreed that this would be a satisfactory match; if it was not one to be embraced with enthusiasm it would be preferable to her being left on the shelf. At the age of twenty-six there was little time to lose. The marriage contract was soon signed, and the brothers continued on their way to Venice.

Once he had arrived there for a final round of bachelor revels, George William decided that he was not ready to consider closing the door on the freedom of a single man. This, Sophia understood, was purely because he had 'attached himself to the first courtesan he met, a Greek woman who had no other claim to beauty except the clothes she wore', and she 'put him in a frame of mind most unsuitable for marriage'.[4] Nevertheless the delicate matter of extricating himself from such a commitment without tarnishing the honour of his family remained. A simple process of fraternal barter was decided upon, with Ernest Augustus taking his place as bridegroom. In order to placate the Princess and her brother, a convention was entered into and signed by both brothers, by which George William agreed he would not marry, so that Ernest Augustus would be more likely to inherit either the Duchy of Calenberg-Göttingen or that of Lüneberg-Grubenhagen (or Celle for short), in which the family also had an interest. The Hanoverian envoy was anxious to point out that as there were two more brothers, one married but without issue and one bachelor who was thought incapable of producing children, Ernest Augustus would probably inherit both duchies in due course.

While it seemed hardly dignified for her matrimonial future to be decided upon like a game of chess, Sophia was prepared to accept this solution, telling her brother as if to save face that a good establishment was all she cared about. If it could be provided by the younger man, it would be no hardship for her to give up one brother for another, and she would be happy to do anything considered advantageous to her interest. She was given to understand, or managed to convince herself, that George William had contracted venereal disease in Venice and was therefore hardly fit to marry, while Charles Louis gallantly told her that he had always thought Ernest Augustus the better man.

The wedding ceremony was fixed for 30 September 1658 at Heidelberg. Given away by her brother Charles Louis, the bride went to the altar in a dress of white silvery brocade, and a large crown studded with the family diamonds on her head. Her train was carried by four maids of honour, and twenty-four noblemen marched before the bridal couple carrying lighted torches bedecked with ribbons matching the colours of their coats of arms, blue and white for the bride, red and gold for the groom. Cannon fired as Sophia and Ernest Augustus were pronounced husband and wife, then they took their seats on canopied thrones opposite each other. A succession of Te Deums followed, and the bride then formally renounced any claim to the Palatinate, a tradition observed by all Princesses of the house on marriage.

The journey from Heidelberg to their home at Hanover was one long triumphant procession, with Brunswick Dukes and their wives coming to pay their respects at every stop. As they reached the gates of Hanover the four ducal brothers, followed by their large retinues, came out to greet the bride and joined her in her carriage. They entered the city to the sound of cannon fire, and next to join in the personal welcome was Sophia's mother-in-law the Dowager Duchess of Calenberg.

In the excitement of her marriage, she did not appreciate, and indeed could not foresee, the impact of an event in which the expatriate English community, as well as her mother, had rejoiced at the beginning of September. Cromwell, who had overthrown their kinsman King Charles I and sent him to the scaffold eleven years earlier, was dead. England's shortlived republican experiment was about to end.

With admirable common sense, Sophia admitted to herself that she did not love the man to whom she was betrothed, but she found him 'amiable' and was determined to be a good wife. For his part he made every effort to be the best of husbands, at least for the first two or three years of marriage. Although he was unable to resist temptation, or more precisely other women, and although she was naturally hurt by his infidelity, she steeled herself to make the best of a bad job. Fortunate was the wife whose husband had eyes for her and her alone.

In personality and interests they were well matched. Less intellectual, Ernest Augustus did not share her passion for theology and philosophy, but he was as devoted as she was to music and opera. They both also enjoyed decorating their homes and landscaping the gardens. Sophia was anxious that she might be unable to have children, but her fears proved unfounded. By the end of 1659 she knew that she was expecting a child. Her husband and his brother planned to go to Italy early the next year, and she and her niece 'Liselotte' (Elizabeth Charlotte), seven-year-old daughter of Charles Louis, visited Queen Elizabeth at The Hague, but only after she was sure that there was no danger of a miscarriage, and she took care to return home in good time not to risk a premature birth through jolting on the carriage journey. She was back home to welcome her husband and brother-in-law, and her husband's presence helped her through the long, sometimes dangerous three-day labour which culminated in the birth on 28 May 1660 of their eldest son and heir George Louis.

While the Prince and Princess were giving grateful thanks for the safe arrival of this child, the cousin to whom Sophia might have been married instead was at the centre of another celebration. Three days earlier Charles Stuart, an exile for several years following the execution of his father, had arrived at Dover, and on his thirtieth birthday, 29 May, he triumphantly entered London, the capital city of a newly restored monarchy, as King Charles II. Fewer than half a dozen lives stood between the crown he wore and Sophia with her newly born son.

Early in the new year of 1661 Sophia, expecting her second child, arranged to visit her brother at Heidelberg, baby George and Liselotte going with her. It was an enjoyable stay, though she was anxious lest any of the family, particularly the Hesse-Cassel branch, might take offence if she paid her respects to Louise von Degenfeld and her son and daughter while Charlotte was still at court. However, she managed to visit them discreetly and she adored these illegitimate children, of which there were to be fourteen in all. Their mother, whom Charles Louis married morganatically and created Raugravine, died in 1677 and their father in 1680, after which Sophia took responsibility for them.

In October 1661 Sophia gave birth to a second son, Frederick Augustus. Two months later Ernest Augustus succeeded as ruling Prince-Bishop of Osnabrück and the family moved to the castle of Iburg. Husband and wife relished having a new palace to plan and build.

To her distress, the next four years saw a succession of miscarriages and stillborn children. She blamed herself for not taking enough care of herself early in pregnancy, but anxiety probably contributed to her nerves and perpetual worry. In April 1664, after recovering from a miscarriage of twins, she set out on a long visit to Italy, leaving the boys, 'Görgen' and 'Gustchen', in the care of her Oberhofmeisterin, or head of staff, Mme von Harling, at Heidelberg. Ernest Augustus had gone on ahead of her. Nearly a year of Italy, travels around the country with longer stays in Venice and Rome, gave her a welcome change of outlook, where she occupied her time with shopping, sightseeing, looking at art collections and meeting interesting people. However, she found that Italian customs, the way of life and their loose morals grated on her, and she regularly suffered from severe stomach upsets which were blamed on the rich food and unfamiliar climate.

Most of all she missed her boys, who were never far from her thoughts. She claimed she would sooner watch their antics than all the plays of the *commedia dell'arte*, and see their faces rather than all the works of art in Italy. Only the desire to be a dutiful wife kept her so long in a distant country; 'what the husband wishes, the wife must also desire.' She was always anxious to receive news of their progress from the Heidelberg nursery, and when told that they had contracted smallpox she was horrified. To her relief the next bulletin reassured her that the attack had only been mild, though she was anxious lest they might be scarred for life and in future she would no longer have pretty boys to love, now she would 'have to love ugly ones'.[5] After her return in February 1665 she decided that in future she would not be parted from her family for so long. Sometimes an irritated Ernest Augustus would declare that she loved their children more than she loved him, a remark with which she might have been disinclined to take issue. A more considerate husband might have realized that he only had himself to blame, for he did not deny himself his right – as he presumably saw it – to take mistresses.

During the next nine years five more children were born. In 1666 Maximilian William (and a stillborn male twin) appeared, followed by an only daughter Sophia Charlotte in 1668, Charles

Philip in 1669, Christian Henry in 1671, and Ernest Augustus in 1674. All seven live children reached maturity, though four would predecease her, three sons on the battlefield.

Most of her husband's mistresses passed like ships in the night, but occasionally one might give Sophia cause for concern. After she had been married for seven years, the pretty and well-mannered Suzanne de la Mansilière began to attract Ernest Augustus's attention. A respectable, pious young woman, she suffered regular fits of conscience lest her 'friendship' with the Duke might be misconstrued. Though anxious that a young woman of such virtue could be a definite threat, Sophia treated the girl kindly, befriending her and providing a shoulder to cry on. At length Mansilière felt she could no longer stay at court and declared tearfully that she would have to leave in order to protect her honour. Sophia was lying in bed after the birth of Sophia Charlotte when the young woman came to apologize for having unwittingly caused such unhappiness and protesting her innocence. Sophia treated her to a few kindly but firm words on the theme of Caesar's wife, while assuring her of her friendship. The more she did so, the more overwrought Mansilière became, until she was so hysterical that Sophia had to get out of bed and call for servants to carry her away. The young woman departed, according to malicious gossips, to bear the Duke's child. In Sophia's opinion it was 'the greatest lie in the world', and she blamed her mischievous sister-in-law Eleonore for spreading stories. She had never liked Eleonore d'Olbreuse, an impoverished member of the French Huguenot nobility, who had made a 'marriage of conscience' with her husband's elder brother George William. Unable to resist her, yet forbidden to marry by the convention of 1658, he had entered what Sophia called contemptuously an 'anti-marriage contract' and sworn lifelong fidelity to Eleonore, who was accorded the title Madame de Harbourg.*

Naturally there were other mistresses, though none troubled her as much. The most notorious was Clara von Meisenburg,

* In 1675 they were legally married and she became Duchess of Celle.

whom Ernest Augustus met and brought home from Paris and for whom he arranged a marriage with the amenable Freiherr von Platen. Sophia was careful not to let show her jealousy of 'that woman', and more than a little relieved when Madame von Platen's good looks coarsened while those of Sophia herself never did.

Sophia was an enlightened mother. Remembering her own unhappy childhood with a remote parent, she insisted that her children should see plenty of her. The men and women who came into close contact with them had to be of a loving and cheerful disposition. People whom she thought excessively religious were barred, as she considered their devotion to their faith went hand in hand with too inflexible and strict an attitude towards small children.

Görgen, she wrote to her brother when the young man was almost an adult, took very much after his father, while Gustchen was 'a real Palatine'. In personality, she wrote in a letter to George William of September 1679, she found her firstborn a responsible, conscientious youth, keen to do her bidding and to please her. Gustchen was naughty and moody, Maximilian was lacking in spirit, while Charles Philip was a reserved *Querkopf* (oddhead). Sophia Charlotte, or 'Figuelotte', and Christian Henry were not keen on their learning, and Ernest Augustus was 'the easiest of all my children', but she thought there was not 'much to him'.[6]

Only on one occasion during his formative years did George Louis threaten to besmirch the family's good name. In the autumn of 1676 his parents found that Figuelotte's sub-governess was carrying his child. While Ernest Augustus was furious at the prospect of such embarrassment and disgrace, Sophia took the matter more calmly. There was no doubt that the mother-to-be had been rather free with her favours, but equally little doubt that the son she bore was exactly like Prince George. The child was not acknowledged, and Sophia warned her errant son to be more careful in future, 'not to have his name bawled from the housetops as the progenitor of bastards'.[7]

In December 1679 John Frederick, Duke of Brunswick-Lüneburg, died suddenly, leaving no son, and Ernest Augustus succeeded him as reigning Duke. With the possibility of union between his duchy and that of Kalenberg or Celle, a marriage between his son and heir and George William's daughter Sophia Dorothea would be an advantageous one to consider. Nevertheless he allowed his wife to assess alternative marriage alliances for their eldest son.

It was probably at the suggestion of her brother Rupert that Sophia, now Duchess of Hanover, proposed that her eldest son and heir George Louis should consider a marriage with Anne, younger daughter of James, Duke of York and heir to King Charles II, whose marriage to Catherine of Braganza had been childless. George went to England in December 1680 and there was speculation on the imminent conclusion of such a marriage alliance, but though he and Anne were introduced to each other, the matter was not seriously discussed. By summer 1682 negotiations began in earnest for a betrothal between George and Sophia Dorothea, and everything was settled by September. A dowry was handed to George in person, so that his young wife would be completely dependent on him. On the death of her parents, all their revenues and possessions would henceforth become his property.

Sophia Dorothea was an attractive girl, albeit at sixteen still rather immature and spoilt. The only surviving child of the 'marriage of conscience', she had in practice been illegitimate until her parents' legal marriage. At the age of twelve she was considered to be flighty, and when love letters were discovered in her possession she was ordered to sleep in her parents' bedroom. This *coquette*, born of a highly irregular marriage, was not the kind of girl Sophia envisaged as a suitable daughter-in-law.

At twenty-two George often seemed to be cold and lacking in passion, though at least one young woman could have testified otherwise. Prepared to put her objections aside for the sake of family harmony, Sophia was looking forward to being a grandmother, as well as having a young companion for Sophia Charlotte. Despite her dislike of the girl's mother she went out of her way to be kind and helpful to her daughter-in-law, and Ernest Augustus was very much taken with her. Her brothers-in-law likewise thought that their eldest brother had been extremely lucky to gain such an attractive wife. Nevertheless George and Sophia Dorothea had known each other for several years and never really liked each other. It was said that when she was told of the older generation's plans shortly before the betrothal, she swore that they would have to drag her to the altar, and when presented with a diamond-studded miniature of her future husband, she threw it angrily against the wall. Nevertheless there was no escaping the path of duty, and they were married in a modest private ceremony on 21 November 1682 in the Duchess of Celle's apartments. Eleven months later Sophia Dorothea gave birth to a son and heir, whom they named George Augustus.

Two years later it was the turn of Sophia Charlotte to consider taking a husband. Her mother had taken considerable care with her education, with a view to her making a great match some day. At the age of ten she and her mother had paid a visit to the French court at Versailles, and King Louis XIV was so impressed by the precocious yet good-natured demeanour and attractive looks of this young girl that he was tempted to consider her as a suitable bride for one of the French Princes once she was old enough. She had inherited her mother's intellectual curiosity and thirst for knowledge, and at sixteen years of age she was well read, a fluent linguist and an accomplished musician. Sophia had brought her up with an open mind in matters of religion and in the profession of no particular faith, and at the age of sixteen she was still not confirmed, in order that she might be eligible to marry the most promising Prince, Protestant or Catholic.

Nevertheless a Franco-Hanoverian alliance seemed unlikely, and several eligible matches with Roman Catholic suitors had been rejected by the time the Electoral Prince of Brandenburg presented himself. His first marriage, to Elizabeth of Hesse-Cassel, by whom he had had a son and a daughter, had ended in her death at the age of twenty-two. Eleven years older than Sophia Charlotte, he was deformed – a childhood spinal injury had left him with uneven shoulders – and of a less than amiable reputation, but he was still heir to the most powerful Electorate in North Germany. As a future Elector he would be well-placed to help press Hanover's case for attaining the enhanced status of an Electorate, and on George William's death Celle would doubtless be absorbed by Hanover. As the bride's mother remarked bluntly, with regard to his physical appearance she 'did not care for externals'. On 28 September 1684 they were married at Herrenhausen, and then made their home in Berlin. Sophia went to be with her daughter for her first confinement the following year. Sophia Charlotte had wanted a midwife from Hanover to be with her as well, but she realized that this would be unpopular at the Berlin court and did not want it to be thought that she was remaining too Hanoverian in her ways.

Sophia's return to Hanover was marked by a rift in the family as a result of what has gone down in history as the 'primogeniture struggle'. It had been tradition that both the eldest sons should inherit the duchy, but Ernest Augustus had decided to introduce a system of primogeniture. He had made a will to the effect that their eldest son George Louis would succeed both George William and himself, instead of sharing the sovereignty with his next brother, Frederick Augustus. The new scheme was now awaiting confirmation by all the younger brothers, who would be obliged to swear allegiance to their eldest brother. Ernest Augustus announced his plans to the family at Christmas 1684.

Though she shared her husband's ambitions for the glory of the house of Brunswick-Lüneburg, Sophia was dismayed by what she saw as his heartlessness. Frederick Augustus was bitterly angry at the loss of his birthright, and his mother eagerly took his side. Torn between loyalty to her husband and the defence of her second son's rights, she tried to persuade the latter that if he agreed to his father's terms without causing too much inconvenience, he might be installed in another duchy of his own. His father's intentions were good, she reassured him as if trying to convince herself at the same time, and he should take care not to offend him. She promised to do what she could, while admitting she had no power over her husband, and that 'he argues that to make the House strong will benefit all its members'.[8] Frederick Augustus was not to be placated, and in high dudgeon he left for Vienna in order to lead a detachment of imperial troops against the Turkish infidels. Soon he was begging his parents for money – he declared that his purse was empty, his regiment was surviving on bread and water, and he dreamt 'of a miracle in the desert'.

Sophia asked her husband to make good the allowance he had denied him, but Ernest Augustus was so angry with his rebellious son that he refused to hear another word about him, let alone help. Sophia dreaded their second son being forced to lead a peripatetic life as a soldier of fortune. The affair created divisions between husband and wife, and the former looked for his comforts with Madame von Platen. Sophia raised no objection when he proposed to take his *maîtresse en titre* on the annual visit to Vienna that year.

Sophia Charlotte's first child, a son named Frederick Augustus, only lived for a few months, and a premature second son in July 1687 was stillborn. At the time she and her husband were in Magdeburg on their way to Hanover, out of harm's way. Dorothea, Electress of Brandenburg, the Elector's second wife, was distrusted by her stepsons, who thought she would stop at nothing in clearing the succession for her own sons. When one of them fell down and suddenly died after eating an orange in her apartments, Sophia Charlotte and her husband, suspecting poison, left the country at once. Sophia's comments about *'la poudre de la succession'* were only meant partly in jest, and the Elector was furious with her for mischief-making as well as with the young couple for their 'hysterical departure'.[9] He ordered them back to Berlin at once. Not till the following year did she succeed in producing a son and heir who survived to maturity, Frederick William.

Soon after the wedding of Princess Sophia Charlotte, the Electoral Prince George Louis went to take part as commander of the Hanoverian forces in their campaign against the Turks, and then proceeded on holiday to Italy. Duke Ernest Augustus, who was also in Italy at the time, had noticed with concern his son's indifference towards his lively, attractive wife, lonely at Hanover with her young son, and as soon as he heard that George Louis was coming he invited her to join them.

Her arrival coincided with carnival time, and with no previous experience of foreign travel she threw herself into this holiday with all the zest of youth. Ernest Augustus was pleased to see his hospitality so well appreciated, but George Louis was irritated by his wife's high spirits and spontaneity. The more others praised her to him, the more annoyed he was, and he resented what he saw as his father's meddling. He was not the only one, for his cousin Liselotte loved tittle-tattle and was ready to believe the worst. She spitefully passed on to the family any gossip she could, notably the boasts of the rakish Marquis de Lassay, a notorious self-proclaimed ladies' man who had bragged of being at Venice at the same time and having an affair with the Princess. To her credit Sophia told her niece firmly that Lassay's tales should not be taken at face value, and that the pretty young wife of her unfeeling, inattentive son was bound to turn heads and attract male admirers in a place like Venice, unless she locked herself away. In spite of everything, by the time they returned to Hanover Sophia Dorothea was pregnant again.

Once they were back, it was evident that George Louis' previous indifference to his wife was hardening into hostility. He took a mistress, the equally young and pretty Melusine von der Schulenberg, his mother's *Hoffraulein*. She was less clever than his wife, yet sufficiently shrewd and calculating to take opportunities as they came, and the cuckolded mother-to-be was too proud to accept his infidelity without complaining. While heavily pregnant she followed him into his study one day, implored him to tell her how she had incurred his displeasure and asked how she could make amends. He told her sharply to hold her peace. A few days later she tried again and he lost his temper, shaking her violently and nearly strangling her. She became ill, there were fears that she might miscarry, and in order to avoid open scandal Duchess Sophia had to intervene. She used what little influence she had with her eldest son to persuade him to visit his wife's sickroom regularly until the danger was over. Unable to refuse, and perhaps troubled by his conscience, George Louis sat there sullen and silent, holding her hand.

In March 1687 a daughter was born and named after her mother. Sympathetic to the young woman's plight, Sophia invited a large house party to her summer residence at Herrenhausen, with her daughter-in-law as one of the guests. While both women had little in common, the Duchess was sympathetic and kind-hearted by nature; her appreciation of the difficulties her own daughter was experiencing at a far from friendly court in Berlin had given her a new understanding of Sophia Dorothea's plight. She took her under her wing, making efforts to broaden her intellectual outlook and interest in world affairs, above all the English situation, pointing out that her marriage would in due course probably lead her to the throne of England as a Queen consort. However, her efforts bore little fruit, for Sophia Dorothea was too immersed in her boredom and self-pity to care about what was still a remote possibility.

To try to hasten her recovery, the Duchess invited her parents over and gave a sumptuous ball in their honour at Leine Palace. The honour of opening the ball fell to the Duke of Celle, who led the dancing with his daughter, and George Louis obediently gave her the next dance. All was affability on the surface, but appearances were deceptive. When Sophia Dorothea complained to her mother of her husband's infidelities and ill-treatment, the Duchess of Celle told her frankly that she would be well advised to imitate the phlegmatic indifference of her mother-in-law and make the best of such a situation.

Adapting to unsatisfactory family circumstances was second nature to Sophia. She had long accepted the impossibility of trying to persuade her husband and Frederick Augustus to understand each other's point of view in the primogeniture struggle, and though her heart still ached for her son, she assumed once more the role of a dutiful wife whose husband's every word was law.

Events across the North Sea gave Sophia cause for concern as well as similarly divided loyalties. As a friend and relation of both the hapless Catholic King James II and his Protestant son-in-law William, Prince of Orange, when the latter entered London as Protector of the Anglican religion in 1688 and the former fled, she found she could not take the side of one or the other. While sympathetic to the cause of English Protestantism she was no bigot, and she thought nothing could be less Christian than to spread stories that the baby Prince of Wales was a changeling. Writing to congratulate the Prince of Orange, now King William III, on his accession, she made a sympathetic yet tactful allusion to the former King James, who had always honoured her with his friendship, stressing that she was sure her frankness 'will give you a better opinion of me, and that you will more readily believe all my wishes for your good fortune'.[10]

The Declaration of Rights, passed in Britain in 1689, debarred Roman Catholics from succeeding to the crown. Married for twelve years, King William III and Queen Mary were still childless, and their heir, the Queen's sister Anne (who might once have become Sophia's daughter-in-law but was now married to Prince George of Denmark), had no living children. The King accordingly nominated Sophia and her issue as his successors, a suggestion which Parliament had yet to ratify. However, in July Anne produced a seventh child, a son William, later Duke of Gloucester. At first it seemed apparent that he would live longer than those who had preceded and predeceased him, and it was confidently believed that he would reach maturity and assure the succession himself.

In the following year Sophia was grieved to lose two of her sons in quick succession. Charles Philip was killed at the battle of Pristina, and the summer carnival at Hanover was cancelled due to court mourning. He had been a brave and talented young man, and she grieved deeply for him. Later that year his brother Maximilian lost two fingers in a shooting accident, but this episode paled into insignificance beside the death of Frederick Augustus in battle. She had always hoped that one day he and his father would be reconciled, and his sudden death revived her resentment of her husband's treatment.

By now Sophia Dorothea had become openly indifferent to her uncaring husband. She had insufficient resources in herself not to become bored while George Louis was away at the war. Her in-laws found her undisciplined, impatient of etiquette which they took for granted, and superficial with her constant preoccupation with dressing to outshine Countess von Platen, whose presence at court she resented. Sophia had made every allowance for her daughter-in-law, but when Sophia Charlotte left home for Berlin Sophia (Electress) remarked that it was a good thing as her daughter would no longer risk being spoilt by the bad example of Sophia Dorothea.

Soon the latter was throwing tantrums and making scenes. George Louis had already sought comfort outside marriage with Melusine von der Schulenberg; the first of their three daughters, Anna Louise, was born in January 1692 and the second, Petronella Melusine, the following year. Sophia Dorothea began a clandestine correspondence with the Swedish Count Philip Christopher von Königsmarck, a colonel in the Hanoverian army since 1689. One of his sisters was married to a Swedish count in her father's military service and was well known to her, and he told her that he had visited her parents' court before he moved to Hanover. He thus reminded her of home; she found his high spirits and good looks irresistible, and his attention flattered her at a time when she knew she was losing her hold over her husband. It stung her that her husband was becoming infatuated with a lady-in-waiting who was slightly younger than herself and inferior in looks as well as rank. Soon the disaffected young wife and mother and the dashing Count were lovers.

While Sophia Dorothea may not yet have been fully aware that Anna Louise and Petronella Melusine were fathered by her husband, it was no secret that George Louis was much more attached to his mistress than his wife. In conversation the latter claimed casually that her husband cared as little for her as she did for him. However, he was concerned for his reputation; ruling Princes regarded a virtuous wife, or at least a discreet one, as their right. At first she probably thought she could control her flirtation with Königsmarck, allowing him to write to her from July 1690 without her replying to his letters in turn. After that it was but a small step to consenting to and even encouraging secret meetings when he came to Hanover at the end of the year's campaign. His poetic, chivalrous temperament appealed to her much more than did her dull matter-of-fact husband, and she began writing to him when he was away.

While the authenticity of what purports to be their surviving correspondence has inevitably been the subject of much debate, modern authorities generally accept that about half still remains and that it can be assumed to be genuine. Around twice a year they sent their letters to the Count's sister, Aurora, and on her death they passed to her elder sister Amalia, Countess

Lewenhaupt, remaining in the family until presented to Lund University Library in the nineteenth century. A few more came into the possession of Sophia Dorothea's granddaughter Louise, Queen of Sweden, and she sent them to her brother Frederick II ('the Great'), King of Prussia, who added them to the Hohenzollern Archives in Berlin. Others were thought to have been found in Sophia Dorothea's room in 1694, either sewn into curtain linings or hidden in playing-card boxes, found and probably destroyed many years later by her son George after his accession to the British throne as King George II.[11] Those still in existence suggest that they had become lovers by around March 1692. References to the act of *monter à cheval* were enough to confirm that they were just as guilty of adultery as her husband and his mistresses. Unwisely they took too many people into their confidence to preserve total secrecy, betraying themselves by pre-arranged signals and glances. Notes left for Königsmarck by her lady-in-waiting, Eleonore von dem Knesebeck, in his hat or gloves were just as easily seen. Soon their affair was common knowledge throughout Hanover.

For the sake of the electoral house's good name, they were both firmly warned that the affair must come to an end. Sophia Dorothea was told by her own mother, by her mother-in-law, and by Sophia Charlotte on her visits to Hanover. Electress Sophia had always liked and admired Königsmarck, understood the mutual attraction between them, and felt morally obliged to try to stop them from playing with fire. Sophia Charlotte replied abruptly to her sister-in-law's teasing reference to her love for music by telling her how fortunate it was 'that my passions are so easily satisfied'.[12] The Count was forewarned by George's brothers, by his fellow-officers and by Field-Marshal Henry von Podewils, head of the Hanoverian army, all of whom valued him as a good soldier. Though the Count liked to call himself 'a poor butterfly burnt by the flame', he gave Podewils his word that they were not having an affair. Nobody believed him, and it was suggested that it would be in their best interests if he sought a military post elsewhere.

Efforts were made to keep Sophia Dorothea with her husband's family when Königsmarck was away on campaign, so she should have fewer opportunities to meet him. Sophia tried to arrange various outings on which her daughter-in-law's presence was required, and she deliberately mentioned Königsmarck's name in conversation from time to time, hoping that this might stop the younger woman from daydreaming about the man who threatened to bring about her disgrace. Too infatuated and too trusting, Sophia Dorothea found ingenious ways of circumventing this, such as complaining that her brother-in-law Maximilian was lodged too near her for decency's sake, or feigning illness. She also asked to stay with her parents at Celle where she felt her movements were less restricted, and George had to permit such visits in order to maintain good relations with them, though he suggested that her absences from Hanover should be as short as possible.

The elder generation were divided in their attitudes to Sophia Dorothea. Her father-in-law, who had always liked her and admired her streak of independence, was reluctant to believe the accusations made against her. Perhaps he resented his boorish son's manners, and felt that if she was cheating on him then the young man was getting no more than his just deserts. By contrast the Electress treated her coolly. Always inclined to be cautious, and knowing there were faults on both sides, she kept her distance from the daughter-in-law who, if not as guilty as her enemies made out, was behaving foolishly in a way which would surely end in disgrace. When Sophia Dorothea returned home her mother welcomed her with open arms, but her father treated her coldly. Though not fully convinced of the charges made against her by the Court at Hanover – that she was obstinate, disobedient, disrespectful to the Elector and Electress, that she neglected her children and was unfaithful to her husband – he made it plain that her behaviour had left much to be desired.

Any intentions she may have had of steeling herself for one last effort at making an unpromising marriage work were shattered soon after her return to Hanover. One evening she was outside with her ladies Fraulein Knesebeck and Madame Sassdorf, and the philosopher Leibniz, watching an eclipse of the moon. Returning towards Herrenhausen in the dark they lost their way, and found themselves at the door of a smaller, newer building. Knowing what they were likely to see, Madame Sassdorf begged her mistress not to enter, but in vain. Suspecting the worst, she walked inside with grim determination, found herself in front of a closed door, and turned the handle. There she came face to face with Mademoiselle von der Schulenburg reclining on a couch, one hand in that of Prince George. His other hand was rocking the cradle in which their second daughter Petronella Melusine, the future Countess of Chesterfield, lay sleeping. A furious exchange ended with George physically attacking his wife again, allegedly attempting to strangle her, and they were only prised apart by her ladies-in-waiting. This time she hoped her parents-in-law might take action, but while the Electress censured her son for his flagrant infidelity, she criticized Sophia Dorothea for her rashness. For once the Elector was less sympathetic, telling her kindly but firmly that all Princes had their weaknesses, and it was her duty to condone those of her husband.

Surrounded by ever more hostile relations, not to mention malicious mistresses who would stop at nothing to humiliate her and have her permanently excluded from court, Sophia Dorothea could hardly be blamed for dreaming of the unattainable. Anything, she must have surmised, would be better than the empty marriage which made her a virtual prisoner at Hanover. She and Count Königsmarck foolishly continued planning a new life together, while left in no doubt that they were risking arrest and imprisonment. Neither had enough money for them to live on; Königsmarck maintained a large household, his financial affairs were in some disarray, and he had run up considerable gambling debts. When she consulted her marriage contract, Sophia Dorothea discovered to her surprise that she had nothing to call her own, and she began trying to secure an independent income from her parents, without divulging her ultimate objective. Unfortunately for her, Celle was then at war with Denmark and her father's surplus financial resources were going into the army's coffers, while her mother only had jewellery for disposal and did not want to risk her husband's displeasure by selling it for no apparent immediate need. While aware that their daughter wanted a divorce, neither parent approved and they tried to dissuade her.

At the Hanoverian court an elopement was much feared. On the accession of Augustus as Elector of Saxony, Königsmarck went to Dresden to claim payment of a three-year-old gambling debt. Unable to pay, the Elector offered his friend the command of a Saxon regiment instead, which was accepted as a measure of security. By now the families found it increasingly difficult to keep the lovers apart and dreaded what would happen when the Count returned from the campaign in the summer of 1694. He had to join his Saxon regiment at Dresden and had instructed his household that everything should be ready for him to depart on 5 July. When he arrived in Hanover he avoided all company, paid no calls, took no steps to resign his commission or to put the affairs of his regiment in order.

Sophia Dorothea had become more wilful than ever, refusing to share the conjugal roof with her husband, pleading constantly for a separate establishment and formally asking to live permanently with her parents at Celle, if her father could be persuaded. George Louis was about to pay a prolonged visit to his sister at Berlin, and he too realized that his marriage was a lost cause. Before his departure he was alleged to have said that there had been enough quarrels; on his return he would write to her father and demand a formal separation.[13] In her misery she returned once more to Celle, but her father had lost patience and refused to let her regard their home as a permanent refuge. While her mother readily agreed to let her wronged daughter stay as long as she liked, the Duke told his daughter that if she did not return to Hanover by a mutually agreed date, she would be permanently separated from her children.

On her return from Celle, etiquette demanded that Sophia Dorothea should stop at Herrenhausen and pay her respects to Electress Sophia. Instead she went straight to her apartments in Hanover, pleading illness. The court was scandalized at this defiance of protocol, and Countess von Platen knew that it would take but little to eliminate her as a member of the family. Meanwhile Count Königsmarck had returned to Hanover to wind up his affairs there. They may or may not have planned elopement; it was rumoured that they had considered running away to France together, but then changed their minds and decided to go to Wolfenbüttel, where they would be welcomed by Duke Anthony Ulric. Certain factions at court suspected that his impending departure for Dresden was a smokescreen for illicit romance with the Elector's wilful daughter-in-law, and hatched their plans accordingly.

During the night of 1 July Königsmarck was seen to enter the Leineschloss Palace and go to Sophia Dorothea's apartments. He never came out alive. What precisely happened that night will probably never be known, but the traditional version has it that he received a note in pencil left on a table in the sitting-room of his house in Hanover that afternoon, informing him that he was summoned to meet Princess Sophia Dorothea in her private apartment at about 10 o'clock that night. The note purported to be hers but was in fact the work of Countess von Platen. That he did not suspect it was a trap designed to lure him could be put down to his ignorance of how much his and the Princess's indiscretions had become the subject of gossip at court during his absence. Disguising himself in shabby clothes, he gave a prearranged signal under the window of her apartment, and she let him in. It was the first time she had seen him for three months, and she told him that the note was a forgery. He told her that a carriage was ready to take them to safety at Wolfenbüttel, and she would have agreed to join him at once if it was not for the matter of saying goodbye to her children. She would do so next morning, and asked him to return with his carriage at the same time on the evening of 2 July.

Nearby Countess von Platen and her courtiers were lying in wait. Her spies had kept her informed of the intended flight, and as soon as Königsmarck had arrived, she went to the Elector's chamber to inform him. With the assistance of four halberdiers, she said, she could catch the young lovers red-handed. To the scheme of capturing and arresting them, he gave his approval, and she hid the men in a chimney recess, locked all the doors out of the Princess's gallery except one near the chimney, and hid behind a curtain. When Königsmarck tried to leave and found his way blocked, he realized what had happened. Outnumbered by four to one he had no chance, but with the sword which he always carried he wounded three of them. However, they overpowered him and stabbed him to death, and as he lay dying the Countess, who had been watching with malicious glee, came and kicked him viciously in the mouth. Having witnessed his despatch, she realized with dismay that the Elector had merely authorized her to bring the Count to justice, and she returned to his apartment panic-stricken. Though angry with her he knew that he was also implicated in the murder, and he authorized her to do what she could to suppress any trace of the night's events. The halberdiers were ordered to throw the body in the palace latrines, cover it with quicklime and brick the wall up. They accomplished their mission silently and by dawn they were all in their beds.

A little over two centuries later, the historian Dr Georg Schnath carried out exhaustive researches in the archives of several European cities. His final reconstruction of that night's events differed little from the above version, except in minor details. The assassins, he concluded, were not halberdiers or guardsmen chosen at random, but four well-known courtiers known to Königsmarck, two of whom he had regarded in the past as troublemakers. Countess von Platen, he suggested, was in the habit of giving instructions on the authority of the Elector without his prior consent, and if she did not actively instruct the men to kill the Count, she may have counted on his signing his own death warrant by instinctively drawing his weapon first and the courtiers striking back in self-defence. Finally, a number of skeletons were found at intervals during the next two centuries, probably those of dead monks from a nearby monastery. Königsmarck's body had probably been put in a sack, weighted with stones, and thrown into the river.

Unaware that anything was wrong, Sophia Dorothea spent the rest of the night packing her jewels and preparing to depart. Expecting her children to pay their usual call the next morning, instead she was informed by a palace official that she was confined to her apartments and under orders not to leave. Her premises were searched, and incriminating letters from Königsmarck came to light. Three days later her lady-in-waiting Fraulein Knesebeck came to tell her that the Count was dead. Fraulein Knesebeck was offered escape by a brother-in-law, but her mistress persuaded her to stay to swear to her innocence, and she was later put under arrest on unspecified charges.

When he had heard nothing from his master after a couple of

days, Königsmarck's secretary Hildebrand went to see Podewils and report his disappearance. Unaware of what had happened, the Marshal assured him that his master was bound to return before long. Reluctant to believe him, Hildebrand sent a message to the Elector of Saxony informing him of the Count's disappearance. His suspicions hardened later that week when court officials broke into the house with a search warrant, forced open Königsmarck's desk, confiscated letters and papers, then sealed the rooms and their contents with the official seal. Königsmarck's sisters were informed that their brother was missing. When they could get no satisfactory answer from the Elector of Hanover, they asked the Elector of Saxony to intervene on their behalf. Believing that Königsmarck must be in captivity, the Elector sent an envoy to Hanover to conduct an inquiry and demand his freedom on the grounds that he was now a major-general in the Saxon army. To this a reply was delivered stating that at the time Count Königsmarck was last seen, he was still a colonel in the Hanoverian army. The Elector could not be expected to release him, even if he knew where he was, and it was inferred that he had disappeared of his own free will.

Rumours were gradually spreading throughout Europe, and the Elector of Saxony reluctantly halted his inquiries after it became apparent that not to do so could threaten a rift between friendly German electorates. Hanoverian envoys were instructed not to discuss it at the courts to which they were accredited, though little else was being talked about. Fraulein Knesebeck was arrested for 'having helped to alienate her mistress's affections from George',[14] but really to prevent her from gossiping. A charge of attempting to murder George Louis with nitric acid was thrown out when she insisted that she used it solely for the care of her personal complexion. She was sentenced to life imprisonment in a fortress at Scharzfeld but escaped after three years.

Meanwhile, once confronted with the correspondence, Ernest Augustus and George William agreed that a divorce must be arranged which suppressed the name of Königsmarck altogether and concentrated on Sophia Dorothea's refusal to cohabit with George. She was removed to Ahlden, in Celle territory, and the foreign diplomats, if told anything at all, were led to believe that she had been caught in flight from Hanover to Bruchhausen to throw herself on her parents' mercy. Initially unaware of Königsmarck's fate, or reluctant to believe that he had been killed, she thought divorce would open the gates to her freedom and to reunion with him. Despising her husband, she insisted she was only too keen to be divorced and firmly refused every attempt at conciliation which the Consistorial Court, made up of experienced ecclesiastical lawyers and civil authorities from Hanover and Celle, tried to bring about.

The only charge laid against the Princess was one of 'incompatibility of temper, added to some little failings of character'. All question of adultery, which might tarnish the good name of Hanover, was omitted. The proceedings were delayed by her refusal to confess giving any offence to her husband. During an adjournment she was allowed to withdraw to Lauenau; although departure to Celle was prohibited, there was no longer any opposition to her leaving the capital of Hanover, though she was not allowed to take her children. In Lauenau she found little rest, for the lawyers kept up their pressure on her, still trying to wear her down and persuade her to confess her sins in order to facilitate a divorce which would do no damage to the reputation of the electoral house. They read her chapters from Corinthians on the duties of married women, and asked her why she was being so obstinate and unorthodox as to disregard the injunctions of St Paul. She would not argue with them, firmly maintaining her innocence. 'If I am guilty,' she declared, 'I am unworthy of the Prince; if I am innocent, he is unworthy of me!'[15] Once the trial was resumed, her defence was always the same, and the court was frustrated at being unable to wring a confession from her.

Prince George's counsel, Rath Livius, accused her on her husband's behalf, of lack of love and obedience towards him; of having falsely charged him with infidelity, to his parents and her own; and of having repeatedly refused to live with him. For this act of disobedience, he asked the judgment of the court. Sophia Dorothea's counsellors, Rudolf Thies and Joachim von Bulow, asked her whether she would return to her husband or abide judgment for disobeying his repeated desire. Her answer was unyielding; she would never again live under the same roof as him.

On 28 December 1694 the marriage was dissolved; as she refused to live with her husband, she was guilty of desertion, and on these grounds alone a decree of separation, or divorce, was recorded. Sophia Dorothea was given the right of appeal, but she contemptuously refused to take advantage of it. As the guilty party she was denied the right to marry again, but her husband, adjudged innocent, was not bound by any such terms. A private arrangement between Ernest Augustus and George William agreed that she should be strictly confined by her father, who would give her an income of 8,000 Thaler a year, to be increased on her father's death to 12,000 Thaler, with a further increase on her fortieth birthday. George was allowed to keep her dowry for the use of their children.

On the conclusion of proceedings in Hanover Sophia Dorothea took tearful leave of her children, whom she expected to see again in due course. Neither of them knew that they would be separated for life. She had assumed that she would be permitted to live with her mother at Celle, unaware that her father had agreed with the Elector that she should be kept a state prisoner in the castle of Ahlden. Not until she was a virtual prisoner there did she realize that she would not be permitted access to her son and daughter, her father did not wish to see her, and her contact with the outside world would be severely limited. Germany was scandalized by the judgment, which was regarded as of doubtful legality, and the sentence as one of wanton cruelty. Some of the other states questioned whether the divorce was really legal.

Henceforth to be known as the Duchess of Ahlden, she was entitled to her own establishment, and the castle was provided with elegant furniture. A household consisting of personal attendants was appointed for her, all having to take an oath to the Elector to the effect 'that nothing should be wanting to prevent anticipated intrigues; or for the perfect security of the place fixed as a residence for the Princess Sophia Dorothea, in order to maintain tranquillity, and to prevent any opportunity occurring to an enemy for undertaking or imagining anything which might cause a division to the illustrious family'.[16] The establishment included two or three ladies-in-waiting, two pages and gentlemen-in-waiting, a marshal, a garrison of forty soldiers, infantry and cavalry. There were also two valets, a butler, three cooks, a confectioner, a head groom and several servant boys, a coachman, fourteen footmen and twelve maids. Allowing the Princess the luxuries to which she was entitled by rank was a clever manoeuvre on the part of the Elector and his son, as it would help to perpetuate the myth that she had retired to Ahlden of her own free will, rather than been expelled from the family.

Though she maintained the staff out of her own allowance, she had no say in their appointment. They were encouraged to spy on her and report anything suspicious to the castle governor, who was under orders from the Elector to watch her every move and ensure that she had no contact with the outside world except through her correspondence. Strict precautions were taken to prevent any attempt at escape. Flanked on one side by the River Ahler and protected on the other by a moat, the castle was surrounded by sentries who kept watch day and night. The Princess was not allowed outdoors, and only when the doctors insisted that it was for the good of her health was she permitted a short walk in the back garden, but never without a guard. She could not ride out or drive through the neighbouring woods without an escort. Even certain parts of the castle were out of bounds to her. When a fire broke out on one occasion, she could not escape without crossing a gallery which was part of forbidden territory to her. Terrified, she had to stand at the entrance of the gallery, clasping her jewel box in her hands, not daring to advance beyond the line until given permission by the proper authority.

Time hung heavily on her hands, but in addition to the letters she wrote she kept a diary recording all her actions and thoughts. Every day she had interviews with each of her servants, from the chief of the three cooks downwards. The church at Ahlden was close to ruin when she began her captivity, but she provided funds for its redecoration and repair, as well as for an organ. After it was reopened for public service she was refused permission to attend. A chaplain had been provided for giving her church services, but even under guard she was not trusted to join with the people of Ahlden in common worship. When she wanted to take part in divine service, the chaplain read prayers to the garrison and household in one room, to which the Princess and her ladies –

placed in an adjacent room where they could hear without being seen – listened, as she was prohibited from active participation.

She was also kept at a distance from her relatives. Not even her mother, the only member of her family who had not disowned her, was allowed to pay her visits, though they were permitted to exchange letters. Yet all contact between her and her two children was expressly prohibited, and they were in effect ordered to forget that they had ever had a mother. Between George and his children the subject was forbidden, and he 'froze' at any mention of her. As he could have remarried if he wished, his granddaughter Wilhelmina of Prussia maintained in her memoirs that Melusine von der Schulenburg was George's morganatic wife, and after he became King his chief minister Sir Robert Walpole was heard to remark – probably in jest mingled with exasperation – that the Duchess of Kendal, as she had become, was as much 'Queen of England as anyone ever was', but English church law as was then current probably prevented him from remarrying while his former spouse was alive.

Part of the reason for her imprisonment was the fear that other unfriendly European powers might find her of use. Denmark and Wolfenbüttel were enemies of Hanover until 1700 and 1706 respectively, while Saxony and Brandenburg were regarded as uncertain allies at best. The country under greatest suspicion was France, but though Louis XIV was theoretically also an enemy of Hanover, it was believed that he would not stoop to intrigues. While he might be prepared to receive Sophia Dorothea in France if she converted to Catholicism, he would not go so far as to play an active role in helping her to escape. Neither did the Duchess of Celle's efforts to alienate William III and Queen Anne from Hanover by asking them to espouse her daughter's cause have any effect. Nevertheless in September 1702, soon after Queen Anne ascended the British throne, the Duchess asked her to intercede and help have Sophia Dorothea freed, on the grounds that her daughter's position was not fitting for the mother of a future King of England.

Although unforgiving, there were limits to George's vindictiveness. In 1698 he gave George William a written promise that the terms of his former wife's confinement and her financial support would not be made stricter on her father's death. He sent her trusted financial advisers and allowed her to keep all surpluses derived from the domains she inherited on her father's death in 1705, as well as relaxing censorship of her correspondence and made it easier for her to receive visitors. He allowed the widowed Duchess of Celle to move from her dowerhouse in Luneburg to the castle of Celle so she would have an easier journey to visit her daughter. He was disturbed by the petition she sent him to be set free on his becoming Elector in 1698, but political dangers attendant on release dictated his refusal.

After her escape from Scharzfeld, Eleonore von dem Knesebeck was so disappointed at Sophia Dorothea's indifference, not to say ingratitude towards her, that she turned against her former mistress. She proclaimed that the Princess squandered vast sums on clothes and personal luxuries while wilfully forgetting her promises to the person who had risked everything to try to save her.

Soon after his son's divorce case the health of the Elector began to fail. It was rumoured that he had caught syphilis from Countess von Platen, a disease which may have caused her own death in 1700, but this may owe more to the embittered aspersions of Eleonore von dem Knesebeck than to any actual foundation in fact. The stories that she had had a brief love affair with Königsmarck in order to lure him to his doom, and also conducted orgies with young men, certainly lack credence. The cause of his illness was more probably strain brought about by the Königsmarck affair, and a series of strokes and heart disease caused by putting on too much weight. As he became more of an invalid the influence of von Platen dwindled accordingly, and he was ready to look more kindly on the former daughter-in-law who, he considered, had been treated too harshly. He began writing her kindly letters, and for a while she hoped that perhaps she might be granted her liberty after all.

The Electress had no faith in doctors, and prepared herself to face the inevitable. In his last months her husband would tolerate nobody else's company. His eldest son and heir had already been entrusted with the day-to-day work of government, including the signing of state papers. She took all her meals in his rooms, spent much of her time sitting beside him doing her needlework or reading to him, only leaving him to take her regular afternoon walk in the garden. He passed away on 20 January 1698, and with him went the Duchess of Ahlden's last fading hopes of attaining her freedom. The widowed Electress was weary but relieved at her loss, wishing to remember the happier times when her husband 'had been himself'.[17]

TWO

'Surrounded by people without pity or justice'

PRINCESS SOPHIA DOROTHEA OF CELLE;
SOPHIA CHARLOTTE AND SOPHIA DOROTHEA,
QUEENS OF PRUSSIA

In his will Elector Ernest Augustus left his widow the estate of Herrenhausen including the surrounding villages, and substantial annual provision for its maintenance. She signed all revenues over directly to George Louis, as his successor, so he would have responsibility for the upkeep of the palace and grounds while she had full use of them for the rest of her life. She lived mainly in her own quarters, the magnificently decorated suite of rooms on the first floor, though she often took meals with her son. His hostess at the palace was now Melusine von der Schulenberg, openly acknowledged as his wife in all but name, and granted precedence over all other ladies at court apart from his mother and visiting royalty. Though she and Melusine disliked each other, to avoid ill-feeling she kept her opinions to herself. She continued in her official position as Electress, as George Louis showed no likelihood of remarrying. Her household remained the same, except for the addition of her husband's secretary who took charge of her accounts and helped her to send the younger Princes regular sums from her private income, as campaigning was expensive and she could not bear to think of them starving while she and their eldest brother were living in comfort at Hanover.

Princess Anne of Denmark's sole surviving child William, Duke of Gloucester, was still expected to follow his mother on the

British throne. Even if he did die during childhood, Sophia knew it was possible that one of the fifty-four Catholics closer by hereditary claim than she and her issue might embrace the Protestant faith in order to take their place in the succession. She never made any secret from King William III of her sympathy for ex-King James II in exile, and knew that James Edward Stuart, whom she was wrongly inclined to regard as the 'Prince of Wales', might be a more acceptable sovereign-in-waiting to the English than she and her children. Once he was older and free of parental control, she knew that he might choose to become a Protestant. Others took up this idea and suggested to James II that William III, a widower since December 1694, in poor health and who seemed unlikely to remarry, should make the boy his heir after Anne, on condition that he was sent to England and raised in the Protestant faith, but James II refused to hear of it. In June 1700 the Duke of Gloucester celebrated his eleventh birthday, suddenly fell ill and was dead within the week.

Three months later the English diplomat George Stepney wrote to Sophia with some trepidation on what he admitted was a delicate matter, but to which he felt he should refer without waiting for Parliament to make its feelings known. He sent a list of all persons who, despite being Roman Catholics, might have a superior claim to the throne to hers by blood. Following the son of ex-King James II, still greatly under French influence, were his younger sister, and the Savoy family who were also of Stuart blood, albeit forbidden by the Declaration of Rights to 'inherit, enjoy or possess the crown'. He wanted to have some idea of her feelings on the matter. She replied that she hoped her life might be long enough to be of service, but there was little likelihood of her surviving two people (King William III and Princess Anne) who were much younger than she though in less robust health, and she feared that after her death her children would be regarded as mere foreigners.

In October she and Sophia Charlotte went to Holland to meet King William III and discuss the Elector of Brandenburg's prospective assumption of the title 'King in Prussia' and also her rights to the English succession. While she felt that the only kingdom to which she could reasonably look forward at her age was the Kingdom of Heaven, she did not want to neglect anything she could do for her house. She still hoped that Parliament would vote her, or more specifically the electoral family, an establishment and annuity such as befitted the heirs to the English throne. Her eldest son the Elector was happy as he was, 'and did not ask for a crown', but there were 'others of whom they might like to take their choice'.[1] He was 'absolute' in Hanover and might be too set in his ways when the time came for him to succeed to the throne of England, unlike the son of the former King James II, who was still young enough to be moulded into the kind of sovereign the English would prefer. Though English and Hanoverian diplomats feared that her plain speaking might do their cause more harm than good, she promised to support Holland against France in return for her official nomination to the English succession, while the Elector of Brandenburg could count on King William III's recognition of his claims to the title of King in Prussia.

Since 1696 the Elector and Electress of Brandenburg had been the guardians of the orphaned Princess Caroline of Ansbach. Born in March 1683, Caroline was the daughter of John Frederick, Margrave of Ansbach, and his second wife Eleanor of Saxe-Eisenach. Caroline's father died when she was three, and the almost destitute Dowager Margravine, left with a daughter and a baby son, married again, to John George IV, Elector of Saxony. He treated her badly, made it clear that he cared more for his mistress than for his wife, and his death from smallpox in 1694 came as a blessed relief for her and the children. She survived him by only two years. The Elector and Electress felt they had been partly to blame for her premature death by encouraging her in this unsuitable second marriage, and they had promised to look after the children should anything happen to their mother. Sophia Charlotte ensured that Caroline would receive a thorough education, and by adolescence it was noticed that she had taken greatly after the Electress in speech and mannerisms.

In January 1701 the Elector was proclaimed King of Prussia and the Coronation took place at Berlin later that month. With tongue in cheek the newly crowned Queen Sophia Charlotte described it as being 'the player-Queen opposite my Aesop'. Their

Coronation service was so long and tedious that at one moment she drew out her *tabatière* for a pinch of snuff, prompting cold looks from her husband and a note ordering her to 'remember where and who you are'.[2]

King Frederick was proud, if a little in awe, of his attractive and talented wife. She tolerated him for the sake of appearances, but they had hardly anything in common by now and her role was of a dutiful consort rather than an adoring or devoted partner. She cared little for the pomp and circumstance of a sovereign court, and discharged the ceremonial duties required of her with indifference. Matters of state meant less to her than matters of the mind, and it was said that 'she preferred rather to live a life of intellectual contemplation and philosophic calm; the scientific discoveries of Newton were more to her than kingdoms'.[3]

Her husband presented her with Lützenburg Palace, just outside Berlin. Here she was able to indulge her love of art, and supervise the layout of her gardens planned on the model of Versailles, with terraces, statues and fountains. She surrounded herself with fine paintings, carpets, rare furniture, porcelain and crystal. Soon the palace was famous not just for its splendid collections but also as a meeting place of talented people. She invited people because of their wit and talent, rather than their wealth or rank. Receptions were held on certain evenings in the week, and all trimmings of court etiquette, ostentation and ceremony were set aside. Intellectual conversations, reading of great books, learned discussions, music and theatricals kept the company late into the night, and sometimes enlightened courtiers went straight from one of these gatherings to attend the King's levee, held at around four in the morning.

Lützenburg attracted the most gifted and beautiful ladies of the court, learned men from every country in Europe, Catholic and Protestant theologians, philosophers, representatives of literature, the arts and sciences, and French refugees who would not normally expect invitations to appear at court. Since the revocation of the Edict of Nantes in 1685, Berlin had become a rallying-place for Huguenots, many of them men of intellectual eminence and noble birth, banished from their native France. They were particularly welcome at Lützenburg, renowned for its partiality to everything French rather than German. Another welcome guest was the young Caroline of Ansbach, and these gatherings had a lifelong influence on her mental development as well as encouraging her to mix with people of interest rather than rank. At these meetings only French was spoken; everything was conducted with such refinement that one of the Huguenot nobility declared that he felt himself once again at Versailles, and asked whether the Queen of Prussia could really speak German.[4]

Electress Sophia frequently came to visit her daughter in Berlin, and was delighted to find that she had taken after her in so many ways. Sophia Charlotte was known behind her back as the 'Republican Queen' as she was considered such a liberal. She would take nothing for granted, her eager and active spirit always wanting to know the truth, even, as her close friend the philosopher Gottfried Wilhelm von Leibniz once complained, 'the why of the why'.

Meanwhile the Duchess of Celle spared no efforts to try to secure the freedom of her daughter Sophia Dorothea. In the spring of 1700 Saxon and French troops marched through Brunswick in the opening campaign of the War of the Spanish Succession. It was feared they might advance on Ahlden; although the danger was negligible, Duchess Eleonore took advantage of the possibility, telling her husband how terrible it would be if French troops occupied the undefended castle of Ahlden and took as hostage a princess whose son might one day ascend the English throne. The only way to avert the danger was for Sophia Dorothea to be transferred to a fortified castle where any attack could be easily repelled, and no castle was better able to meet this contingency than Celle.

It was an argument which neither the Elector nor his advisers could dismiss out of hand. Much as he resented the idea of doing anything that might give his former wife any measure of liberty, he gave his grudging consent, while reminding the Duke of Celle of his solemn promise never to see his daughter again. Bernstorff, chancellor of Celle, was ordered to keep an eye on the Duke and attempt to influence him against any weakening in case he tried to effect a reconciliation.

One evening in April 1700 the Duchess of Ahlden was escorted to Celle. She and her retinue arrived late at night and were sent to their special quarters at once. As the arrival was kept quiet, the court was not supposed to take any notice of it, but her mother visited her regularly and they doubtless discussed the chances of her staying indefinitely. In July Liselotte wrote rather maliciously to her aunt, the Dowager Electress, asking whether the Elector would send the Duchess of Ahlden back to the castle or allow her to remain where she was; 'I hear that the Princess leads a very solitary life, but all the same she is splendidly dressed, and when she takes a walk on the ramparts at Celle she always covers her face with a veil. I imagine she hopes to touch the heart of her husband by her decorous life, so that he may take her as his wife again.'[5]

Unfortunately for her the French threat, which had purposely been exaggerated by her mother, was short-lived. Once the troops had retreated from their foray into Brunswick territory, the Elector told the Duke of Celle to arrange for the return of his daughter to Ahlden. The Duchess insisted on retaining her daughter, claiming at first that the danger was not over, and then saying that her daughter was too ill to be moved. At length she ran out of pretexts, and the Duke felt honour-bound to stand by his agreement with the Elector, unpalatable though it may have been. For Sophia Dorothea her last chance of freedom had gone.

In June 1701 the Act of Settlement was passed, naming Electress Sophia and her heirs, on condition they were Protestants, as successors in order to end further speculation in England and Europe. James Cresset, the English envoy at Hanover, brought her the official notification, and she wrote to thank King William III, saying that though it was 'now the fashion for Electors to become Kings, we await that event without impatience here, and pray with all our hearts "God save the King"'.[6] While realizing that several of her friends and supporters in England were keen for her to make an appearance over there, she remarked tactfully to her advisers that it would seem strange for somebody of her age to walk behind two people, young enough to be her children, neither of whom (particularly Princess Anne) would find her presence especially agreeable.

Otherwise she would be delighted to be with the people among whom she was raised at her mother's court, although they might find her a novelty at first but soon tire of an old woman. In August a deputation from England led by Lord Macclesfield arrived in Hanover to present her officially with the Act of Settlement. Several days of entertainments and dinners were arranged, leading up to a full carriage procession for a ceremony at Herrenhausen in which Sophia, standing under a canopy with her ladies standing on her right, received Lord Macclesfield in her presence chamber as he bowed, knelt to kiss hands and presented her with her copy of the document, on sheets of vellum and bearing the seal of King William. In the evening the Elector was invested with the Order of the Garter. After Macclesfield's departure Sophia arranged for English lessons to be given to younger members of the family.

The religious writer John Toland, who accompanied the deputation to Hanover, praised her remarkable health and mental bearing, noting that although now over seventy she still walked and held herself like a young lady, 'has not one wrinkle in her face, which is still very agreeable, nor one tooth out of her head, and reads without spectacles, as I have often seen her do, letters of a small character, in the dusk of the evening'. He was equally impressed with the breadth of her reading material and her fluent conversation in five languages. Best of all, she was

> so entirely English in her person, in her behaviour, in her humour, and in all her inclinations, that naturally she could not miss of anything that peculiarly belongs to our land. . . . She professes to admire our form of government, and understands it mighty well, yet she asks so many questions about families, customs, laws, and the like, as sufficiently demonstrate her profound wisdom and experience.[7]

The death of King William III in March 1702 and accession of his sister-in-law, the constantly ailing Queen Anne, brought her one step nearer the throne. Anne was suspected of favouring those who had opposed the late King, whom Sophia had always regarded as a friend. This, and King Louis XIV of France's proclamation, when the death of King James II occurred in

France in September 1701, of his son as King James III, gave Sophia cause for concern. However, formal letters assured her and the Elector of Queen Anne's friendship and affection, and Anne declared in her accession proclamation that she intended to follow all her predecessor's policies.

While Sophia might say regularly that she had reached the age when she must 'prepare to meet my maker rather than turn my thoughts to a worldly crown',[8] she began hoping for recognition of her status as heiress apparent in the form of a regular allowance from Parliament, and she was not above insinuating that this should be voted. This, she believed, would set the seal on her position as 'Princess of Wales'. Moreover she would welcome any additional income, as she wanted to provide for her younger sons, particularly Maximilian and Christian. The former was forever in debt, no matter how much she helped him out, while there was less to spare for Christian than she wished. Yet there was no sign of a grant, nor of any invitation to England, and she resigned herself to the fact that the English court evidently did not desire her presence. At least she could content herself with the inclusion of her name in the English liturgy. However, there was one less claim on her purse when Christian, aged thirty-one, was driven into the River Danube during the battle of Munderkingen in 1703 and drowned.

In the autumn of 1704 Electress Sophia spent two months with her daughter at Lützenburg. The King of Prussia had the greatest respect for his mother-in-law, who liked his love of pageantry and etiquette, and plenty of festivities were staged in her honour. The Electress also took a keen interest in Caroline of Ansbach, who regarded the Queen, fourteen years older than she, more like a beloved elder sister. In 1704, the year of her twenty-first birthday, her hand in marriage was sought by Archduke Charles, titular King of Spain and heir to the Emperor, whom he later succeeded. The Elector supported his suit, and negotiations were in progress while the Electress was at Lützenburg.

Charles's succession to the throne was not guaranteed, and there was also the problem of Caroline's religion. She would have to enter the Roman Catholic Church, an action which would clash with her support of liberty of conscience in matters of faith.

Though a Protestant himself the King of Prussia had little sympathy for her scruples on this issue, feeling that young princesses should be prepared to adapt their religion to political exigencies, and he urged her to accept Charles. The Queen of Prussia had every confidence in the young woman to make up her own mind, and tactfully refrained from expressing an opinion.

Electress Sophia was most impressed by Caroline, who was taking after her only beloved daughter in so many ways. She was convinced that she would make the right wife for her grandson George Augustus, and she encouraged her to resist all pressure from the King. With relief she wrote to Leibniz in November 1704 that most people at Hanover applauded the Princess's decision, 'and I have told the Duke of Celle that he deserves her for his grandson. I think the Prince [George Augustus] likes the idea also, for in talking with him about her, he said, "I am very glad that you desire her for me."'[9] Her sympathies were with the young woman, clearly worried and upset by the pressure being exerted on her, though she stood her ground. The King of Prussia was furious with Caroline, and she found the atmosphere so unpleasant that for a while she contemplated leaving Berlin and returning to Ansbach, where her brother John was now Margrave, until his temper had cooled. For a time it seemed as if she might become betrothed to her quarrelsome, headstrong cousin Frederick William, only surviving child of the King and Queen of Prussia. While the Queen would have liked her as a wife for her son, the King had other ideas, though he did not oppose the scheme in case his alternatives fell through, but neither young person cared much for the other and it came to nothing.

Queen Sophia Charlotte's health had lately been indifferent, and the bane of her life was her husband's avaricious, ambitious *maîtresse en titre*, Mme von Wartenberg, wife of the Prussian Prime Minister. She was angry that Mme von Wartenberg wanted to become an intimate of herself as well as of her husband, and took great pleasure in irritating her and the King by addressing her in French, which she could not understand. For some time differences between the courts of Prussia and Brunswick-Lüneburg had prevented Queen Sophia Charlotte from visiting Hanover, but by the end of 1704 relations were improving.

Despite severe weather and the King's disapproval, in January 1705 she set out for Hanover, but the journey proved too much for her in her poor state of health. At Magdeburg she fell ill and took to her bed. Though she rallied enough to continue, she had a relapse on reaching Hanover. A tumour in the throat was diagnosed, and when the doctors told her they could do nothing more, she bravely resigned herself to the inevitable. A French chaplain at Hanover offered his services but she politely declined on the grounds that she had devoted twenty years of study to religious questions, and he could tell her nothing she did not already know. A sobbing lady-in-waiting was urged not to pity her; 'I am at last going to satisfy my curiosity about the origin of things, which even Leibniz could never explain to me, to understand space, infinity, being and nothingness; and as for the King, my husband – well, I shall afford him the opportunity of giving me a magnificent funeral, and displaying all the pomp he loves so much.'[10] She died peacefully, aged thirty-six.

Sophia had been suffering from a severe cold and was confined to her apartments at the time. Reassured by messages that the Queen of Prussia was improving and out of danger only hours before she died, she was denied the opportunity to say farewell to her only daughter, and it was George who stayed with her till the end. He admired his sister's stoic acceptance of death and the way in which she refused the proffered ministrations of the clergy, but he was stricken with grief at the loss of one who was in the prime of life and paced his room for five days and nights, kicking at the wainscoting as he tried to regain his composure, refusing food and company.

Some ultra-conservatives at Berlin had resented her liberal views and intellectual activities, and it was rumoured that courtiers, acting in league with them, had poisoned her with diamond powder before she left Berlin. At the post-mortem, it was revealed that 'her stomach was so worn that a finger could be thrust through at any place'.[11] Sophia wrote to her son-in-law, now a widower twice over, that she had lost 'what I loved most in the world',[12] and he renamed Lützenburg Charlottenburg in her honour. Caroline was also desolate at losing this beloved member of the family. 'Heaven, jealous of our happiness, has taken away from us our adored and adorable Queen', she wrote to Leibniz in March. 'The calamity has overwhelmed me with grief and sickness, and it is only the hope that I may soon follow her that consoles me.'[13]

The death of the Queen of Prussia left the Electress Sophia with three surviving children. At seventy-four she knew she could not count on succeeding to the crown in person, and felt she was too old to travel to England in the near future. Nevertheless she saw no reason why she should still not ascend the throne, particularly given the poor health of Queen Anne, thirty-five years her junior.

While the disconsolate Caroline returned to her brother's palace at Ansbach, Sophia became increasingly convinced that her grandson George Augustus, now twenty-one and seven months younger than his young cousin, could find no better bride than her. A strikingly handsome and extremely intelligent young woman, she would surely be claimed by one or other of the Protestant courts of Europe unless Hanover staked a claim to her first. King Frederick thought that without his wife to strengthen her resolve he could easily put pressure on her to reconsider marriage with Archduke Charles, or perhaps his own son Frederick William. Fortunately the Margrave of Brandenburg-Ansbach told her that he resented the King's efforts to interfere, and he gave her his full moral support. If her regal guardian in Prussia was threatening her, she was welcome to make her home in Ansbach again for as long as she pleased.

While the Elector respected his mother's judgment, he decided that it would be as well for his son to see Ansbach in disguise, under an assumed name, and meet the Princess to see if they were mutually attracted. He wished to spare him the misery of a coldly arranged state marriage, as well as keep the family's intentions from the King of Prussia. George Augustus was immediately captivated by Caroline, and in July 1705 they were betrothed. To Sophia, it was 'predestination at work', but the King of Prussia was as angry as they had expected. Trying to reconcile him, Sophia wrote that Caroline was clearly meant for one of her grandsons, but 'Your Majesty must have thought her too old for your son, or you would hardly have let her get away'.[14] When he was inclined to agree, somewhat against his better judgment, she teasingly remarked that perhaps he had had an eye on Caroline as a wife himself, a remark which infuriated him.

There was one notable absence from the celebrations. The elderly Duke of Celle, who had reached his eightieth year in good health and spirits, died of a chill caught while out hunting, and the Duchy of Calenberg passed into the hands of the Elector of Hanover as previously arranged. Mourning was not allowed to delay the wedding, in case the King of Prussia tried to prevent the match. On 2 September Princess Caroline and the Margrave of Ansbach arrived at Hanover, and that evening the wedding was solemnized in the chapel at Herrenhausen. The bridegroom, it was noticed, distinguished himself by sleeping throughout the wedding sermon. Even so it was soon apparent that this marriage would be more successful than the ill-fated union of his parents. For the first few months, George Augustus seemed so besotted by his wife that he could hardly bear to let her out of his sight.

Furthermore the thwarted Prince Frederick William of Prussia visited the court of Hanover the following year and became betrothed to George Augustus's sister Sophia Dorothea. She had been brought up by governesses, overseen by her grandmother Electress Sophia. Such descriptions of her in childhood as still survive testify to a gentle-mannered girl with fair brown hair and blue eyes, which were, in the rather extravagant words of one anonymous observer, 'the admiration of the poets, and the inspiration even of those whom the gods had not made poetical'. Toland paid tribute to the young woman's lively personality, noting that

> In minding her discourse to others, and by what she was pleased to say to myself, she appears to have a more than ordinary share of good sense and wit. The whole town and court commend the easiness of her manners, and the evenness of her disposition; but, above all her other qualities, they highly extol her good humour, which is the most invaluable endowment of either sex, and the foundation of most other virtues.[15]

This match met equally with Electress Sophia's approval. She hoped, rather too optimistically, that the aggressive young Prussian who had often bullied his cousin George Augustus in boyhood had matured and would make a worthy husband. A vast collection of clothes was ordered from France for Sophia Dorothea, and King Louis XIV remarked that he wished all German princesses would have such extravagant trousseaux, as it was so good for trade. A round of celebrations for a proxy marriage at Herrenhausen in November before the bride's departure for Prussia did nothing to alleviate her homesickness, and despite the King's impatience, hoping that his future daughter-in-law's horses would gallop all the way, Sophia considered it just as well that she was travelling slowly, 'for if she arrived as red-eyed as she left, His Majesty would hardly be overcome by her beauty'.[16] Eleven days later she and the Crown Prince were married at Berlin.

Although ready to act the adoring husband at first, Frederick William was always ready to find other feminine company while she was busy presenting him with children. Between 1707 and 1730 she produced no fewer than fourteen, of whom ten survived to maturity. Her first son, Frederick Louis, was born in November 1707, but at the celebratory cannon fire for his christening he had a severe fit from which he never fully recovered, and within a few weeks he was dead.

Crown Prince Frederick William was ever preoccupied with money, and his wife resented his parsimony. For her a royal court meant endless extravagance, lavish entertainment, balls and receptions for visiting sovereigns and all that went with it. Tall and well-built, with the passing years she became more matronly and, as her contemporaries discreetly noted, her waist 'rapidly increased in amplitude'. Armchairs were enlarged in order to support her weight; her demeanour, it was said, was 'noble and majestic', while 'her features were strongly marked and not one of them was good'.[17] When she chose she could be amiable and affable to those around her, but most people at court found her pride as Queen and as a daughter of the house of Hanover rather overbearing. She made herself unpopular with her love of gossip, and her husband's friends found her a bore and a snob who evidently looked down on the Hohenzollerns. Her rooms in the palaces at Berlin were decorated with curtains and upholstered furniture. Queen Sophia Charlotte had got her own way partly by stealth and partly by charm of personality, but the haughty Sophia Dorothea never had the same tact.

Nevertheless she still had her captive mother's interests very much at heart. She had not seen the Duchess of Ahlden since she was a child, and often reproached herself unfairly for not being in a position to do more for her. While she was asking Electress Sophia for information about the life of her mother, her mercenary husband showed interest in his mother-in-law for a rather different reason; to be more precise, her financial assets. When they returned from a Hanoverian visit to Berlin he sought legal advice as to whether the Duchess of Ahlden was entitled to bequeath her property to her children, or whether it would revert to her former husband if she predeceased him. Advised that it would not, he worked to win her goodwill by hinting that he might be able to use his influence with his father-in-law to obtain her release. With her father's death in 1705 the surveillance on her at Ahlden Castle became more stringent, and whereas requests to see her children had previously been met with a non-committal answer that it might be possible in due course, now they were firmly refused. While holding out the promise of freedom, in order to encourage her to leave more of her wealth to her daughter in Berlin than her son in England, he took care not to antagonize the Elector of Hanover by asking him to release the former wife whom he hated so much.

The Crown Princess of Prussia began corresponding regularly with her mother, letters being passed through the widowed Duchess of Celle who was always prepared to act as a willing go-between. She assured her mother that the Crown Prince was helping as much as he could. From her captivity, Sophia Dorothea the elder clutched at straws and trusted him. She did not hesitate to flatter him, writing in a letter, undated but thought to be from 1709, asking him 'to continue to favour me with your friendship which is so precious to me', and assuring him of her 'boundless gratitude for the interest you take in everything that concerns me'.[18]

By this time Caroline was expecting her first child and on 1 February 1707 she gave birth to a son, named Frederick, the first of eight children (not counting a stillborn son) who would be born to the couple during the next seventeen years. Their eldest daughter, Anne, followed on 2 November 1709. George Augustus tactfully wrote to Queen Anne in England, requesting permission to name the child after her, and inviting her to be a godmother. The Queen sent her good wishes through an envoy, and a letter with a small present for her godchild. She nominated the Duchess of Celle, the child's maternal great-grandmother, to act as her proxy. Whether this was done out of courtesy to her or out of pure devilry is not known, but Dowager Electress Sophia had never altered her bad opinion of the Duchess, and the Elector George was displeased by this reminder of an episode from the past which he heartily wished to forget. Queen Anne's gesture, if well-meant, did nothing to soothe ruffled feelings.

Two more Princesses were born to Caroline at Herrenhausen. Amelia Sophia Eleanor, always known in the family as Emily, followed on 10 June 1711, and two years later to the day there was a third daughter, Caroline Elizabeth. Caroline was a kindly mother, though never indulgent, and her daughters always respected her. Sophia doted on her great-grandchildren, showering them with presents. Sometimes she gave them items bought at the fairs in Hanover, sometimes purses, baskets, chair covers or altar cloths she had made or designed herself. It was an eternal source of sadness that Sophia Dorothea's first two sons died as babies, but Electress Sophia adored her granddaughter Sophia Dorothea's eldest daughter Wilhelmina, who she decided looked just like Sophia Charlotte.

While George Augustus was devoted to his wife, he was a typical man of his time and soon took a mistress. Henrietta Howard, the eldest daughter of a Norfolk baronet, was married to a dissipated spendthrift of uncertain temper, who made no secret of the fact that he had married her for her money. Virtual poverty and an unsavoury reputation necessitated a move from England to Hanover where the cost of living was much less. Mrs Howard befriended the Dowager Electress Sophia and was introduced to her grandson and his wife. A well-read and amiable young woman who admitted to an interest in the teachings of Leibniz, she was appointed a *dame du palais* by Caroline, and soon became close to George Augustus. The ladies accepted the situation as quite natural; Caroline found her a pleasant change from the coarse, ill-read Hanoverian ladies who had previously comprised most of her social circle, while the Electress remarked that if Mrs Howard became her grandson's mistress she would surely help him improve his English; if he was to inherit the throne of England one day, he had to be familiar with the language.

Caroline spent many a happy hour in the rooms of her grandmother-in-law at Herrenhausen, surrounded by her lovingly acquired collection of books and porcelain, and intelligent guests, among them Leibniz, and the composer and *kapellmeister* George Frideric Handel, as well as princes and generals from throughout Europe. Georg Schütz, the Hanoverian envoy to London, regularly sent Sophia new books from London so she could keep well informed of English thinking, but she rarely did more than dip briefly into the volumes, telling him sagely that everything had been said before, 'and it is only the way in which it is said that's different'.[19] She insisted on being still addressed as Electress, as Royal Highnesses, she said, were 'becoming very common', and Queen Anne forbade the use of the title Princess of Wales.

In The Hague and Hanover it was believed that the British ministry was still plotting to subvert the Hanoverian succession even after James Stuart's declaration in March 1713 that he would never change his own religion, though he promised not to interfere with the Anglican beliefs of his potential subjects.

Towards the end of 1713 Queen Anne was seriously ill once again, and there was more general and growing speculation as to her successor, in Britain as in Europe. Her speech from the throne on 2 March did not mention the Hanoverian succession; Sophia heard from friends in England that she was increasingly conscience-stricken at the fate of her half-brother, and desperately wanted to nominate him as her heir. It was natural, Sophia admitted, as he was closer to the Queen than she was. Her crown, she assured everyone, would come in the next world, 'though if I were twenty or thirty I might have more to say'.[20] But George decided the moment had come to act, and he arranged for the

Duke of Marlborough to have full powers from Hanover to defend the succession should James invade England on Queen Anne's death. He also sanctioned the question which Schütz put on Sophia's behalf, as to whether the Electoral Prince, as Duke of Cambridge, should not have a writ enabling him to take his seat in the House of Lords. In 1706 George had opposed his mother's desire to let George Augustus go to England. Now an open move would at least help the Whigs and Hanoverian Tories to counteract measures which they feared might be taken in favour of James. The Privy Council found no legal grounds on which to refuse the writ which was issued, but to mark Queen Anne's intense displeasure Schütz was forbidden the court. The Queen then wrote three strongly worded letters, to the Electress, to the Elector and to the Electoral Prince, warning them that any attempt on their part to set foot on English soil during her lifetime might lead to most undesirable results.

Despite the pleas of Sophia, Caroline and Leibniz, George was shrewd enough not to send his son over. He was not afraid of defying Queen Anne, but he was jealous lest his son become the centre of attention, and made an excuse that Schütz had acted without orders in going to England to present the request. Such a move was no longer essential as he had succeeded in giving his supporters in England the lever they wanted.

The rest of his family were greatly disappointed by his decision. Prince George Augustus was increasingly frustrated with his idle, purposeless existence at Hanover. Despite his place in the English succession he had not yet been granted a seat in the Hanoverian Privy Council; he had no regimental command, no place in the council of war, and little chance of further military action in the immediate future. Knowing how he longed to be of service Caroline was irritated with her father-in-law, and Sophia was furious, though her anger was directed mainly at Queen Anne.

Now in her eighty-fourth year, Sophia was beginning to look more frail. For a few years she had been troubled by recurrent bouts of erysipelas, but was impatient with medical science and its practitioners. It was far better, she thought, to die suddenly, than to have 'doctors and clergymen muttering over me without being able to do any good'.[21] Still she defiantly told everyone that she

The Georgian Princesses

would outlive Queen Anne, and that the words 'Queen of England' would be inscribed on her tombstone, even if ill-health prevented her from crossing the North Sea. 'I care not when I die,' she said, 'if on my tomb it be written that I was Queen of England.'[22] In support of her claim to longevity she quoted an old Dutch proverb, *Krakende wagens gaan lang* ('Creaking carts last long').

However, her anger with Queen Anne's action probably hastened her own demise. Queen Anne's letter was delivered to the Electress on the evening of 6 June 1714 when she was playing cards. She got up from the table, and when she had read the letter she became greatly agitated, complained of headache yet still went outside, pacing up and down the garden for about three hours before retiring for a disturbed, miserable night. The next morning she still seemed unwell but improved during the day, and by 8 June she had apparently recovered her composure. Nevertheless the gesture rankled deeply, and she ordered that the Queen's letters to herself and her grandson should be published, though the Elector, reluctant to inflame the situation further in England, refused to allow his to become public property. 'This affair will certainly make me ill – I shall never get over it,' she told everyone. 'But I shall have this gracious letter printed, so that all the world may see that it will not have been by my fault, if my children lose the three kingdoms.'[23]

She dined as usual with the Elector, and late in the afternoon took her customary daily walk in Herrenhausen gardens, and despite warnings that it was overcast and looked likely to rain, sending the porters with their sedan chairs away, accompanied by Caroline and some of her ladies-in-waiting. According to one account she began to talk to her granddaughter-in-law about the letters, becoming more and more excited, increasing her walking pace as she did so. Suddenly she went very pale and collapsed. Another version has it that a sudden heavy downpour drove them to seek shelter, and while waiting for the rain to stop, she felt faint and collapsed in the arms of one of her ladies. The party took her back to her apartments and spared no effort to try to revive her, but the looking-glass they held to her lips remained unclouded. She was already dead.

On being notified of her death, Queen Anne commanded a general mourning, and reluctantly inserted the Elector's name in the Book of Common Prayer as heir to the throne in place of his mother. Aware of his apparent indifference to the English succession, she anticipated little trouble from him, and his mother's demise came as a relief. On 27 July (OS)/7 August (NS) she was told that the Electoral Prince, George Augustus, was not coming over to England, and answered wearily that 'that gave her no uneasiness now'. Four days later she fell into a coma and passed away, aged well beyond her forty-nine years. She had denied Electress Sophia the chance to wear the crown, even if *in absentia*, by barely two months.

In October 1714 Caroline, now Electoral Princess of Hanover and Princess of Wales, left Herrenhausen to join her husband and father-in-law who had gone to England together after the latter's accession to the throne as King George I. Her youngest daughter Caroline, not yet two years old, was unwell and stayed behind to recover, while Anne and Amelia were sent to The Hague in the care of their English tutor, and their mother followed a few days later. After an emotional parting with her brother the Margrave of Ansbach, who rightly suspected that they would never meet again, the Princess and her daughters crossed the North Sea together. Anne would later marry the Prince of Orange and make her home on the European mainland, but for her sister and mother it was the only sea voyage they ever undertook, and they were destined never to leave England.

Caroline's duties as Princess of Wales began soon after her arrival in London. She had to fill the vacuum left by the lack of a Queen Consort the best she could, with the disadvantage that no Princess of Wales could ever really replace a Queen. In her case her difficulties were compounded by the jealousy of the King, who suspected her of trying to win popularity at his expense. By tact and diplomacy she managed to avoid the royal displeasure though her husband the Prince of Wales, keen to secure popular favour, was less successful. Nevertheless she retained better personal relations with King George I than her husband, as her father-in-law admired her strength of character as much as her personal charm. With her fine skin, fair hair, bright blue eyes and healthy complexion, she was clearly an improvement on his ugly, elderly mistresses. She was far more intelligent than they, and tactful enough not to show off her superior intellect to those who might feel themselves out of their depth with her. When she found that King George had given up attempting to understand the documents passed to him which he signed without a glance, she told him jestingly that he had become lazy. He replied that he was busy from morning till night, only to be told that people said the ministry did everything, and he nothing.

At her first appearance at the English court, declared one observer, the Princess 'came into the drawing-room at seven o'clock and stayed until ten. There was a basset table and ombre tables, but the Princess sitting down to piquet, all the company flocked about to that table and the others were not used.'[24] At once she charmed all who were presented to her by her grace and affability. The next morning the Prince and Princess of Wales walked round St James's Park with several ladies from court. During the next few days she appeared at the Drawing-Rooms every evening, and complained that she scarcely had time to get her clothes together for the Coronation, which took place at Westminster Abbey on 20 October. As there was no Queen Consort, neither the Princess of Wales nor the peeresses walked in the procession, but the Princess watched from her seat in the abbey.

From her late mentors Queen Sophia Charlotte of Prussia and the Electress Sophia, Caroline had absorbed a commanding intellect and appreciation of arts and literature, as well as learning how to influence men around her who were unequal to her in intelligence, without appearing to do so. Some courtiers were inclined to treat her as a mere cypher, knowing that she had no influence with the King and suspecting she had none with her husband either. Others shrewdly recognized her abilities, and saw that in the reign of the next King George she might be the secret power behind the throne. Even now she was the first lady in the land, and more popular than her husband and father-in-law. Taller than both and imposing in presence, she had an excellent memory for faces and names, and was good at keeping her feelings to herself. Her love of the arts, letters and science brought her respect, her lively spirits, affability and sound judgment of character, all worked in her favour.

The Prince and Princess of Wales settled at St James's Palace. Tactfully they only recruited English men and women to their household staff. Unlike the King, both spoke English well, though in her immediate circle Caroline usually talked French. She tended to avoid writing in English, and generally employed her daughters as secretaries instead when the need to write it arose. Full of praise for England, on one occasion she said that she would 'as soon live on a dunghill as return to Hanover'.[25]

In the summer of 1716 Caroline was expecting another child, which would be her first to be born in England, and in July the court went from St James's to Hampton Court. She and her husband decided they would like her confinement to take place there. Their doctors and court officials decided otherwise, as by October the days were getting shorter and the roads were too bad for ease of transport. It was a difficult pregnancy and on at least one occasion she was in danger of miscarrying. Her ladies were tired out by her long walks, and wished she would take more care of herself. The result was a stillborn prince, and for a while the exhausted mother was close to death herself.

Determined to take better care of herself during her next pregnancy the following year, on 20 October 1717 she gave birth to a son, named George William. His short life was destined to be overshadowed by the most disagreeable episode in relations between herself and her husband on one hand and the King on the other. The Prince of Wales invited his father to be godfather to this little grandson, and wanted his uncle, the Bishop of Osnabrück, as the second godfather. But the King insisted that the traditional right of the Lord Chamberlain, the Duke of Newcastle, to be the Prince's godfather, should be honoured. The Prince and Princess of Wales hated Newcastle, and, after the ceremony, the Prince of Wales accused him of having acted dishonestly, and called him a rascal, declaring that 'I shall find you out', meaning that 'I shall find time to be revenged on you'. The Duke thought the heir to the throne had said he would 'fight' him, and in alarm told the King that he had been challenged to a duel.

The King placed his son and daughter-in-law under house arrest, banished them from St James's and sent them to set up their own court at Leicester House, ordering them to hand their children over to his guardianship.

They missed their three daughters and baby son desperately, and one evening they came to visit them without seeking prior approval from the King. It was an emotional meeting; the Princess fainted with shock, while the Prince sat and cried like a child. Even so they failed to move the King, who intimated through the hated Newcastle that in future the Prince and Princess must always ask personally to see the children, and permission would be granted once a week.

The young Princesses felt the separation just as badly. Eight-year-old Anne lamented that they had a good father and good mother, yet they were like charity children. The King did not visit them, she added; 'he does not love us enough for that.' As the eldest daughter she became an intermediary between parents and grandfather; she sent a basket of cherries from Kensington to her father, and little notes to her mother assuring her that they were well, all passed to the Princess of Wales secretly through her lady-in-waiting Charlotte Clayton. Charlotte herself was not permitted to see the Princess, and they had to resort to subterfuge; a helpful servant in the royal household informed her that the Princess would meet her in a garden house at the end of a terrace so that nobody would see her. Few members of the household dared to risk the King's wrath, but their sympathies were overwhelmingly with the heir and his wife and their unfortunate children who were suffering the most. Once his anger had cooled, the King had relented enough by the end of January 1718 to let the Princess of Wales see her children unconditionally once more.

By this time baby George William was ill, and within a few days he was dead. An inquiry was set up to prove that his death had been due to natural causes unconnected with the separation from his mother, and a post-mortem established that he had been born with a polyp on his heart, yet it was scant consolation to the Princess to be told that he was too sickly to have had any chance of survival.

As the royal palaces of Windsor, Hampton Court and

Kensington were forbidden to the Prince and Princess of Wales, they had to seek a summer residence elsewhere. They chose Richmond Lodge, which provided a welcome haven from the appalling stench given off by London streets in summer. By this time the Princess was expecting another child, but shortly after their arrival at Richmond she suffered a miscarriage.

In the winter they returned to Leicester House. During their two and a half years of semi-banishment their relationship with Robert Walpole improved. One of the most able members of the House of Commons, he had been quick to appreciate the extent of the Princess of Wales's influence over her husband and the importance of securing her goodwill. At the same time he and the other ministers appreciated how important it was for the royal family to be reunited. The royal debts were by now over £600,000 in excess of the Civil List, and a reconciliation would help to restore public credit as well as the family's popularity. The Prince and Princess of Wales were more amenable; the former had been left with heavy debts after purchasing Leicester House, while the latter was determined to have custody of her daughters once more. Still angry with her father-in-law for his cruel behaviour, she was a loyal wife, but as a mother she would do almost anything to have her children back. She informed Walpole firmly that it would be 'no jesting matter' to her; 'you will hear of this, and my complaints, every day and hour, and in every place, if I have not my children again.'[26] Lord and Lady Cowper, her lady of the bedchamber and her husband, advised her to hold out for the children, as if she failed to regain them 'she would never have a faithful friend again nor be thought a good mother'.

The King was reluctant to be pushed into making peace with the son whom he heartily disliked. Fortuitously Anne fell ill with smallpox, and for a few days the doctors feared that she might not survive. The shock of their baby brother's death had brought the three sisters closer together, and the King knew that the death of a second small grandchild while under his care would be on his conscience. He let the Princess of Wales visit her at once, and soon afterwards a public reconciliation took place. The King was reluctant to accept that anything had changed; he refused to allow his son and daughter-in-law use of the royal palaces, and would not let them come back to live under the same roof as him, which was no hardship to either party. He grumbled about having to part with his granddaughters, and nominally they remained under his care, but ministers persuaded him to ease all restrictions gradually until they were in effect restored to their parents who were allowed to see them as often as they wished. A formal notification of reconciliation was sent to foreign courts throughout Europe, and the domestic quarrel which had almost become a public scandal was officially over.

However, it was soon apparent to Caroline that the King had gained more than his son and she, as the children stayed in his household under the care of Lady Portland. They were permitted only to visit their mother at Leicester House and Richmond Lodge, and appear with her at the opera in the royal box on rare occasions. The Princesses always retained great affection for their mother, but assimilated some of the contempt for their father freely expressed at the King's court. Apart from the placid, sweet-natured Princess Caroline, they were inclined to speak with a lack of respect for him thereafter. They liked their grandfather, and enjoyed walking with him around the gardens at Kensington while he inspected improvements in progress, such as the building of new paths alongside the lawns, and rare plants being cultivated in the nurseries for transfer to Hampton Court.

Three more children, all healthy infants, were born to the Prince and Princess of Wales at Leicester House. In April 1721 there was another son, William Augustus; in February 1723 another daughter, Mary; and in December 1724, the youngest child, Louisa. The last birth was difficult for Caroline, now aged forty-one, and she suffered an umbilical rupture in the process, the after-effects of which would trouble her increasingly the rest of her life.

For the next few years the Princess of Wales immersed herself in her intellectual and gardening interests. When not reading or engaged in conversation with great minds of the day, enjoying contemporary novels such as Defoe's *Robinson Crusoe*, and Swift's *Gulliver's Travels*, she oversaw improvements and the planting of new trees in Hyde Park and gardens at Kensington, St James's and Richmond. During the years of waiting for the throne her husband became fussy and over-critical, but he and the Princess knew better than to provoke the irascible King or cross him more than necessary. She was more philosophical, happy to occupy her time gardening or reading and being with their children.

The girls were delicate, frequently suffering from colds, bronchitis, swollen neck glands and convulsions. She and her husband refused to accept the customary remedies recommended by court doctors, such as laudanum and gin. When Lady Mary Wortley Montagu told her how the Turks had 'ingrafted' smallpox to render it harmless, she allowed her younger son to be inoculated the same way. Despite criticism from doctors and clergymen who claimed she was meddling in the ways of Providence, she begged for the lives of six condemned criminals from Newgate, who had not had the disease, to be spared on condition they underwent inoculation as an experiment. It was such a success that six charity children underwent the same treatment, and in April 1722 she had Amelia and Caroline inoculated as well.

As eldest daughter of the Prince and Princess of Wales, Anne, the Princess Royal, had somewhat exalted ideas of her status, and was becoming vain, arrogant and ambitious. One day she informed her mother that she wished she had no brothers, so that she would be able to succeed her father on the throne. On being reproved by the Princess, she retorted, 'I would die to-morrow to be Queen to-day.'[27]

When King Louis XV of France was seeking a bride, a betrothal with the Princess Royal of England seemed a good way of helping to reconcile the two countries which had so often been enemies. A marriage contract was drawn up and matters were virtually regarded as settled until the French court insisted that the future Queen Anne of France should be received into the Roman Catholic Church. The house of Hanover could not afford to be compromised by such a Catholic connection, and no more was heard of the matter.

As a young girl Anne made a lady-in-waiting stand beside her every night, reading aloud until she fell asleep. Once she took so long to do so that the unfortunate lady fell asleep herself in the middle of a chapter. The Princess of Wales deplored this high-handedness in her daughter, but knew better than to scold her; she decided to give her a taste of her own medicine first. The following night she called Anne to her bedside and asked her to read aloud. When the Princess reached for a chair she stopped her, saying that if her daughter read standing she would be able to hear better. The reading began, with Anne pausing from time to time, complaining that she was tired, or her throat was dry. But the Queen would not let her stop; the reading entertained her, and she was not yet tired of listening. At last the Princess began to cry, saying that she felt very faint. Now her mother decided that the girl had learnt her lesson, and she scolded her for having behaved so badly the night before.

Although imperious, Anne was talented and very clever. When she was only five, her governess noted that she spoke, read and wrote German and French very well, had a good knowledge of history and geography, spoke English prettily and danced well. Soon she became skilled at painting, embroidery and fluent Italian, singing, playing the harpsichord, and composing instrumental pieces. When she was aged eight Handel was appointed her music master. It was not a post he accepted lightly, and since he had left Hamburg, he said that nothing on earth could make him teach music; he made 'the only exception for Anne, flower of princesses'.

While the Prince and Princess of Wales had been settled in England with their daughters and younger son, the elder son Frederick had been left behind in Hanover to be looked after by servants and tutors under the supervision of his great-uncle, Prince Ernest Augustus. King George I thought he should be brought up in the ancestral home and have some knowledge of the Electorate. Hanoverian subjects might feel slighted by being left without a younger representative of the family among them. When Frederick reached the age of eighteen, Walpole, by now chief minister, told the King that unless he brought his grandson over to England, Frederick might never set foot in the country. He believed that the Prince and Princess of Wales were intent on making him Elector of Hanover after the King's death, and nominating their younger son William as the Prince of Wales' successor in England. The King dismissed the scheme, saying that Frederick, at eighteen, was old enough to make up his own mind on the matter.

Nevertheless the question of finding him a wife could not be postponed indefinitely. Alliances between the houses of Hanover and Hohenzollern had created a precedent which the King's daughter Sophia Dorothea, Queen of Prussia, was happy to maintain. Between her and her brother who would shortly reign as King in Great Britain, there was little love lost. For his sister, the courtier Lord Hervey noted, 'he had the contempt she deserved, and a hatred she did not deserve'.[28] Now nearly forty, a determined woman known disrespectfully behind her back to foreign ambassadors as 'Olympia', she had made the best of a bad job in her marriage to the brutal King Frederick William. Yet several years at the court of Berlin had only reinforced her belief that the Hanoverians were superior to the Hohenzollerns, and a feeling that living in Prussia was akin to being in exile. The cultured court of Herrenhausen was more to her taste than the barracks-like atmosphere at Berlin, and her insistence on raising their children in the French manner, rather than the German, led to many a difference between husband and wife.

If he resented her airs, graces and innate sense of superiority, she deeply regretted the absence of the stiff ceremonial, great fêtes and heavy pomp of her own court. She suffered from his bad manners, was repelled by his wild hunting parties, his gluttony and drinking sessions, and the crude jokes he enjoyed with his court jester and soldier-cronies. The more she tried to persuade him to refine the court, the more he resented what little pomp and ceremony there was at Berlin, and he abolished court dress in favour of military uniforms of rough domestic cloth.

Only when he left on one of his inspection tours, could she breathe with relief, and made up for lost time by organizing hastily improvised banquets and balls. Otherwise she would complain bitterly about him, and made no effort to keep her feelings from her children, particularly Frederick and Wilhelmina, who shared her aesthetic traits, artistic leanings, love of comedies, operas, ballets, masquerades and tournaments, everything which their father derided as 'godless things increasing the kingdom of the devil', and were soon turned against their father. They saw that their parents were at loggerheads, and took on their mother's love of gossip and telling tales about members of the household. They were silent and reserved at table in their father's presence, knowing that it only irritated him all the more. She was too frightened of her husband and his temper to make a stand on behalf of any of their children, but her private apartments were a convenient place of refuge into which they were always invited to escape. According to the ambassadors, hers were the only comfortable rooms in the palace.

It had long been her dearest wish that her nephew Frederick should marry her daughter Wilhelmina, and that her artistic, dreamy son Crown Prince Frederick, heir to the Prussian throne, should marry one of his cousins in England. The Princess Royal, who shared his passion for music, or the horse-loving hoyden Amelia, would be equally suitable as a wife and the next Queen of Prussia. King Frederick William told his wife angrily that he would not have a daughter-in-law 'who gives herself airs, and will fill my court with intrigues as you do'. As for their son, he was 'only a sniveller, and rather than marry him off I'll give him the strap. He has a horror of me, but I can bring him to heel.'[29]

The Crown Prince was ready to marry Amelia or anybody else, if it would give him independence from his brutal father. As for Frederick at Hanover, he declared that he was quite in love with Wilhelmina, whom he had never seen, but she did not care for the idea of marrying him. The Queen of Prussia had talked about him so much, that her daughter felt she would dislike him on sight. The Queen told her that he was 'a good-natured prince, kind-hearted, but very foolish; if you have sense enough to tolerate his mistresses, you will be able to do what you like with him'.[30] This would not be the husband of her dreams, Wilhelmina decided; she wanted somebody to whom she could look up and respect.

King George I was more receptive to the idea. On one of his visits to Germany he came to see Wilhelmina, and decided that she would prove a satisfactory ornament to his dynasty, but suggested to the parents that the two parties at seventeen and fifteen respectively were too young to be married yet. Queen Sophia Dorothea pointed out that her nephew in Hanover had a mistress already, and her father relented. Without consulting the

Prince and Princess of Wales, he assured her that the marriage would take place on his next visit to Hanover, in 1727.

Marriage in the younger generation was not the only family problem on the mind of Queen Sophia Dorothea. In 1725 she was approached by her mother's representative and chief financial adviser, Count de Bar, to negotiate her liberty. The defeat of Jacobite invasions and plots, in which the Duchess of Ahlden might have been used as an unwitting pawn against her former husband in London, had meant that she could no longer be considered as a danger. But the Queen found sadly that her plan (and she felt also that of her father) was unacceptable at Ahlden. The prisoner did not merely want forgiveness by grace, but a repudiation of the 1694 verdict to acknowledge that she had been unjustly treated. If this was not freely offered she would prefer to rely on 'the plans of her trusted friends'[31] to gain her freedom, presumably the Jacobites. The daughter told her mother that she did not dare to speak about the amnesty until the project she and her husband had at heart, the double marriage between two of their children with two of her brother's, was secured.

The Duchess of Ahlden did not favour the marriage project. As she had no say in anything, her views were of no account and she knew it, but she may have deliberately taken a negative view as her former husband was in favour. However, she wrote to the Queen of Prussia to tell her so, and as the Queen was always kept on a tight rein by her frugal husband, she probably needed ready money to buy the favour of influential people towards the double-marriage scheme. It was obvious that she could expect no such financial assistance from her mother. She then tried threats; having promised her mother that she would intercede with King Frederick William to obtain her release from King George I, she sent word to Ahlden that she would no longer do so unless the double-marriage deal came off. The Duchess of Ahlden refused to reconsider. Realizing she had gone too far, the Queen sent a message through Ludemann, the bailiff of Ahlden, in which she assured her mother of her filial devotion and affection. To show her good intentions she sent along presents, including miniatures of two of her many children. The Duchess of Ahlden kept the miniatures but coldly returned the presents.

Count de Bar had been a devoted servant of the Duke of Celle, and after the Duke's death joined his daughter's household. Debonair as well as aristocratic, he knew how to flatter her, and wooed her with small presents which he brought back from his journeys throughout Europe. He won her over and she trusted him implicitly, as she did Ludemann, his assistant. As both travelled frequently on matters pertaining to her business, or so they assured her, they could take letters and presents between her and the Queen of Prussia in and out of the castle without the governor's knowledge. King Frederick William tolerated his wife's correspondence with her mother, though as he prized good relations with King George I he knew the latter's compliance could not be taken for granted. Sometimes the Queen feared his uncertain temper and passed a short verbal message to one of the Prussian privy councillors or attendants, who would relay it in similar fashion to Bar or Ludemann.

Neither man was motivated solely by sympathy for the captive Duchess of Ahlden. Had she not been a very rich woman with no opportunity of keeping a close watch on her finances herself, but dependent on those whom she felt she could trust, they would not have risked so much in helping to facilitate this unofficial and frequently troublesome exchange of correspondence. As men of the world, they did not hesitate to take advantage of their position of trust to keep back some of her revenue that passed through their hands. In a better position to observe matters from the outside world, the Queen of Prussia became suspicious of their dealings and warned her mother. At length she was persuaded that Ludemann had betrayed her trust, but she would not hear a word against Bar, who had become indispensable to her and was the only person from the outside world who could still come to visit. When she faced him with her daughter's accusations, she accepted his explanations without doubting his word. She continued to confide in him, bemoaning Ludemann's treachery as an affair which had caused her very deep and poignant grief, and shows me the deplorable and dangerous condition wherein I am placed – a condition which is getting worse and worse. I am surrounded by people without pity or justice, and their number is daily increasing. I am incessantly exposed to their calumnies, false suspicions, and ill-turns. They now have it more than ever in their power to invent words and actions which they attribute to me, and so strive to blacken my reputation.[32]

Throughout the years the Duchess of Ahlden had always clung to the hope that one day she would regain her liberty. The Jacobite rebellion of 1715 had given her grounds for optimism, particularly when pro-Stuart agents tried to take advantage of questions raised by the Königsmarck affair and the possibility of her innocence by soliciting the support of King Charles XII of Sweden, who had aspirations towards invading Scotland and restoring the house of Stuart to the throne. In 1718 three Scottish gentlemen had tried unsuccessfully to gain access to Ahlden to greet Sophia Dorothea as 'Queen of Great Britain'. Although these plans came to naught after King Charles's death, she would not regard her cause as hopeless.

Despite lack of exercise, she had remained in good health. Though the castle afforded her plenty of comfort, despite her dignified bearing through the years she still longed for freedom, the chance to travel and meet other people without any restrictions. As over thirty years – more than half her life – had elapsed since her divorce, she had grounds for justification in thinking that she had paid dearly for what could easily be passed off as a youthful indiscretion. Even if her former husband could not be persuaded to show leniency, at the age of sixty-six he was unlikely to live for much longer, and then perhaps her day would come. Even escape, perhaps with Bar's connivance, was a possibility. 'I picture myself becoming a monster losing its sight, but I have hardly thought about it', she wrote in August 1726. 'I doubt whether Heaven, in exchange, will be pleased to open certain eyes. I am entirely ignorant of what is happening in the world except what I learn from the ordinary political news. I am guarded, and more pains than ever are taken to prevent my learning anything.'[33]

Bar had convinced her that he could use part of her funds at Amsterdam to purchase aid in securing her escape. Meanwhile, far from making any plans to give the trusting Duchess any such help, let alone financial assistance of any sort, he was busy appropriating most of the money he had realized from the sale of her bonds. When proof was brought to her of his fraudulence she allowed court proceedings to be brought against him, but this final act of deception broke her spirit. Everyone in whom she had placed her confidence had been taken from her or else had betrayed her.

During the last years of her life she had the best medical care available with her own resident doctor, and visits by court physicians from Hanover who examined her regularly to report on her state of health. But now, deserted and forgotten, she took to her bed with depression, or what her puzzled contemporaries described as 'something like brain fever'. Surgeons and physicians were sent to Ahlden to try to nurse her back to health, but she had lost the will to live. By October she was seriously ill, and passed away on 13 November 1726, aged sixty.

King George I was known to be superstitious. Some years earlier a well-known French 'prophetess' was recommended to him for her power to foretell the future, and he commanded her to read his to him. Somehow Duchess Eleonore induced her to tell him something which would help her daughter at Ahlden. Accordingly she warned him to take good care of his former wife if he wanted to live for a long time, as he would not long survive her.

The courts of Hanover and Prussia went into mourning, Hanover in deference to the memory of the Duke and Duchess of Celle, Prussia in deference to a Queen whose mother was known to have left her a large inheritance. In London her death was treated as of no consequence, with the *London Gazette* making only a brief allusion to the death of the Duchess of Ahlden. The day the King received the news, he went to the Haymarket Theatre to see an Italian comedy, accompanied by two of his mistresses, and the following day he commanded a special performance at the King's Theatre. Though angry that his daughter and the court of Prussia had gone into full mourning for her mother's death, he was powerless to do anything about it.

Meanwhile his former wife's body was put in a lead coffin and left in the Ahlden vaults, awaiting his instruction about the funeral arrangements. None came for some weeks, during which time her will was seized and destroyed, so that all her property would go to her former husband, instead of her son and daughter. The household was disbanded and her furniture dispersed, while some of her papers were destroyed and the rest, packed in strong cases, sent to Hanover. Early in the new year an envoy from the King went to Ahlden with orders for the governor to bury the Duchess in the castle garden. That winter the River Ahler had overflowed, turning the garden into a swamp, and as it was impossible to dig a grave, several attempts were made to sink the coffin into a waterlogged hole but in vain, and it was returned to the castle vaults. King George was informed, and later he gave instructions to transfer the coffin to Celle and bury it in the ducal vaults of the church. It was carried there by night, taken to the vaults and deposited without ceremony. Later a small tablet was affixed to one corner, with her name, and dates of birth and death, but none of her titles.

The Prince of Wales was not allowed to make any public demonstration of grief for his dead mother. It was a matter which rankled with him and with the Queen of Prussia, who mentioned sadly in a letter to him her regret that neither of them had ever been able to persuade their father to let their mother leave Ahlden.

THREE

'Her will was the sole spring'

PRINCESS CAROLINE OF BRANDENBURG-ANSBACH, LATER QUEEN CAROLINE, AND HER DAUGHTERS

On 3 (OS)/14 (NS) June, a few weeks after his former wife's burial, King George I left London for Germany, intending to meet Queen Sophia Dorothea of Prussia at Herrenhausen and discuss the double-marriage project. In accordance with custom, petitioners could wait for the King along his route and hand petitions into the coach. One such document which he apparently received in this way, soon after arriving in Germany, was a letter written by the Duchess of Ahlden the night before she died, protesting her innocence and his injustice to the end, cursing him and summoning him to appear before God's throne and justice within a year and a day of her own death. This letter, which she had then passed to one of her attendants,[1] was given to a member of the King's entourage on the royal coach as he proceeded to Osnabrück, tired after a rough crossing and suffering from indigestion. The story may have been fabricated by his son or his son-in-law, neither of whom had any reason to remember him with affection. Nevertheless he had a seizure in the carriage, and when they reached Osnabrück he was dying. By the time his servants put him to bed he was unconscious, and died shortly after midnight on 10 (OS)/21 (NS) June 1727.

Four days later the news reached London and Sir Robert Walpole informed the new sovereigns, now King George II and Queen Caroline. Once the former was convinced that it was not a practical joke, he curtly ordered the minister to go and take his directions from Sir Spencer Compton, Speaker of the House of Commons. Accepting gracefully this apparent dismissal from high

office, Walpole left the royal presence, knowing that his influence
with the woman who was now Queen would see him back in
office before long if he was careful. Her relations with her father-
in-law's First Minister had not always been amicable; she was well
aware of his unflattering references to her figure behind her back,
and she had been irritated at his failure to secure the speedy
return of her children from the late King's surveillance.
Nevertheless she was impressed by the way in which he kept her
informed on public affairs, and she knew the country was in safe
hands while he was in power. Any attempt her husband might
make to assert his prerogative for the sake of it and put another,
less experienced parliamentarian in charge could be dealt with,
and though he had verbally been promised the chief post by the
King, Compton agreed to serve under Walpole.

Court mourning ended soon after the burial of King George I
in Leineschloss Church at Hanover, close to Electress Sophia, and
the new King and Queen were crowned at Westminster Abbey on
11 October. On their accession they gave up Leicester House, and
made St James's Palace their London headquarters. The King
disliked Windsor Castle but it appealed particularly to Queen
Caroline, who often stayed there during his absences in Hanover,
and she arranged a valuable collection of china in one of the
recesses of the picture gallery. Kensington Palace was their
favourite, and the Queen took particular interest in improving and
altering the palace gardens.

In effect the next ten years were to be virtually the reign of
Queen Caroline in all but name. Once her husband became King,
observed Lord Hervey, formerly gentleman of the bedchamber to
the Prince of Wales during his father's reign, now the Queen's
vice-chamberlain and unofficial court jester, 'the whole world
began to find out that her will was the sole spring on which every
movement in the Court turned; and though His Majesty lost no
opportunity to declare that the Queen never meddled with his
business, yet nobody was simple enough to believe it'.[2] She
became adept at managing him without his being aware of the
fact. Much as he might scold or contradict his wife in public
whenever she expressed an opinion, in private he always deferred
to her. In spite of his vanity, he was shrewd and cautious enough

not to make foolish mistakes. Years of bullying and being treated with coldness by his father had left him with a sense of insecurity; and he knew he was no match for his wife's superior intellect or her talent for dealing with people. It was no exaggeration to say that she governed the kingdom through Walpole, with whom she devised a way of controlling the King. The Chief Minister discussed affairs of state with her, and once matters were decided between them, she undertook to bring the King round to their point of view. She would always appear to agree with him, even when he announced his intention of doing something different, and then gently talk him into her (and Walpole's) point of view. Ministers soon realized that if anything required the King's consent, they merely had to persuade Walpole. He would convince the Queen of their argument, she would speak to the King and persuade him that the idea was his, and the minister's recommendation would come back to him in the form of a royal command.

Her liberal restraining hand worked well on Walpole, who had always been ready to argue for the impeachment or exile of political opponents during the previous reign, or execution of Jacobite peers. With her instincts to urge mercy wherever possible, respect freedom of speech in Parliament, and the freedom of the press, her influence was decisive. She was wise enough to conciliate opposition members who professed loyalty to the Stuarts, her theories on democracy, the popular will and civil liberty having been learnt in her youth from Sophia Charlotte, Queen of Prussia.

Each time her husband went to Hanover she was invested with the full powers of Regent. Since her arrival in England she had been shocked by what she learnt about the prisons, and on her husband's accession she strove to bring about some reform of the penal system. Aware of injustices and anomalies in criminal law, she took it on herself to err on the side of clemency wherever possible, and she was reluctant to sign death warrants. When it was in her power as Regent she chose to have prisoners released early, she intervened to mitigate penalties for debtors and other minor offenders, and took a keen personal interest in action to remedy the deplorable condition of public prisons. During her second regency in 1732 she pressed for an inquiry to be instituted into the system of abuses, particularly of gaolers and warders who aided the escape of rich prisoners while subjecting the poorer ones, unable to pay the extortionate demands made of them, to additional insult and oppression. She was horrified by the select Commons committees' revelations of ill-treatment and inadequate nourishment in prison. While she found Walpole disinclined to any sweeping reform of legislation unless demanded by political expediency, at least she could persuade him to sanction more vigorous inspection of prisons, with punishment for gaolers found guilty of cruelty.

With such principles and remarkable tact, she knew how to dissuade Walpole if he should persist with what she considered any unsound measures. When he introduced an Excise Bill in Parliament in 1733, a scheme which would reduce the land tax while increasing excise duties on wine and tobacco, the opposition attacked it vigorously, as did many of his friends and colleagues. Initially the King and Queen supported him, respecting his courage in the face of increasing parliamentary hostility, but at length Queen Caroline felt it prudent to ask advice from others. Warned by Lord Scarborough that if the Bill was not dropped there would be mutiny in the army, she urged Walpole to withdraw it. Later that week he announced in Parliament that he intended to postpone the measure for two months, and no more was heard of it.

While King George was not strictly faithful to her and had Mrs Howard as a mistress, the Queen knew better than to complain. Mrs Howard was unambitious and easily manageable, and when she grew weary of being his constant companion the Queen was sorry to see her leave court.

By middle age she suffered increasingly from gout, and with regular pain in her ankles she found walking difficult. Knowing her husband's impatience with illness in himself and in others, she kept her troubles to herself as far as possible. When they were particularly severe she would bravely plunge her hot swollen feet into a bowl of cold water to reduce the swelling so that she could fit her walking boots on and trail obediently round the gardens with him. Augustus II, Elector of Saxony, whom she had known in her youth, sent her a wheelchair which she sometimes used at Drawing-Rooms when the effort of standing proved too much.

Queen Caroline was affable to nearly everyone with whom she came into contact. Unlike her husband, she possessed the royal gift of always saying the right thing, eager to ask after other people's children, their activities, interests and welfare. When guests were invited to dine, she was tactful enough to point them out discreetly to servants by name if she thought they had not drunk enough, not because she wanted them to imbibe themselves into insensibility, so much as from the good hostess's belief that a man who was conspicuously sober must have spent a very disappointing evening.

The only person with whom she did not get on well, sadly for all concerned, was her eldest son Frederick, Prince of Wales. The 'double-marriage' plans made by King George I and the Queen of Prussia had come to nothing, as King Frederick William of Prussia was determined not to have Amelia of Hanover for a daughter-in-law, and his daughter Wilhelmina shared his lack of enthusiasm for Prince Frederick. Increasingly impatient with the delay, Frederick sent an aide from Hanover to plan an elopement, but news of it reached King George II, who promptly ordered a stop to it and summoned the Prince to England forthwith.

Frederick had not seen his parents since their departure from Hanover in 1714. At first Queen Caroline seemed more glad than the King to have his company, and she regarded his practical jokes indulgently. The King regarded him with some reserve, till he found the mild young man seemed inoffensive enough. But gradually the Prince came to distrust his mother, whom he saw to be more intelligent and more devious than his father. He also resented their unashamed favouritism of his petted younger brother William, and suspected that if it had been within her power, she would have tried to nominate him as heir to the throne instead.

Normally so perceptive and far-sighted, Queen Caroline sorely misjudged her eldest son in her efforts to control and influence him through her devoted protégé and the notorious troublemaker Lord Hervey, who was initially a friend of Frederick. When the latter was created Prince of Wales in 1729, both men shared a mistress, Anne Vane. Hervey, and perhaps the Queen, condoned the liaison at first, as they hoped that she might pass them useful information about the Prince. Hervey foolishly sent the Prince a ribald, rhyming letter about the Queen and the Princesses. The Prince rightly resented such disrespect from a man who owed almost everything he had to his position as a member of the royal household, and they fell out. Hervey disowned Anne Vane, and for several months he was out of favour at court. Nevertheless he soon worked his way back into the good graces of the King and Queen, while the increasingly independent-minded Prince of Wales never did.

Of the three elder daughters of Queen Caroline, Anne, the Princess Royal was the cleverest, as keen a reader as her mother, and a competent painter. Before the rest of the family rose each morning she was usually up herself, busy at her paints, her books and sewing. She had a good singing voice, and under the tutelage of Handel she had learnt to play the harpsichord well, and compose instrumental pieces. Enthusiastic but impatient at the card table, she irritated others by rapping her knuckles as she played, particularly if they were too slow for her.

As an adult she was close to her mother but not her father. To Hervey she complained regularly about the King's vanity, his tedious military reminiscences, his boasting of his success with other women, and his bullying of the Queen. He could bear major misfortunes well, she conceded, but in a bad mood he was 'the devil' to anyone who came near him, and usually for some trivial reason such as a page powdering his periwig badly, or a housemaid setting a chair in a different place.

Amelia, known as Emily in the family, was an active, extroverted young woman. She was better looking than her elder sister, and some at court found her more clever though her intellectual interests and accomplishments were less marked, while her ready wit made her the most popular of the sisters. Lady Pomfret, writing to Mrs Clayton in 1728, called her the oddest, or at least one of the oddest princesses that ever was known; she has her ears shut to flattery and her heart open to honesty. She has honour, justice, good-nature, sense, wit, resolution, and more good qualities than I have time to tell you, so mixed that (if one is not a *devil*) it is impossible to say she has too much or too little of any; yet all these do not in anything (without exception) make her forget the King of England's daughter, which dignity she keeps up with such an obliging behaviour that she charms everybody.[3]

Several minor German Princes sought her hand in marriage after the failure of her betrothal to Prince Frederick of Prussia, and she rejected them all. She became the family flirt, enjoying affairs with the Duke of Newcastle and the Lord Chamberlain, the Duke of Grafton, a grandson of Charles II, a liaison which caused endless gossip and some irritation to the Queen, who pretended to treat his over-familiarities as a joke but was privately angry with him. The Princess and Duke went hunting together two or three times a week, riding away from the rest of the party. Once at Windsor their attendants lost them altogether, and they did not return to the castle until long after dark. Everyone imagined they had gone together to a private house. The King was in Hanover at the time, and the Queen scolded her daughter thoroughly, threatening to tell him on his return. Walpole dissuaded her, saying that it would do the Princess harm, and the Duke would not care. Throughout her life she was happiest when hunting, and she became increasingly eccentric with age. At church she shocked members of the congregation by arriving in riding clothes and carrying a dog under each arm. Like her father, she loved fresh air and was impervious to cold. Her health was better than that of her sisters, and she survived them all.

The third sister Caroline was considered less pretty and too fat. Shy, good-natured and passionately loyal to her eldest sister, she adored reading and drawing. Well known for her good nature and piety, she was her mother's constant companion in later years. 'Send for Caroline, and then we shall know the truth',[4] was the constant refrain of her trusting parents. While Emily hated Lord Hervey, Caroline's admiration for him bordered on infatuation.

That he was a married man with eight children, and had been notorious for liaisons with good-looking young men in the past before and during his marriage, seemed to make no difference to her hopeless passion.

Bored with life at her father's court, and keen to avoid the nightmare of a spinster's life under the reign of a brother whom she detested, Anne was anxious to find a husband, and King George was equally anxious to see her married off. In 1733 she was aged twenty-four. With her long face, disfigured by smallpox and bulbous eyes, she had never been attractive, and like her mother she was becoming fat. Most of the other contemporary Kings were Roman Catholics, and the few German princelings who might have been suitable for her or her sisters were thought too insignificant for someone as imperious as she. Among the few eligible Protestant suitors was William IV, Prince of Orange. Nearly two years younger than Anne, he was grossly deformed, and in the words of the ever-malicious Hervey, 'almost a dwarf'. When Queen Caroline sent Hervey to the Prince, under orders to come back and tell her 'without disguise what sort of hideous animal she was to prepare herself to see', he was able to tell her that her future son-in-law, notwithstanding his physical appearance, had a pleasant enough manner.

As far as the Princess Royal was concerned, according to Lord Hervey, it was not merely a choice between this Prince and any other, 'but between a husband and no husband – between an indifferent settlement and no settlement at all; and whether she would be wedded to this piece of deformity in Holland, or die an ancient maid immured in her royal convent at St James's'.[5] When King George warned her of his physical shortcomings, she said that she would marry him, even if he was a baboon, to which he retorted that she would 'have baboon enough'.[6] In 1733 a betrothal was arranged, and William arrived at Greenwich early in November. His future wife's demeanour was detached to the point of chilliness. Far from expressing any excitement at the arrival, she sat calmly in her apartment at St James's playing her harpsichord.

The wedding was to take place within a few days of the groom's arrival, but almost at once he collapsed and fell seriously ill with pneumonia. For some weeks his life was in danger, and none of the family came to see him. Fear of infection may have been one reason, as an epidemic of smallpox was raging throughout London, and one of his suite died. Another, rather hard-hearted theory, was that the King may have merely been rather inflexible in observing the royal rule that he intended to make clear the fact that the Prince of Orange was 'nobody' prior to his marriage with the daughter of the King of England, and he could only become somebody through alliance with the royal family. After the Prince had been allowed a few weeks to convalesce the wedding was rearranged for 14 March 1734 and took place at the Chapel Royal, St James's, the bride showing the same impassive demeanour throughout. After the ceremonies they had a brief honeymoon at the Dutch House, Kew, and then returned to London.

Once the time came to leave her childhood home for Holland, the Princess of Orange seemed oddly reluctant to make the break, and Queen Caroline was particularly distressed to see her depart. 'My sadness is indescribable', she wrote to her daughter within hours of the newly wed couple leaving for Gravesend and then Holland; 'I never had any sorrows over you, Anne, this is the first, a cruel one.' The King, she assured her daughter, sent his affectionate greetings, and was 'worse than us all', and she ended with a plea to love her 'always as tenderly as the most affectionate mother flatters herself that you do'.[7]

On their arrival in Holland the Prince and Princess of Orange took up residence at Leeuwarden Palace. Almost at once Anne reverted to her childhood habits of petty tyranny over servants and ladies-in-waiting, thinking nothing of keeping them standing or reading to her until they were fit to drop. Her arrogance was resented by the Dutch, from whom she never concealed her opinion that they were inferior to the English. She preferred to keep her own company, surrounded by her music and books. William evidently felt he had done his duty by marrying and providing a means of ensuring the succession in due course, and for the sake of peace and quiet he was prepared to leave her to her own devices.

Early that summer he went to war, leaving behind a young wife who was increasingly homesick and expecting a child. As she fondly imagined that any son of hers might inherit the thrones of Hanover and England one day, particularly if both her brothers remained unmarried, she did not want her confinement to take place on foreign soil – in other words, outside England. When she divulged her intentions to her husband he was aghast, warning her that this would create a most unfavourable impression on his people. Yet she was not to be dissuaded and, swearing her attendants to secrecy, she planned a journey back to England. By the beginning of June she was comfortably installed in her old home at Kensington Palace. Almost at once she realized how much she had missed the place, and threw herself happily into taking part in functions at her father's court, attending Handel's concerts, and quarrelling with her elder brother.

Queen Caroline was delighted at her daughter's return, but King George made no attempt to conceal his irritation. At first her husband treated this aberration with indulgence, but presently he sent one of his gentlemen to inform her that he would be at The Hague in two weeks' time to meet her. Tearfully she prepared for the journey to Harwich and thence to Holland, but on her arrival at Colchester she was handed a letter saying that her husband would be unable to meet her as planned. This was a perfect excuse for her to return to Kensington. A few more weeks of increasingly heated communication between her, her husband and her father, and an ultimatum led to her return to Holland by the end of the year.

The following spring, her *accoucheur* had to break the news to her that she was not with child after all. Miserable and homesick, she talked hopefully of returning to England again for the summer. However, her protracted stay the previous year had put everyone else on their mettle against such an eventuality. Even Queen Caroline, more ready than most to find excuses for the eldest daughter whom she missed greatly, warned her that she was now William's wife; 'God has given you skill and judgment, you are no longer a child.'[8]

With the sovereign's eldest daughter married, it became imperative to find the Prince of Wales a suitable wife. In 1735 he was aged twenty-eight, and the choices were narrowing. Charlotte

Amelia of Denmark, one of the few Protestant Princesses left, was recommended by the King, but further investigation revealed that she was a mentally retarded dwarf, and therefore quite unsuitable. Hardly anybody was left apart from Augusta of Saxe-Gotha, a shy and plain but otherwise satisfactory young woman. Betrothal negotiations were concluded by April 1736 when the seventeen-year-old Princess arrived at Greenwich, still clutching her doll for comfort.

Augusta had led a very sheltered life, and little thought had been given to her education. Her mother had assumed that as the Hanoverians had been on the British throne for over twenty years, everybody in England would be speaking German by now. As a result she had learned no English, and knew very little French. However, she made a pleasing impression on everyone with her quiet and modest good sense. She was probably too overawed to do anything else. The Prince of Wales was delighted with her, and for all his faults he remembered his manners, obviously to try to compensate for the lack of notice which everyone else had taken of her. He met her at Greenwich, took her up the Thames in his barge to the strains of musical accompaniment, supped and dined with her in public, and did not leave her until 2 o'clock the next morning. When she was introduced to her future parents-in-law she sank humbly to their feet, thus making an excellent first impression.

The wedding ceremony was held at the private chapel at St James's by the Bishop of London at 9 in the evening. A salute was fired in the park outside as the hands of the couple were joined at the altar, to announce the news to the people. While the marriage did nothing to ease the immediate tension between the Prince and his parents, the Princess made a good impression on everyone, and nobody had a word to say against her.

This pleasant state of affairs did not last long. Shortly after the wedding the King visited Hanover, leaving behind strict instructions that the Prince and Princess of Wales should not dine in public nor attempt any 'progress' through the country. As usual Queen Caroline was appointed Regent in the King's absence, and the Prince was bitter at not being granted any share of the responsibility which he felt was his by right as the future sovereign.

He seemed determined to put his wife up to various discourtesies in order to tease his mother. Against her better judgment she invited them to dine once or twice a week, as well as to music and cards in the evening at Hampton Court. The Princess came to these latter functions, but not the Prince, though he was obliged to come to dinner. Such meals were rather unpleasant for all concerned. The Queen found her daughter-in-law extremely dull, and complained of her son's silly jokes. An afternoon with them, she complained afterwards, made her feel as tired as though she had carried them around the garden on her back.

When they all attended divine service in the chapel at Kensington Palace, the Princess of Wales always deliberately entered late, and had to squeeze past the Queen, until the latter could not put up with it any more and ordered her daughter-in-law's chamberlain to ensure that, if the Princess was unable to arrive on time, she must enter the chapel through another door. This was not good enough for the Prince, who told his wife that if she found the Queen had arrived at chapel first, she should not enter at all but return to the palace. Such petty behaviour only widened the breach between the Queen and her son, but as she knew he was always to blame, she was wise enough not to hold her daughter-in-law responsible. The young woman might be dull and lacking in personality, but she was harmless and evidently free of malice. 'Poor creature!' the Queen would exclaim; 'were she to spit in my face, I should only pity her for being under such a fool's direction, and wipe it off.'[9]

The regency was a trying one for Queen Caroline in other ways. In Edinburgh two smugglers were sentenced to be hanged, and after one had been executed crowds surrounded the hangman and pelted the guards with stones. The other prisoner escaped and on the orders of Captain Porteous, commander of the town guard, troops fired on the crowd, killing some and wounding many more. Porteous and his soldiers escaped; he had long been notorious for his violent methods of quelling crowds, and the magistrates sided with the people and ordered his arrest on a charge of murder. He was tried, found guilty and sentenced to death. Believing that rough justice had been done, the gentry of Edinburgh forwarded a signed petition to Queen Caroline asking for clemency. She requested a reprieve for six weeks to give time to consider whether a royal pardon would be appropriate. The angry Edinburgh mob stormed the prison, dragged him from his cell and hanged him before troops could come to his rescue. Infuriated at this usurpation of authority, the Queen's patience was exhausted. Rather than submit to such an insult, she threatened to the council that she would make Scotland a hunting-ground, to which the Duke of Argyll answered diplomatically that he would take leave of Her Majesty, 'and go down to my own country to get my hounds ready'.[10] It was felt that the people of Edinburgh should be severely punished. Scottish peers in the House of Lords came to the defence of their countrymen, and a nominal fine was levied on the city, while the Provost of Edinburgh was disqualified from holding office again.

It was a difficult Christmas that year for Queen Caroline. The King had stayed in Hanover longer than usual, and she feared that the attraction of his new mistress, Baroness Amelia von Walmoden, was responsible – and her pride was correspondingly wounded. Her letters to him accordingly became shorter, the usual four dozen pages being replaced by a perfunctory seven or eight. Friends looked on her injured pride and indifference with concern, fearing that any attempt to reproach the King would arouse his anger, and her power over him would lessen. Walpole was sanguine enough to understand that the King's respect for his consort's judgment and ability was too deeply ingrained, but not everybody else was so confident.

In December the Princess of Orange gave birth to a stillborn daughter, and her own life hung in the balance for some time. The Queen wrote to tell her 'how I have suffered and my joy at receiving you back from God, whom I thank with all my soul. I have you and that is enough. May He grant you renewed strength and make you a happy mother of a family.'[11] The King was nearby at Helvoetsluys, but even when told of his eldest daughter's dangerous condition he refrained from making the short journey necessary to see her. To make matters worse for the Queen he was prevented from returning to England on time by severe weather at sea, and when he ordered the captain to set sail regardless their ship ran into such a heavy storm that word reached St James's that the vessel had been lost at sea with all hands and passengers. After eight months' absence he returned to England in January 1737, shaken but glad to be alive.

That spring the news for which the family had waited so long was confirmed. The Princess of Wales was *enceinte*, but not until June did the Prince inform his mother that a child would be born to them and that the confinement was expected in October. She duly congratulated them, but on putting some searching questions to her daughter-in-law she was greeted with a persistent 'I don't know.' At once her suspicions were aroused, and she wondered whether a spurious child was going to be foisted on them. Her son had hinted the previous summer that his wife was expecting, but nothing ever came of it, and she wondered whether he was capable of begetting a child.

The Prince of Wales intended the confinement to take place in London, while his parents stipulated that the Princess should remain at Hampton Court, so they could witness the event and satisfy themselves that the child was genuinely hers. In July the King, Queen and prospective parents all moved to Hampton Court and dined together in public as normal. By the time the King and Queen retired to bed after their regular game of cards, the Princess had gone into labour. The Prince had decided that nothing would prevent the child from being born at St James's, away from the parental eye, maybe out of sheer obstinacy and a refusal to be ordered about, maybe as he had feared that they might try to do away with the child. Though it was unlikely that they would have stooped to such depths, apparently the Princess of Wales also shared his paranoia, alarmed at their obvious preference for the Duke of Cumberland to her husband. They set out and, though she moaned in agony, begging for them to return to Hampton Court, he pressed on and they reached St James's about 10 p.m., and she was carried upstairs to bed, shrieking with pain. Within an hour she had given birth to a daughter, with only two Lords of the Council present as witnesses.

Some three hours later the King and Queen were woken with the news that their daughter-in-law was in labour. Once they had realized that they had been outwitted they were furious. Assembling a party including Lord Hervey, their daughters

Amelia and Caroline, and a few lords-in-waiting, they went to St James's. Queen Caroline softened as soon as she laid eyes on her granddaughter, but all of them treated the Prince with coldness. A few days later the King and Queen accepted the invitation, which they considered theirs by right, to become godparents to the infant, named Augusta after her mother. Afterwards the King decided that the time had come to teach his son a lesson. Following consultation with Lord Hervey and Walpole, he charged him with concealing all knowledge of the pregnancy until within a month of the baby's birth, and with having exposed the Princess and her child to great peril by moving them precipitately. The Prince would no longer reside in the King's palace, until he manifested a just sense of 'duty and submission', and was ordered to leave St James's Palace as soon as it could be done without causing inconvenience to the Princess.

This marked the nadir of the Prince's relations with his parents. The King declared that his son must be a changeling, while the Queen told Hervey that her son was 'the greatest ass, and the greatest liar, and the greatest canaille, and the greatest beast, in the whole world, and I most heartily wish he was out of it'.[12] The King bore no ill-feeling towards his daughter-in-law, who would undoubtedly suffer from any punishment of her husband. She wrote to him expressing her regret for what had happened, and to offer her services as mediator in the quarrel. He replied how sorry he was that she should have suffered on account of her husband's folly, and that only by his own actions could the Prince seek forgiveness. Three days later the Princess wrote to the Queen, explaining the 'facts' about the so-called concealment of her condition. Her doctors and the midwife had assured her that she would not be brought to bed until mid-September, and when the labour pains began she thought she was suffering from colic. It grieved her greatly that her husband's conduct was so misunderstood by his mother and father. They were convinced that she was only writing at her husband's instigation, and they refused to accept or believe her explanations.

By the late summer of 1737 Queen Caroline was in poor health. A difficult year had taken its toll, and she had long kept secret from everyone except her husband the umbilical rupture resulting from the difficult birth of her last child. Ever since his accession to the throne she had fought against gout and physical weakness. In August she was so ill that rumours of her sudden death swept London, and the shops began withdrawing their bright clothes, substituting black dresses for mourning until they were reassured of the false alarm. Though she recovered sufficiently to take part in a walkabout with the King at Hampton Court, she was not well enough to attend the christening of her granddaughter. In accordance with their normal routine she and the King left Hampton Court late in October and celebrated the King's birthday at St James's on the 30th.

One morning the following week she was seized with violent internal pains, and retired to bed, getting up that afternoon for a Drawing-Room which the King had offered to postpone. By the end she could barely stand, but assured the King that she was only suffering from a temporary indisposition. He spent the evening playing cards, and on his return he was upset to find her so ill. In the next morning the fever subsided and the doctors thought she was better; but she knew otherwise. Commiserating with her daughter Caroline, a chronic invalid suffering from severe rheumatic pains, she tried to comfort her with the certainty that 'we shall soon meet again in another place'. At her request the King held his usual Drawing-Room, and Amelia took her mother's place. Towards evening the Queen worsened, and cried aloud to Caroline, 'I have an ill which nobody knows of.'[13]

The next day it was impossible to conceal the severity of her illness. At Kew the disgraced Prince of Wales enquired whether he might come and see her. The King insisted that 'the rascal' should not be allowed to 'come and act any of his silly plays here . . . he wants to come and insult his poor dying mother, but she shall not see him'.[14] That afternoon the Queen asked whether her son had wanted to visit. When the King told her what had happened she accepted his decision, saying she had no wish to see the Prince again. Too weary to argue, she sent a message of forgiveness to her son through Walpole, saying she would have seen him with pleasure but such an interview would have embarrassed the King.

Her worsening condition the next day did not prevent her from attempting to conceal the true cause of her illness and the King begged her to let him tell Dr Ranby about the rupture, but she denied it. Nevertheless he sent for Ranby, who examined her and said he must operate. No longer able to keep her secret, the Queen turned her face to the wall, and wept for the first and last time. Two more surgeons were summoned to assist with the operation, but years of reticence and neglect had done their work, and it was too late for effective treatment.

Next day the wound was mortifying and increasingly painful. Dr Ranby declared that she could not survive for long, and she sent for her husband and children (except for the Prince of Wales), asking them not to leave her until she died. To Caroline she commended the care of the younger children, entreating her not to let the 'vivacity' of Louisa 'draw her into any inconveniences, and to do what she could to support the meek and mild disposition of Princess Mary'.[15] She told Louisa, at thirteen the youngest, to 'remember I die by being giddy and obstinate, in having kept my disorder a secret.'[16] To the Duke of Cumberland she asked that he should be a support to his father at all times, and try to make up for the vexations caused him by his elder brother.

To her husband she gave the ruby ring he had placed on her finger at the Coronation, and said that he must marry again. Between sobs, he promised her, '*Non, j'aurais des maîtresses!*' '*Ah, mon Dieu! Cela n'empêche pas*,'[17] she sighed. When Walpole returned from his wife's funeral at Houghton, Norfolk, to be warned of the severity of the Queen's condition, she told him she had nothing to say to him, 'but to recommend the King, my children, and the kingdom to your care'.[18]

For two days she appeared to hold her own, and the physicians hoped that she might recover after all. On the Thursday a change for the worse took place and she suffered much pain, but she bore it all without complaint. To his daughters, Hervey, and the physicians and surgeons, the King spoke repeatedly of how she was the most wonderful wife man ever had, while he continued to scold her. If she kept on constantly shifting around, he would ask how the devil could she expect to sleep if she would never lie still. When she lay still, he complained that she was staring like a calf that had just had its throat cut. If he had bullied her into eating and she threw it up immediately afterwards, he would ask her roughly why she had called for a thing if she did not want it; if she did like it, why give it away? His constant praise of the Queen's fortitude was mixed with that of his own, and soon Amelia was 'sick to death of hearing of his great courage'.

On the morning of 20 November she asked one of her physicians how long she was likely to last, and he assured her she would soon be at rest. She took her leave of the King and thanked him for all his goodness to her. That night he was sleeping fitfully at the foot of the bed, and Amelia lay in a couch-bed in the corner. The death-rattle in her throat began, and she begged them to open the window. 'Pray,' she ordered with her dying breath, and Amelia began to read some prayers. Caroline held a looking-glass to her lips, but no sign of moisture appeared. The King knelt down and kissed the face and hands of his wife several times, before their daughters led him away to their apartments.

He spoke incessantly about her for several days, weeping the whole time. One morning on waking he sent for Baron Borgman, who had a portrait of the Queen which she had given him, reputed to be a better likeness than any in his own possession. He asked that it be placed on the chair at the foot of his bed, and that he then be left alone until he rang the bell. Two hours later the bell rang and the Baron returned. 'Take the picture away,' the King said, calm and dry-eyed. 'I never yet saw a woman worthy to buckle her shoe.'[19]

With the death of Queen Caroline the shy and retiring Augusta, Princess of Wales, became first lady of the land. She had never attempted to influence her husband or father-in-law, but one of her sisters-in-law was less scrupulous. From Holland the Princess of Orange wanted to visit England for her mother's funeral, but her sisters were so alarmed at the effect her presence might have on the King that they begged Prince William to dissuade her from coming. While he managed to delay her long enough for her not to attend the obsequies, she was so determined to try to exert some influence over her father that she came to London on the pretext that a stay in England would benefit her health. Never one to be fooled by his imperious eldest daughter, the King rejected her offers of condolence and advice so fiercely that she returned without spending a second night on British soil.

Meanwhile the Princess of Wales, her husband and their infant daughter were still at Kew, barred from the royal palaces, as the King had been as Prince of Wales twenty years earlier, and as a city residence Frederick rented Norfolk House, in St James's Square, from the Duke of Norfolk. By Christmas 1737 the Princess was expecting a second child, and on 4 June 1738, two months prematurely, she gave birth to a son who was baptized privately that evening lest he failed to survive. Christened George William Frederick, he was placed in the care of a wet-nurse, Mary Smith, who proved to be his saviour. He lived to be eighty-one.

Neither the Prince nor Princess of Wales was unduly troubled by the King's hostility. A formal reconciliation of sorts between father and son, done largely for show, did nothing to change relations between them. Husband and wife became popular by default, for although there was some sympathy for the King he was tolerated rather than popular. While Frederick had occasional mistresses, his wife accepted the situation without complaining. They were both seen regularly at the opera in London, and taking the waters at Bath. They enjoyed taking part in private theatricals, and spent much time together, absorbed in their shared gardening and artistic interests, especially the Prince's involvement in cataloguing his paintings and sculptures. The upbringing and education of their growing family also took much of their attention. A second son, Edward, later Duke of York and Albany and Earl of Ulster, was born in March 1739, followed by a second daughter, Elizabeth Caroline, in December 1740. Four more children followed, namely William, later Duke of Gloucester and Edinburgh and Earl of Connaught, in November 1743; Henry, later Duke of Cumberland and Strathearn and Earl of Dublin, in October 1745; Louisa in March 1749; and Frederick, destined to die at the age of fifteen, in May 1750.

By the new year of 1751 the Princess was expecting a ninth child, the one her husband would not live to see. One wet spring day he was working in his garden at Kew, got himself soaked to the skin and caught a cold which turned to pleurisy. On the evening of 20 March he had a severe fit of coughing, called out, '*Je sens la mort*', and fell back dead. He was aged forty-four.

Often derided as stupid and a characterless nonentity, the Princess of Wales had matured fast since the days when the sheltered, ill-at-ease girl barely out of the nursery had been brought to England to meet and marry a prince of whom she had known nothing. She knew that many of her husband's faults had arisen from being driven into foolishness by his parents' ostracism. Grief-stricken as she was at the loss of a husband and father who had given her nearly fourteen years of happy family life, she knew she owed it to his memory and to the future of their children to do everything within her power to achieve a better relationship with the irascible, lonely old King. Above all it would not do for the fatherless twelve-year-old George, now first in line to the throne, to look on his grandfather as an enemy.

On the day after the Prince of Wales's death, she wrote tactfully to the King in French to assure him that her overwhelming sorrow 'does not make me the less sensible of the great goodness of Your Majesty', and she commended herself and her children to his 'paternal love and royal protection'.[20] He sent her a kindly message by return, and came to visit her at Leicester House. While he refused to behave like a hypocrite and put on an extravagant display of grief for the son whom he had cordially disliked, he had nothing but sympathy for his son's wife, whom he considered had had to suffer much for her husband's wilful and reckless behaviour.

Later that month the King recommended to Parliament the appointment of the Princess of Wales as Regent and guardian of her son. While he personally would have preferred to nominate the Duke of Cumberland, he knew there was strong feeling against the Duke and that Parliament would have opposed such a measure. It was decided that the Princess would be assisted by a council composed of Cumberland, the only Prince of the blood who was of age, the great officers of state at the time of the King's death, and four others whom he would personally name. Members of the council could be removed only by consent of a majority in the council, or an address by both Houses of Parliament, and certain acts of sovereignty (the dissolution of

Parliament, the creation of peers, and the appointment of judges) could be exercised only with the advice of the council. The Princess accepted this arrangement, satisfied that as surviving parent of the next King she, and not the brother-in-law whom she had feared since her marriage, would be Regent. To argue with the King and his ministers, she knew, would benefit neither herself nor her son, and only strengthen the Duke's case.

The King was sympathetic to her case for being made Regent. While honest enough to admit that as a father, he was naturally inclined to prefer the Duke of Cumberland, he liked and respected his daughter-in-law, notwithstanding her lack of political experience. This would not matter as a council, he told his ministers, would be there to assist her, particularly where cases of treason were concerned; women, he said, were 'apt to pardon'; he himself was inclined to mercy, and it would be better if she had 'somebody to refuse for her'.[21]

Nearly four months after her husband's death, on 11 July 1751, the Dowager Princess of Wales gave birth to a ninth child, a daughter. To please the King she named the child Caroline, after the late Queen, and Matilda, in honour of the Queens of the Angevin monarchy.

The birth of this Princess was the one happy event in what was otherwise a year of one mortality after another. In October the King's eldest daughter Anne, Princess of Orange, who had inherited much of her father's obstinacy and pomposity, was left a widow when her husband died of a stroke. King George II wrote to her with more affection and sympathy than he had shown her for many years, begging her not to doubt 'the very sincere share I have in your great affliction', and assuring her she would always find in him 'a father who will cherish you tenderly'.[22] Even so, she was hard-headed enough to remember the British government's policy which she firmly believed had been responsible for Holland's humiliation in recent years, and when the envoy Earl Holderness arrived from England to express his condolences in person he was granted a cold reception.

In December Queen Louisa of Denmark, the youngest and prettiest of the King's daughters, who had inherited much of her mother's charm and strength of personality, suddenly passed

away. Married in 1743 to Crown Prince Frederick of Denmark,
who ascended the throne as King Frederick V three years later,
she had stoically endured an unhappy marriage while too proud to
admit it. At the time of her marriage she had declared that, if she
should become unhappy, her family would never know. In eight
years of marriage she gave birth to two sons and three daughters.
Since the seventh month of her first pregnancy she had suffered
from a strangulated hernia, the agony which her mother had
concealed for so many years, and her first son died in infancy. The
second son, born in 1749 and named Christian (like the elder
brother who died before his birth), was an imbecile who
nevertheless succeeded to the throne in due course and went on
to contract what would prove to be a disastrous marriage with one
of his English cousins. Like his sisters, Prince Christian was
deprived of his mother at an early age. She was carrying a sixth
child when complications ensued, the result of the trouble which
she had bravely neglected in spite of her mother's death-bed
warning, and died aged twenty-seven.

As the King remarked sadly, it was 'a fatal year for my family'.
In a rare moment of sentimentality, he confessed that he did not
love his children when they were young; 'I hated to have them
running into my room; but now I love them as well as most
fathers.'[23]

The Dowager Princess of Wales was not a strong personality. She
had been a model wife in making herself totally subservient to her
husband, accepting unquestioningly his opinions and attitudes,
even his occasional infidelities, as well as his view that a husband
should never talk to his wife of politics. One need look no further,
he told her, than his own father the King, who was the laughing-
stock of his ministers for having allowed his Queen to govern him.
After her husband's death she devoted herself entirely to the care
and upbringing of their children. Her relationship with his family
was governed solely by his opinions; he had feared his father and
been deeply suspicious of his favoured younger brother, and out
of respect for his memory she needed no persuading to adopt his
views faithfully. She made it clear to his friends that her husband's
politics were to be buried with him, and she burnt his private

papers. Never having concerned herself with politics during his lifetime, she had no intention of starting now. Her only care was for her children and particularly for the new heir apparent, who was made Prince of Wales in April.

As a result the honeymoon period between the King and his daughter-in-law did not last long. By the end of 1752 she was complaining to George Bubb Dodington, one of her late husband's confidants, that she was not deceived by her father-in-law's civility or his intention to keep them short of money. Since he had profited by £30,000 per annum by his son's death, why was he putting 'their money into his pocket'? Should the innocent suffer, she asked Dodington, angered by his leaving his son's 'inconsiderable' debts unpaid. The rest of her in-laws were no better, she insisted; the Duke of Cumberland, 'her great, great fat friend', and his sister Princess Amelia, were doing her 'all imaginable mischief'.[24] As the King had always been mean about money, he told her, her best course would be to take no notice of it. In fact money still owing to servants for wages, and to tradesmen for goods supplied, was paid by the exchequer in due course, but some of the Prince of Wales's debts had been incurred through his political ventures and the King could hardly have expected to meet these as well.

The Prince of Wales had taken a lease of Leicester House, Leicester Square, in 1743, and shortly before his death he settled Princes George and Edward and their household next door in Savile House. His widow continued to live at Leicester House with her younger children, and her elder sons next door. Savile House remained the town house of George, Prince of Wales, until his accession to the throne, and in the country he lived near her at Richmond Lodge, Kew. When the King was away in Hanover he assisted his mother at her weekly Drawing-Rooms.

As an adolescent George was inclined to be shy and backward. Lady Louisa Stuart, daughter of the Earl of Bute, thought that Edward had always been the favourite son, praised and petted at the expense of his elder brother. Yet the Dowager Princess of Wales was dissatisfied with the progress both were making in their education; in October 1752 she wished that George was 'a little more forward and less childish at his age', and in February 1753, after Earl Harcourt had resigned as his governor to be replaced by Lord Waldegrave, she told Dodington that she was not satisfied that either George or Edward had 'much improved' since their father's death.[25]

Worries about her sons' development were not the only anxiety the Princess had to face. Whenever King George II visited Hanover, after the death of Queen Caroline, he always left a Council of Regency to exercise the authority of the Crown during his absence. In April 1755 he set out for Hanover again, to make arrangements for its defence. His relations with Prussia, an ally of France, were uncertain, and in the event of an Anglo-French war he feared for the safety of his Electorate. Although the council had not included any other members of the royal family, with war and the threat of invasion imminent, it would have been impossible to exclude the Duke of Cumberland, Captain-General of the army. As the Prince of Wales was still short of his majority, the Princess was anxious lest the elderly King, now aged seventy-one, should die in Hanover as his father had done. By the Regency Act of 1751 she would become Regent, but if the King died abroad, how could she be sure that the Duke would step down and hand his authority over to her? With the nation on the verge of war, Parliament was more likely to choose him than her. As he was president of the Regency Council she could not trust him not to repeal the Act, put himself forward as his nephew's Regent, and perhaps even, following in the footsteps of King Richard III, remove his nephew from the succession altogether.

Fortunately for her peace of mind, the King returned safely in the autumn of 1755, and there was no war. He returned with the intention of arranging a betrothal between Princess Sophia of Brunswick-Wolfenbüttel, eldest daughter of the reigning Duke, Charles I, and his grandson George. However, the Princess of Wales considered that her immature eldest son was too young to think of marriage. She also felt that Sophia was a determined young woman under whose spell he would surely fall, and any influence she had over him would soon be destroyed. In addition, any marriage alliance planned by her father-in-law would automatically be suspect in her eyes. She readily believed that he was endeavouring to advance his own private interests in Hanover, and at the same time she had hopes of promoting the claims of her own flesh and blood, perhaps suggesting her fourteen-year-old niece Frederica Louise, only surviving daughter of her eldest brother Frederick, reigning Duke of Saxe-Gotha, as a suitable bride for her son when the time came. In the end, all marriage negotiations were placed on hold as England became preoccupied with the Seven Years War.

In widowhood the Dowager Princess had one dependable ally, the Earl of Bute. Appointed a lord of the bedchamber by the Prince of Wales on his marriage, he remained in the household after his master's death, being appointed groom of the stole. After her husband's death she was lonely in a country of which she knew little, having led a comparatively sheltered married life, and Bute was of inestimable value in the selfless moral support he gave her. A faithful servant, well educated, happily married, good-looking, he was the one contemporary of the Dowager Princess who seemed able to put her at ease. Her natural reserve and stiffness vanished whenever he was around, observers noticed, and in her voice was heard 'a mellowness in her German accent', according to Horace Walpole.

Even before the death of the Prince of Wales, there were rumours about their 'intimacy'. That they were intimate in the sense of mutually trusting friends there was no doubt; but despite the excited imaginations of contemporaries, there is no evidence that they committed adultery. Yet even one or two members of the household did not shrink from taunting her to her face. When scolded by her mistress for immodesty Elizabeth Chudleigh, one of Augusta's maids of honour, retorted, '*Votre Altesse Royale sait que chacune a son But.*'[26] In their efforts to silence scandalous gossip, they arranged that he should visit her secretly by the back stairs, a precaution which in the eyes of some only added to the probability that their liaison was not free of scandal.

It only took the assertions of one or two gossips that they were lovers for the charge to stick and blacken her name for posterity. Early in the next reign satirical prints and newspapers, recalling the adulterous affair of King Edward II's wife and her lover, portrayed them as a reincarnation of Queen Isabella and Roger Mortimer.[27] Bute undertook charge of Prince George's education, and the stern moral lessons he inculcated in his pupil were enough to dispel any impression that – unless he was an incorrigible hypocrite as well as the soul of discretion – there was any way that he and his employer could ever have had an illicit relationship.

By the time the Dowager Princess of Wales celebrated the reaching of majority of her eldest son, in June 1759, it must have seemed that the King was almost indestructible. At the age of seventy-five he was deaf and almost blind, and had outlived most of his generation as well as several of the next. In June 1757 he had lost his sister Sophia Dorothea, Dowager Queen of Prussia and widow of King Frederick William I. Whatever her faults she had been a devoted mother, and her eldest son, who now reigned as Frederick II ('the Great'), was brokenhearted, as he wrote to his elder sister Wilhelmina that 'all the other losses in this world may be redressed, but those occasioned by death are beyond remedy'.[28] In her old age she had become peevish and tedious, but he only remembered the times when she had protected him against his father's rages, and seemed such a glamorous and enlightened person. She had left a wish not to be buried with her husband.

At the end of 1757 another daughter, the hypochondriac Caroline, had passed away at the age of forty-four, gently but firmly declining to see any member of her family. Having been the constant companion of her mother, she suffered more than anyone else by the Queen's death, and gradually became a complete invalid. The family had regarded her as an irredeemable hypochondriac for so long that Amelia, writing to Anne in Holland, mentioned that Caroline was better, 'though pray don't mention it to her, for she only allows of not being worse'.[29] Generous to a fault, she gave much to charities, and after Lord Hervey's death she ensured that none of his children would ever want for anything. Increasingly reclusive in her last years, she simply lost the will to live. Towards the end she seemed to take comfort in the knowledge that release would not be long in coming, telling her servants, 'I feared I should not have died of this!'[30]

Less mourned was the widowed Princess of Orange, whose health was failing. The only one of the princesses to take after their mother in her artistic and intellectual interests as well as her political intelligence and capacity for hard work, she lacked Queen Caroline's charm and ability to win friends or champions where they were needed. She had paid conscientious attention to her duties as ruler after her husband's death, doing more work in a day than her chronically misshapen husband could in fourteen, according to William Bentinck, a member of the Dutch court since her marriage. Nevertheless arrogance made her her own worst enemy; 'day by day her personal credit and the love of the people is lost.'[31] She succumbed to dropsy in January 1759.

Of the daughters of King George II and Queen Caroline, only Mary, who had married Prince Frederick of Hesse-Cassel in 1740, and the spinster Amelia, were destined to outlive their father. After the birth of the youngest of three sons, Frederick, in 1747, Prince Frederick of Hesse-Cassel walked out on his wife and family. After a long silence, she received a letter from him to say that, prior to their marriage, he had been greatly attached to a well-born Catholic lady and had asked her to marry him, but she rejected him as he was a Protestant, and begged him to espouse the Catholic faith. Fearing the reaction of his subjects, he held out for a long time. When he informed her a little while later that he was about to marry a daughter of King George II of England, and tried to visit her to explain, she shut the door in his face and forbade him to come near her house again. However, he persuaded her to come and visit him if he should fall ill and be about to die, and promised that he would do the same for her.

Shortly before the birth of his third son he was informed that she was dying. On her death-bed she asked him to become a Catholic, 'that their Souls might be united in Heaven'. As he did not have the heart to refuse, he wrote to his wife. A furious King George II ordered his daughter to return to England, and never to live with her husband again. She replied that 'it was Her Duty to remain in the situation in which it had pleased God to place Her; but that she would make her *own terms* for the sake of her sons, as they were brought up Protestant'.[32]

Amelia was content to remain a spinster to the end of her days. She acted as the hostess of her brother the Duke of Cumberland whenever he was in England at his home, St James's, and later at

Cumberland Lodge. When noblemen sent out invitations for parties at their country houses, it was always understood that brother and sister should be invited together. When he was on military service abroad she followed his campaigns with interest, and she worried about him whenever he was at the front. It must have been a source of some relief that his premature ill-health, partly attributed to wounds sustained while fighting at the battle of Dettingen in 1743, gradually curtailed his military career.

In Holland Anne had constantly fretted about the plight of her spinster sisters at home, but any tentative moves towards matchmaking cut no ice. 'I sometimes believe you think that unmarried women have no places in heaven,' Amelia wrote to her with some asperity, 'for you think nobody can have the least happiness without being tied from morning to night to a creature which may tire one's life out.'[33]

Of the Dowager Princess of Wales's four daughters, the second and third were sickly infants who never seemed likely to reach maturity. Elizabeth, Horace Walpole wrote, had a figure that was 'so very unfortunate, that it would have been difficult for her to be happy, but her parts and application were extraordinary'. By the age of eight she had not been taught to read as her health was so poor, but she gave promise of being an artistic child with a lively mind. She particularly enjoyed participating in theatrical performances, even though she was so frail she could not stand upright unaided but had to lean against the side-scene, and learned parts in plays simply by hearing her brothers and sisters rehearsing them. 'She went to her father and mother, and begged she might act. They put her off as gently as they could – she desired leave to repeat her part, and when she did, it was with so much sense, that there was no denying her.'[34] She died of an inflammation of the bowels at the age of eighteen in September 1759, and thereafter Louisa rapidly became an invalid.

The eldest, Augusta, who had made her entry into the world in such unpropitious circumstances, was ironically the only one who would live to a reasonable age. Sharp-witted, bold and argumentative, she was also plump and put on weight without any effort, but her mother's admonitions that she must think of her figure and eat more sparingly had no effect.

The youngest, Caroline Matilda, was the only really attractive one of the family. With her golden hair, large blue eyes and natural gaiety and charm of manner, she put all her sisters in the shade. Like Elizabeth she took to learning naturally, and proved good at memorizing speeches, even whole scenes, from the plays of Shakespeare and Addison. Like her brothers and sisters, she spoke French and English well, and later learnt Italian.

On 25 October 1760, three weeks short of his seventy-seventh birthday, King George II collapsed at Kensington Palace, and as he lay dying, the footmen summoned Amelia. Unwell herself at the time, she was almost deaf and her eyesight was failing. When she entered the chamber she thought her father was speaking to her, and her servants had difficulty in making her understand that she was too late to do anything. At length she realized what had happened, promptly despatched messengers to fetch the doctors, and wrote to the young nephew of twenty-two who had until then been Prince of Wales and was now King George III.

FOUR
'Easy, civil, and not disconcerted'

AUGUSTA, PRINCESS OF WALES; QUEEN CHARLOTTE

If Augusta, Dowager Princess of Wales, had ever nursed ambitions to become the power behind the throne, the accession in October 1760 of her diffident eldest son as King George III, with his sheltered upbringing, would have smoothed her path. Some thought she and her favourite, the Earl of Bute, were ready to take on this role without scruple, but it is doubtful whether she ever really wanted to wield any such influence. While she may have been somewhat at the mercy of Bute, there is nothing to suggest that, left to herself, she had any political designs.

There was, however, one matter of pressing importance which united Parliament, people and the Dowager Princess of Wales; His Majesty should find himself a wife and Queen as soon as possible. In youth he had fallen for a Quakeress, Hannah Lightfoot, and was said to have secretly married her. He was also thought to be infatuated with Lady Sarah Lennox, sister of the Duke of Richmond and a great-granddaughter of King Charles II, but she was related by marriage to the ambitious parliamentarian Henry Fox, a personal enemy of Lord Bute, and the Dowager Princess did not want her son to marry anyone who might set him against her dearest friend. A young Protestant bride was the answer, and she still tried to canvass the claims of her niece Frederica of Saxe-Gotha, though she was said to be too intellectual, too interested in philosophy, deformed and unable to bear children. As she died unmarried in 1776, aged thirty-five, any reservations on health grounds were probably justified.

A list of suitable names was drawn up. Most were rejected for one reason or another, mainly either *mésalliances*, age or reports of

95

character defects, and the last to be added, Princess Sophia Charlotte of Mecklenburg-Strelitz, was eventually chosen. Aged seventeen, she was the eighth child and second surviving daughter of Duke Charles of Mecklenburg-Strelitz, who had died in 1752. Of the ten children born to him and his wife Elizabeth Albertina, a princess of Saxe-Hildburghausen, three sons and a daughter had died in infancy. She and King George were third cousins, their mothers both being great-granddaughters of Ernest I, Duke of Saxe-Gotha. Well educated, particularly in history, botany and theology, she spoke French fluently, and most important of all she had no interest whatsoever in politics. Her family had led a frugal life in their small North German duchy, unkindly known by contemporary wags as 'Muckleberg Strawlitter'. Initial reports of her appearance were not flattering; she was said to be small, thin and dark, with a nose tilted upwards and a large mouth. The King told Bute that she was 'not in every particular as I could wish, but yet I am resolv'd to fix here'.[1]

On 8 July 1761 the betrothal of King George and Princess Charlotte was announced, and two ladies were sent from court to Mecklenburg-Strelitz with the honour of escorting her and her servants to England. On their nine-day crossing she hid her nervousness behind a friendly exterior, chattering cheerfully and playing English tunes on the harpsichord while the others suffered from seasickness. They landed at Harwich and continued their journey by road to St James's, arriving on 8 September, where she met her husband-to-be for the first time. Horace Walpole saw how nervous she was, watching her as 'she grew frightened and turned pale' when she saw the Palace. 'Her lips trembled as the coach stopped. But she jumped out with spirit, and has done nothing but with great humour and cheerfulness. She talks a great deal – is easy, civil, and not disconcerted.'[2] Her future lady-in-waiting, Mrs Papendiek, found much to say in her favour, admitting that though she was 'certainly not a beauty . . . her countenance was expressive and intelligent. She was not tall, but of a slight, rather pretty figure; her eyes bright and sparkling with good humour and vivacity, her mouth large, but filled with white and even teeth, and her hair really beautiful.'[3]

That same evening a few hours later she and King George were married at the Chapel Royal, St James's. She was still trembling nervously as the King's brothers, the Duke of York and Prince William, led her up the aisle, the Duke comforting her with a gentle 'Courage, Princess, courage!' After supper she played the harpsichord and sang while guests in the drawing-room awaited supper. She spoke a little French to them and German to the King before excusing herself on account of tiredness, retiring to a private supper with him, and then to bed. Two weeks later they were crowned at Westminster.

On the day of her arrival the King had warned his wife to 'never be alone with my mother: she is an artful woman and will try to govern you'.[4] Their first year of marriage was overshadowed by Augusta's efforts to dominate and crush any signs of independence in her daughter-in-law. King George was too much in awe of his mother to defy her and stand up for his wife, or to try to stop his unmarried sisters from mocking her for her lack of sophistication. Such lively spirits as this plain but eager-to-please young Princess had when she came to England were soon tempered by this cruel behaviour. While some found her a warm-hearted young woman of charm, intelligence, wit and sensitivity to people's feelings, others told a different story of a harsh, short-tempered and excessively strict Queen. Overruled, insulted, a stranger in her husband's kingdom, she soon learned to take refuge in defensive chilliness. It was not surprising that she became morose, embittered and unpleasant, not to say cruel, to those under her control, particularly her daughters whom she kept standing behind her chair until they fell asleep on their feet, in years to come.

She was discouraged from making friends among her husband's subjects; no English ladies were allowed to approach her without first obtaining permission from her German attendants. Later she would speak guardedly of her husband's strict manner on her arrival in England, which prevented her from becoming acquainted with people from the outside world. Aware that she had led a rather cloistered existence, she spoke without resentment, subjugating her own inclinations as all good wives should to her husband's wishes. Some thirty years later, she confided to Earl Harcourt that she still remained fearful of 'medling in Politics *which I abhor equal to Sin*'.[5] Another twenty years after that, when she did not have long to live, she recalled to Lady Harcourt, her lady of the bedchamber, that she was 'most truly sensible' of the King's strict manner at the time of her arrival in England, to prevent her from making acquaintances; 'for he always used to say that, in this country, it was difficult to know how to draw a line, on account of the politics of the country; and that there never could be kept up a society without party, which was always dangerous for any woman to take part in, but particularly so for the royal family'.[6]

While she was keen to assure Lady Harcourt that she knew her husband was right, and that she was deeply thankful for such an example, the general view was that he deliberately deprived his young wife of company and virtually kept her a prisoner, 'in order to prevent her from being corrupted by the poisons of the age'.[7] At St James's and at Richmond Lodge, their summer residence, she saw and mixed with few people other than ladies from the court, the wardrobe and bedchamber women who attended her, and Dr John Majendie, a canon of Windsor, who gave her lessons in English. In time she learned to speak the language with fluency, though with a pronounced German accent. She kept up her harpsichord-playing, and took singing lessons from Johann Christian Bach, son of the renowned composer. When the King was present they played piquet and backgammon together, and when he was away she busied herself with her needlework. Sometimes he read to her in the afternoon while she worked. Exercise, air and a light diet were important to them. The King ate mostly vegetables and a little meat, and drank wine sparingly, while the Queen preferred 'the plainest and simplest dish, and seldom eats of more than two things at a meal'. In matters of the wardrobe, it was noticed, 'while the nobility are eager to supply themselves with foreign trifles, her care is that nothing but what is English shall be provided for her wear'.[8]

She and the King were quick to ensure the succession. After eleven months of marriage, on 12 August 1762, a son and heir, George Augustus Frederick, was born. A second son, Frederick, followed one year later. In 1764 she had a miscarriage, but over the next eighteen years there were thirteen more children.

The Dowager Princess of Wales still had three unmarried daughters, Augusta, Louisa and Caroline Matilda, to care for. Shortly before his death, King George II had considered a match between his granddaughter Augusta and Charles, Hereditary Prince of Brunswick-Wolfenbüttel. The family was aggrieved that their daughters should have been passed over in favour of a daughter of the humble duchy of Mecklenburg-Strelitz when King George III sought a bride, particularly as their Princes were fighting in the Seven Years War as allies of England. In order to strengthen the alliance King George and his ministers felt obliged to reopen the marriage question, and after the war the proposal was ratified and a marriage contract was drawn up. Charles was accordingly betrothed to Augusta, and he arrived in England in January 1764 to be presented to the King, the Queen and the Dowager Princess of Wales. On 16 January the marriage took place in the council chamber at St James's Palace, and they left for Germany at the end of the month.

The Princess, reported Richard Spry, captain of her yacht, was a good sailor; she was 'surprizingly chearful notwithstanding the badness of the Weather, and never once shew'd the least apprehension of danger'.[9] The bride and her youngest sister Caroline Matilda took their leave of each other in tears, and the latter was told shortly afterwards that her own marriage would come next; she must be ready to leave England within the next two years. Augusta had an earthy sense of humour and always retained her sense of the ridiculous, a trait which might have been admirable but for her exalted birth, and one which she would in due course hand down to her notorious daughter with appalling results.

Her first impressions of Germany in a letter to King George III of February 1764 dealt in detail on the peculiar manner of the Germans she had met, including the brother-in-law of one of her husband's family who 'holds his glass between his legs, and a lady today [who] put her fan while she dines in the same place'.[10] Her readiness to make fun of the Germans, to whom she gave the impression that she regarded them as her inferiors despite her own German blood on both sides, did not endear her to the people of Brunswick. Over the years she remained homesick, and returned to England whenever she could, starting the following year when she accepted an invitation to become godmother to her nephew Prince William Henry, born in August 1765, the third of King George and Queen Charlotte's brood of fifteen.

By 1763, when she was still only twelve, Caroline Matilda's future had already been planned. King Frederick V of Denmark, who had remarried after the death of his beloved first wife Louisa, youngest daughter of King George II, was seeking a bride for his son and heir Christian. The younger Louisa had been chosen to follow in the footsteps of her namesake, her shortlived aunt, but King Frederick's envoy Count Bothmar, noting her frailty, saw that she too was not destined to live long or produce healthy children, so the more lively, pretty Caroline Matilda was considered instead. The King insisted that his youngest sister could not be married until after her fifteenth birthday, and even then she would be too young to go to a strange country. Determined not to let go of this prize, Bothmar pressed the case. Europe was still overshadowed by bitter rivalries engendered by the Seven Years War, and the King was persuaded that an Anglo-Danish marriage would be a valuable bastion against French influence and a reassurance of British power and influence in northern Germany and the Baltic area.

The Dowager Princess of Wales believed that her youngest daughter was fitted to be a queen, unlike the sickly Louisa. Questions were therefore raised about the marriage dowry and marriage treaties. Had they known anything about Prince Christian, it was unlikely that he would have agreed so readily. At the age of sixteen the imbecile Christian was badly brought up, debauched, probably venereally infected, too fond of drink, and displaying signs of mental derangement. However, the long-serving envoy Walter Titley had always been treated by King Frederick as a friend, and he can hardly have been unaware of these traits. If he was sacrificing the future happiness of an innocent British princess in order to advance his own career, it probably weighed no more than momentarily on his conscience.

There were parallels between the marriage of Caroline Matilda and that of her great-grandmother Sophia Dorothea of Celle, but at least the former was destined to be released from her sorrows at a mercifully early age. She and her sisters had no companions but each other and their ladies, as strictly chosen by their mother; she was even isolated from her older relatives, and forbidden to accompany her spinster aunt Amelia to Bath. Until her journey to Denmark she had never left London, except for visits to Windsor and Kew. When the kindly Amelia tried to console her by saying that soon she would be making longer and more interesting journeys, the sad reply was that 'surely it would be happier for me to stay where I am than to go so far for a Prince I have never seen'.[11]

On 10 January 1765 the betrothal was announced in Britain and Denmark, yet the Princess had never seen anybody outside the family until she sat for her wedding portrait to Joshua Reynolds. King Frederick V told Titley that he was delighted with the portrait, which hung in his son's dressing-room at Copenhagen, where the husband-to-be examined it repeatedly in great detail and with 'inexpressible pleasure'. King George III formally required parliamentary approval of the forthcoming union, to take place once they were of marriageable age, and was told that such a strengthening of the anti-French and Protestant cause would greatly please the nation. It was expected that the wedding would be within about two years.

Over the next few months Caroline Matilda received congratulations with a forced smile. She took no interest in the trousseau being prepared for her, and was regularly in tears. Her mother lectured her on the duties of royal personages, reminding her that she too had been despatched to a foreign country to marry a prince whom she had never met and saw only a day or so before their wedding ceremony. Did the Dowager Princess of Wales know anything about the idiot who was to become her son-in-law? At length the girl busied herself in working with local charities, visiting her mother's tenants, and gardening at Kew.

On 13 January 1766 King Frederick V died and Christian, aged sixteen, ascended the throne. The date of the marriage was therefore brought forward; Caroline Matilda's proxy wedding was arranged for 1 October, and her departure for Denmark fixed for the following day. The ceremony took place at Carlton House at 7 p.m., with her brother Prince Edward representing the bridegroom. As the ominous date drew closer, she became more miserable. She was still only a child of fifteen, but King George III and his mother assumed that she would settle down after a period of homesickness to become a contented, or at least dutiful, wife and mother. She was warned that Queen Consorts of Denmark were not permitted any attendants from abroad in their entourage; when she reached the borders of Denmark she would have to part with all her ladies, and be surrounded by strangers, who might not even speak the same language as she. She had learnt German in childhood, though it had not been thought necessary for her to learn Danish.

Privately the King was uneasy about the marriage, partly on grounds of his sister's extreme youth, and partly as he had his doubts about their cousin the King of Denmark, though it was probable that some of the less palatable truths about his fellow-sovereign had been carefully withheld from him. On the eve of her departure he wrote to her, addressing her in the third person: 'I think I can no way so essentially show Caroline my real affection for her than in giving her a few hints that may perhaps be a means of preserving her from the precipices into which she may also very probably fall.' She should take care, he went on, to avoid meddling in politics, and show all due respect to her husband's mother and to his grandmother Juliana Maria.[12]

Her greatest grief on leaving England was the parting with Louisa, who was gradually succumbing to tuberculosis. Since Augusta's marriage they had become much closer, and Caroline Matilda must have envied her sister who was allowed to stay in England, and realized that they would never meet again. Her journey across the North Sea was prolonged by storms, and the yacht did not reach Rotterdam until 11 October. While travelling through Holland and Germany she managed to master her feelings and appear gracious, radiant and smiling in public. Only at the final stage of the journey, when she had to leave her English suite and give herself to the care of her Danish attendants, did she break down in tears again.

On arrival she was hailed enthusiastically by the English envoys at Copenhagen and the Danish court alike, and the wedding took place in the palace chapel at Christiansborg on 8 November.

Titley reported that the King showed 'a most lively understanding' and Mr Cosby praised 'the masterly ease and dignity with which he expressed his sentiments'. However, Christian was deformed and very small with a slight, childlike figure; his head barely reached her shoulder. It was gross flattery towards a king who was already suffering from the early stages of schizophrenia, and probably saw his wife as only a momentary diversion, to be treated like a mistress and sent away when he tired of her. Only the French ambassador was honest enough to tell his government that he thought the Princess had 'produced hardly any impression on the king's heart; and had she been even more amiable, she would have experienced the same fate. For how could she please a man who quite seriously believes that it does not look well for a husband to love his wife?'[13]

By the spring of 1767 the Queen was *enceinte*, and in January 1768 a son, Frederick, was born. He was so delicate that at first he seemed unlikely to live for long. At one particularly anxious stage, the doctors recommended that he should be baptized privately in his mother's bedchamber at once, but against the odds he responded to attention and survived. Soon after his birth his parents were leading almost separate lives. King Christian's progressive mental illness resulted in extraordinary bouts of self-masochism, visiting brothels, and spending nights on the town, returning in the early hours of the morning completely drunk. He took a mistress, with whom he might be seen walking about arm in arm, and she generally dressed as a man, often in naval uniform. Only when his advisers told him bluntly that there would probably be revolution in Denmark if he did not moderate his behaviour was he persuaded to dismiss her.

Even those at court who pitied the Queen felt that she was partly to blame for the estrangement from her husband by not accepting his every word as law. They did not appreciate that he was approaching a state of severely diminished responsibility. The only thing to be done, they felt, was to send him abroad 'for his studies', and separate him from his people for a while. In the spring of 1768 the King set out for a few months of visiting England and France, conspicuously without the Queen. She was bitterly upset, and begged the King to let her go. It would be her last chance to see her dying sister Louisa, and she desperately wanted to stay with her mother and brothers again. If she insisted on forcing herself on him, her husband declared, he would not go, and as usual he was allowed his own way. When he returned home in January 1769 his wife greeted him at Roskilde, and for a time their relationship seemed to improve. During his absence she had taken to dressing in male riding costume, wearing a scarlet coat and buckskin breeches. Though the more strait-laced were highly critical, her new attire appealed to the King's tastes. As his tutor Reverdil said, he approved of anything which appeared to militate against court etiquette, and he was impressed with her unconventional dress, even though he said she was far too small to be dressed as a man – an odd remark in view of his own stunted growth.

In October she became seriously ill. The problem was never conclusively diagnosed; she believed it was dropsy; others at court thought it must be a venereal complaint caught from her husband. It was probably the spleen, or *ennui*, as it was called at the time, or in more modern terms a nervous breakdown, to which her husband's bizarre behaviour had undoubtedly contributed. At first she refused the court doctors' prescriptions, and would not even let them examine her. All she wanted to do was turn her face to the wall and die. A deeply penitent King Christian begged her to consult Dr Johann Struensee, his new physician-in-ordinary. She took no notice, suspecting the doctor had been responsible for introducing her husband to a new mistress, Madame Birsette Gabel, who suddenly died in childbirth. King George III wrote to tell her firmly that it was her duty to obey her husband in order to resume her position as wife, mother and Queen.

Further apologies from King Christian for his ill-treatment of her weakened her resistance, and reluctantly she allowed Struensee to see her. His charm and respectful demeanour won her over, and within a fortnight her health was completely restored. Politically ambitious yet enlightened, Struensee had come to dominate the impressionable King, whose schizophrenia was becoming more and more evident. He would have to be ruled by somebody, he confided to the Queen, and it would be in the best interests of everyone if she was the person. King Christian trusted his physician implicitly, dismissed his former advisers and installed him at the head of a secret cabinet.

By the time of her youngest daughter's marriage, the Dowager Princess of Wales was living quietly at Carlton House in London and Kew Palace in the country. Queen Caroline Matilda was seen increasingly in Struensee's company in public, and when whispers turned to scandal, a concerned King George III discussed the matter with his mother and the Duke of Gloucester. It was arranged that they would visit the Duke and Duchess of Brunswick, then summon King Christian and Queen Caroline Matilda to meet them on their way back to Copenhagen, so that the Dowager Princess might speak firmly to her youngest child, warn her of her disloyalty and perhaps help to effect Struensee's dismissal. The Duke of Gloucester had already visited Denmark the previous year, and found his sister in low spirits, fearful of her prospects for the future.

The Dowager Princess's first meeting, at Brunswick with her eldest daughter, Augusta, was not a success. Although the younger Augusta had done her best to keep up appearances since her wedding and departure for Germany, telling her family in England that there was 'both confidence and amity' between her husband and herself, and that 'No two people live better together than we do, and I would go through fire and water for him',14 in fact she had never ceased to blame her mother for forcing her into what was in reality a disastrous marriage.

The second meeting was to be with Queen Caroline Matilda. Although she had agreed to see her mother, at the last moment she had second thoughts. She sent her grand marshal to say that she was ill, and with regret she would have to cancel the meeting. As a compromise her mother, who had heard that she was in the habit of getting up to hunt at five in the morning, and retiring at midnight, replied that they had better meet at Lüneburg, which was closer to Copenhagen. Struensee advised her to accept, and she and King Christian joined the Dowager Princess in the last week of June 1770. The mother was astonished at the change in her daughter, whom she had known as a gentle little princess appalled at the thought of her future and distressed at the prospect of going into what she had regarded as tantamount to exile. Now she was a cold, haughty young consort, insisting that as Queen of Denmark she would not be advised or scolded by her mother. As it was impossible for her to have Struensee dismissed from their presence, the Dowager Princess addressed her daughter in English, only for the latter to say that she had completely forgotten the language of her own country and could not understand a word. Her mother then continued guardedly in German, with a general statement on the duties of a queen. Caroline Matilda listened unmoved, replied that it was too late in the evening for further discussion, and then left the room.

Early next morning the Dowager summoned her daughter to her room, and asked her if she really intended to dismiss her husband's Prime Minister, adding that this would be disastrous to the Anglo-Danish cause. The Queen retorted coldly that she should be allowed to govern her kingdom as she pleased. When her mother criticized the granting of favours to Struensee and pointed out that she was risking public disgrace, the Queen replied with a mocking reference to Lord Bute. King Christian joined them and made a rather incoherent reference to the possibility of his mother-in-law and the Duke of Gloucester visiting them in Copenhagen, but the elder woman angrily refused. They took formal farewell of each other that afternoon, perhaps realizing that mother and daughter would never meet again.

Queen Caroline Matilda was aware of the King's increasingly confused mental state, and her indiscretions continued apace. She insisted on Struensee's presence at all gatherings, allowed him to ride in her coach and walk with her everywhere, and let him shower her with gifts. When she gave birth to a daughter Louise in July 1771, everyone believed him to be the father. He had made enemies at every level of society, and people were beginning to feel sympathy for the cuckolded King. When it was rumoured that Struensee was planning to bring about the King's abdication, if not his death, in order to marry the Queen and assume supreme power as Regent with the infant Frederick as King, they decided enough was enough. Under the Dowager Queen Juliana Maria and her decrepit son, Hereditary Prince Frederick, a conspiracy was hatched to get rid of the all-powerful minister. The occasion was to be immediately after a masked ball at the Frederiksborg Palace on

17 January 1772. Early the next morning the conspirators gathered in the Queen Dowager's apartment, and were let into King Christian's room through a secret entrance, where he was woken and immediately feared for his life. His stepmother assured him that he would come to no harm providing he signed the papers they had prepared. With little comprehension of what he was doing he signed orders for the arrest and imprisonment of Struensee, his right-hand man Count Brandt, and his own wife.

The Queen and her daughter were imprisoned in some discomfort at Kronborg, while Struensee and Brandt were likewise confined in harsh conditions. An investigative commission set up by the government found that among other charges, Struensee's 'unlawful intimacy with the Queen had gone so far as is possible between two persons of different sex'. By challenging the King's powers and issuing edicts which lacked the royal signature Struensee had broken the fundamental law of the land. In prison he was comforted by a new-found faith transmitted to him by a Lutheran pastor, Dr Munter. Christian readily signed the death warrant of the Chief Minister who was his wife's lover. The Queen was declared to be divorced, and sentenced to life imprisonment in the castle of Aalborg.

Now seriously ill and with not long to live, the Dowager Princess of Wales forbade her attendants to mention the name of her youngest daughter who had brought such disgrace on the family ever again. Though ill-informed gossips and suspicious ministers were only too ready to blame their misfortunes on supposed 'meddling' on the part of somebody who was in no position to defend herself from scurrilous assertions, the Dowager Princess of Wales had no influence over her son the King, and never tried to exert any. Her last years were saddened above all by the death of her surviving unmarried daughter, the tubercular Louisa, and the unhappy marriages of the other two.

King George and Queen Charlotte visited the Dowager Princess of Wales three evenings a week, Sunday, Tuesday and Friday, while she came to see them on Wednesday. Not long after her fiftieth birthday in November 1769 she became unwell. Cancer of the throat was the last in a line of sorrows to crown a life which had seen more than its royal share of struggles. In November 1771 the King reported sadly to his brother the Duke of Gloucester that she was visibly losing ground, 'and it is impossible you can figure to yourself how much she is reduced since you went abroad'. A week later he wrote that 'her speech grows less intelligible, she hourly emaciates, and has dreadful faintings towards night, which must soon put an end to a situation that it is almost cruel to wish to see her long continue in'.[15]

When she realized she was dying she asked for her daughter Augusta to come from Brunswick and be with her, and the Duchess came and remained until the last. Duchess Augusta and King George had never been close, while Queen Charlotte still resented the arrogant manner in which her sister-in-law had treated her prior to her marriage. Throughout her stay in England the Duchess was treated coldly, being lodged in a furnished house in Pall Mall while one of the Queen's relatives on a visit from Mecklenburg was granted his own apartments at Buckingham Palace. At a court function one of the Queen's ladies-in-waiting courteously allowed the Duchess of Brunswick and her lady precedence in front of her, a gesture which earned her a stiff reprimand from the Queen as 'the Princess [*sic*] of Brunswick has nothing to do here, and I insist on your recovering the precedence you gave up'.[16]

The younger Augusta's marriage had been popular in Britain where her husband was recognized as one of the allied commanders in the Seven Years War, but he was unashamedly unfaithful to his wife. Only private persons, he told his cronies, could be happily married, 'because they can choose their mates'.[17] His unhappy mate bore his treatment with dignity and refused to complain. Yet despite the impression she gave to the contrary, Augusta was privately bitter about her unhappy family life, disillusioned with her husband's unashamed infidelities and the shortcomings of her children. Of their brood of six, two exhibited clear signs of mental derangement from early infancy, and a third was born blind. Yet to her brother in England she wrote repeatedly of her husband's kindness and her happiness in marriage; he was 'monstrously fond of me and I am a happy woman'. Her family in England saw through this façade; in 1771 when she came to nurse her mother, the King wrote to the Duke of Gloucester that she seemed much graver than formerly, 'and I should rather think by her whole manner that it goes on but coldly between her and the Hereditary Prince, though she has not dropped the most distant hint of it'.[18]

In Germany they were about to lose one of their last two surviving aunts. Mary, Landgravine of Hesse-Cassel, who to all outward appearances disappeared from the pages of history with her estrangement from her Catholic husband, passed away at Hainau in January 1772 at the age of forty-nine.

The dying Dowager Princess of Wales stoically kept to her normal routine to the end. When the King and Queen came to see her on the evening of 7 February 1772 she was confined to bed, but insisted on getting up and being dressed to receive them, though she could no longer speak. The King noted afterwards that they 'had the melancholy scene of knowing she could not last, but that it must not be taken notice of as she did not choose to think so'.[19] She retired to bed at her usual hour and the King and Queen, realizing the end was not far off, stayed in the house all night. At 6 a.m. the next day her lady-in-waiting went to wake her and found that she had passed away.

To add insult to injury, the Duchess of Brunswick was left nothing by her mother. Smarting after the humiliating way in which her family had treated her after what was an errand of mercy, she left England in high dudgeon. To make amends the King reluctantly advanced her a small sum of money and paid the cost of both her journeys. Had all contact ceased between the courts of Brunswick and St James thereafter, it would have been greatly to their advantage. Two years later their embattled sister in Denmark wrote to King George III about Augusta's problems and the Duke of Brunswick's ill-health, probably a minor stroke, which left him a changed man. Since the beginning of his illness, she had been saddened by the alteration in his behaviour towards her. 'She does everything in her power that it should not appear in public, and has always so many attentions for him that it is impossible to remark that they are not well together.'[20]

The Duchess of Brunswick's marital difficulties were nothing to those of the tragic Queen Caroline Matilda. Despite their late mother's strictures, King George III could hardly ignore the harsh treatment to which the Danes had subjected her. After her divorce he felt obliged to try to rescue her from perpetual imprisonment, but baulked at letting her return to England. Queen Charlotte refused to let her come home, saying that she would sooner leave Britain herself than receive her.[21] Nevertheless he demanded that she should be returned to his protection and her marriage portion repaid. To their sister Augusta he expressed his hope in May 1772 'that by mildness she will be brought back to the amiable character she had before perverted by a wicked and contemptible court'.[22] A fleet was sent to Danish waters, and under threat of force she was released and allowed to take refuge at Celle, in her brother's Hanoverian dominions, where she was granted £5,000 a year by the British government. She was treated as a queen and as a daughter of England, and her brother sent instructions that everything should be done to make her comfortable and happy. He advised her to continue behaving with circumspection as she had been doing to her credit during her misfortunes, as it was 'the most effectual means of showing what a blessing you might have been if those that had surrounded you had possessed any principle of honour and integrity'.[23]

She agonized over her children, and dreamt of a revolution in Denmark which would restore her to the throne. King George advised her to dismiss such ideas, counselling patience at least until 'the present horrid people that manage that kingdom' were removed by death or 'the intrigues of some new party'. If she was careful enough to lead an exemplary life, he suggested, she would by degrees find herself at length restored to public favour, and her son would come forward in her defence; 'the only dignified as well as safe part for you is to give up all thoughts of that country, at least till your children can be in a situation to come to your assistance'.[24]

The unhappy ex-Queen of Denmark did not lack champions, foremost among them a young Englishman, Nathaniel Wraxall, who aspired to overthrow the government of the Queen Dowager and restore Caroline Matilda. With extreme reluctance, King

George III gave his half-hearted endorsement of her restoration and undertook to authorize his representative in Copenhagen to announce his approval, once it had been successfully accomplished.[25] Wraxall came to England early in April 1775, but the King refused to see him. Instead he warned his sister in a letter of 23 April 1775 that, if he was to get her safely out of Denmark, he would certainly not undertake to assist in restoring her to the kingdom. He could not

> say any more than if the Danish nobility shall at any time bring the King to recall you with that eclat and dignity that alone can make it advisable for you to return to his kingdom, I shall not only not prevent your going but support those who have been accessory to it; but from what I have declared I cannot either enter farther into the affair or be entrusted with the plan on which they mean to act.[26]

Perhaps fortuitously, a few days later Caroline Matilda was seriously ill. When an epidemic of either typhoid or scarlet fever broke out in Celle, a page boy at the castle developed feverish symptoms and died. She had been particularly attached to him, and before her ladies could stop her she went to see the body. Within a couple of days she had taken to her bed and the doctors despaired for her life. Infection had intervened to bring the prospect of eternal rest to an unhappy young woman who had nothing to live for. Shortly before midnight on 11 May 1775 she passed away in her sleep, aged twenty-three.

Those who had known her well agreed that it was a merciful release. Her favourite clergyman Pastor Lehzen told a friend that he never remembered 'so easy a dissolution, or one in which death lost all its terrors . . . She fell asleep like a tired traveller.'[27] Two days later her funeral took place in the church at Celle, where the people draped themselves and their shops in black as they wept for their 'beloved and good Queen'. On her death-bed she had protested her innocence of all charges made against her to the last, and left a letter to King George III in which she told him that she died willingly. 'But more than all else, and even than death, it pains me that not one of all those whom I loved in life is standing by my dying bed, to grant me a last consolation by a pressure of the hand, or a glance of compassion, and to close my eyes in death.'[28]

The last survivor among King George II's children, Amelia, was the only one to inherit his robust health and attain anything approaching his great age. A lifelong spinster, she had been the constant companion of her surviving brother the Duke of Cumberland, who had fought a battle with ill-health and obesity for some years before dying of a stroke at the age of forty-four in 1765.

In 1752 she had been appointed Ranger of Richmond Park. Less accommodating than her parents, she wanted to keep the park closed to the public, retaining it as the sole preserve of the royal family and select guests. When the public insisted they had a right of passage through the grounds she would not listen, until they took legal action and her advisers told her that her case could not be defended in common law. Yielding with bad grace, she gave orders for rickety old ladders to be placed against the walls so that people could pass through the park at their own risk. After another court case she was compelled to have a proper gateway erected. Disgusted at this victory for democracy, and declaring that the downfall of England commenced with the opening of Richmond Park, she resigned her position.[29]

Thereafter she became a querulous, inquisitive old woman. Perhaps, noted her mother's earliest biographer, 'this was due to the crossing of her young affections, and her nature, driven back upon itself, grew warped in the cramped atmosphere of the court'.[30] In her old age Bath always provided a ready place of diversion where she could indulge in her love of gossip and cards, playing night after night for high stakes, taking snuff all the time. One night at the public card room at Bath, an elderly general sitting next to her helped himself to a pinch of snuff from her box on the table between them. Without a word she stared defiantly at him, then beckoned her footman, ordered him to throw the snuff in the fire, and bring her a fresh box.

To the end she continued to visit her stables and see her beloved horses every morning, never getting in or out of her carriage at the front of the house, but always in the back yard. She

Princess Sophia, c. 1660.
(Mary Evans Picture Library)

Electress Sophia, c. 1710. (Mary
Evans Picture Library)

Sophia Dorothea of Celle, wife of George Louis, Electoral Prince of Hanover, c. 1685. (Mary Evans Picture Library)

Queen Sophia Charlotte of Prussia. (The Royal Collection © 2000, HM Queen Elizabeth II)

Queen Sophia Dorothea of Prussia. (Mary Evans Picture Library)

Caroline, Princess of Wales, engraved by Walter Colls, after the painting by Sir Godfrey Kneller.

The family of Frederick, Prince of Wales, 1751. Augusta, Princess of Wales, wears a veil in mourning for her husband, who had died earlier that year and whose portrait is in the background. The children, left to right, are (back) Princes Edward and George, later King George III; Princesses Augusta, Caroline Matilda (in her mother's arms), Elizabeth and Louisa; (front) Princes Henry Frederick, William Henry, and Frederick William. (The Royal Collection © 2000, HM Queen Elizabeth II)

The Music Party: *Anne, Princess Royal; Princesses Amelia, Caroline, and their brother Frederick, Prince of Wales, c. 1733, by Philippe Mercier.* (The Royal Collection ©
2000, Her Majesty The Queen)

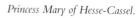
Princess Mary of Hesse-Cassel.

Queen Charlotte, c. 1763, studio of Allan Ramsay. (Scottish National Portrait Gallery)

Queen Caroline Matilda of Denmark (standing) and Princess Louisa, 1767 (The Royal Collection © 2000, Her Majesty The Queen)

Princesses Charlotte, Augusta and Elizabeth, by Thomas Gainsborough, 1784. (The Royal Collection © 2000, Her Majesty the Queen)

Princess Charlotte of Wales, c. 1816, engraved by W. Fry, after the painting by Thomas Lawrence. (Mary Evans Picture Library)

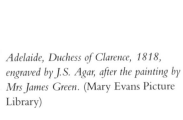

Queen Caroline, c. 1820, Samuel Lane. (Scottish National Portrait Gallery)

Adelaide, Duchess of Clarence, 1818, engraved by J.S. Agar, after the painting by Mrs James Green. (Mary Evans Picture Library)

made generous gifts to various charities in her last years, and was an indulgent great-aunt to the young sons and daughters of her nephew King George III, regularly inviting them to her home at Gunnersbury House, where they played riotous games of skittles for hours on end.

By October 1786, at seventy-four, she knew she was dying, and asked her physician, Dr Warren, 'how long he thought her existence might be prolonged'. He told her that 'her dissolution would probably take place within three or four days, but it was within the limit of possibility her life might be extended to a week'.[31] From that moment she concentrated on arranging her affairs, taking care to provide for all her servants. After her death at her London house in Cavendish Square on 31 October, her nephew was rather piqued to find that she had left nothing to her relatives in England, and the main beneficiaries had been her nephews in Hesse-Cassel, the sons of her sister Mary.

By this time there was a new generation of Princesses. Queen Charlotte's fourth child and first daughter, also named Charlotte, was born on 29 September 1766. Five more followed over the next seventeen years – Augusta in 1768, Elizabeth in 1770, Mary in 1776, Sophia in 1777, and Amelia in 1783. The Queen's childbearing spanned twenty-one years, from the birth of the Prince of Wales in August 1762 to that of Amelia exactly twenty-one years later. Most of her confinements gave her no trouble, but she suffered particularly from depression during her fourteenth pregnancy in the summer of 1780. A combination of anxiety over the behaviour of the Prince of Wales, who only extricated himself from an affair with the actress Mary Robinson after the King had had to give him the money to buy back some compromising letters, and the anti-Catholic riots in London instigated by Lord George Gordon, told on her nerves. Uncharacteristically she wrote in September to her brother Charles, now Duke of Mecklenburg-Strelitz, that no prisoner 'could wish more ardently for liberty than I do to be quit of my burden and to see the end of my condition, if I knew it was for the last time I should be happy'.[32] Sixteen days later she gave birth to Alfred, a sickly prince who lived for only twenty-three months.

By the standards of the day, she had become 'a proper mother' by losing one of her brood of fourteen, but worse was to come. In May 1783 Octavius, the eighth son of nine, a particularly handsome-looking boy aged three, and the King's favourite child, suddenly fell ill and died within forty-eight hours. Saddened at the loss of her 'two dear little angels', Queen Charlotte was pregnant for the fifteenth and last time that summer. To her brother she complained that life was 'monotonous and burdensome'[33] with only her children's society for company, and she must have known that this would be her last confinement.

Born in August 1783, the baby of the family was named Amelia after her elderly great-aunt. When she was two Mrs Delany recalled spending evenings at the Queen's Lodge 'with no other company than their own most lovely family', sitting round a large table, with the younger members of the family drawing and working, and above all 'the beautiful babe Princess Amelia bearing her part in the entertainment, sometimes in one of her sisters' laps, sometimes playing with the King on the carpet'.[34] A year later Fanny Burney saw her royal father doting upon her, and she described him taking her in his arms, kissing and playing with her. She was the apple of his eye, and remained so throughout her short life.

The Princesses' upbringing was largely the responsibility of their mother and their much-loved governess, Lady Charlotte Finch, who was appointed to the household in 1762 and stayed for thirty years. The King's drawing master, Joshua Kirby, was responsible for introducing Thomas Gainsborough, a close friend, to the royal family. Gainsborough taught the Princesses the rudiments of painting and drawing, and when he was painting the series of family portraits which now hang in the Queen's Audience Room at Windsor, he spoke with rapture of the royal children, telling his friends that 'he was all but raving mad with ecstasy in beholding such a constellation of youthful beauty', and that 'the sweetest, the most lovely female countenance of the youthful group always appeared to me to be that of the Princess Royal'.[35]

Charlotte, the Princess Royal, and Elizabeth became the most proficient artists in the family, and several copies made by them survive in the Royal Collection. From copying, and perhaps tracing, drawings Elizabeth developed into the most prolific of the sisters, and later published lithographs, etchings and mezzotints, many of mythological scenes. She also designed, worked and supplied items of interior decoration at the Queen's House, Kew, and later Frogmore, where she helped to design garden buildings, and painted flower murals in the upper room of the Queen's Cottage. Sophia became an accomplished horsewoman, while Augusta and Amelia inherited their parents' love of music.

Lacking spontaneity with her children, the Queen was always stern with her daughters. In later years they would complain about her, while always speaking affectionately of their father. Mrs Mary Harcourt, sister-in-law of the Queen's lady-in-waiting, thought she kept them at 'too great a distance', and another lady at court doubted whether she had ever possessed any maternal feeling at all. Mrs Charlotte Papendiek, daughter of one of her pages, found Charlotte, the Princess Royal, very shy, 'and under restraint with the Queen', but 'out of the Queen's presence she was a different being'.[36]

At home they were expected to join their parents for breakfast at the Queen's House, Kew, taken punctually at 9 o'clock, the youngest being brought in by the wet-nurse. They were given milk, or sometimes tea, and dry toast. The morning was spent at lessons and in a walk in the gardens, regardless of weather. Dinner followed at 3 o'clock, after which they all joined in the garden for games. Charlotte was particularly proud of her cricketing skills, though hockey and football were played as well. There was also a model farm in which they were expected to work, including a small field for them to sow and reap wheat, which they ground and used for making bread. At 5 o'clock they gathered again at their parents' apartments to read, write, or 'make improving conversation', before the governesses took them off to a light supper and bed at 6.30.

Once they had their own 'establishments' the Princes and Princesses seldom saw their parents, and never informally, only meeting during their Sunday afternoon walks. During the season they were taken to London on Thursdays for the Drawing-Rooms, and on reaching the age of ten they were expected to attend evening parties for music and cards at Kew or Windsor. When summoned to be present at royal games of whist they had to stand behind the Queen's chair, and sometimes fell asleep in that position. Unless offered a chair themselves they could not sit down, and when leaving their parents' presence they had to walk backwards. Conversation was limited, as the Queen strongly believed that children must not speak to their parents unless spoken to first.

Even into adulthood almost every hour of the Princesses' days were planned, and permission was needed for the pursuit of any activity other than those normally prescribed and permitted. A governess or lady of the household had to be in the room whenever a man, even a tutor, was present. No excursions were permitted unless closely chaperoned, and they could read no work of fiction unless the Queen had approved it first. While their brothers soon gained their liberty in the outside world, their own lives were often likened not unfairly to those of novices in a well-regulated convent. Attending court, accompanying their parents to and from Windsor, and on their visits to country houses and to Weymouth, or spending their time with the Queen walking, doing needlework and reading became part of their routine, with card parties, visits to the theatre and concerts as special treats. It was, however, no more dull than the life of most upper-class ladies of the age.

Apart from their tutors, courtiers and equerries, they generally saw no men except for their brothers. As a result they lavished no little affection on them, particularly on the eldest, the Prince of Wales. Their father loved having them at home with him, finding them better company than his none-too-obedient or argumentative sons, and perhaps the unfortunate experiences of his eldest and youngest sisters made him think that his daughters would be happier unmarried and staying at home. Only three of his six daughters married, all after the age of thirty, and between them only one ever had any children – a stillborn daughter. Did their father, and their mother, ever wonder whether they might want a home and family of their own?

If King George III had enjoyed better health, all of them might have taken husbands and produced children in the normal course of events. It was their tragedy as well as his that he became seriously ill a few days after his fiftieth birthday in June 1788. A series of severe abdominal spasms and a bilious attack were the first manifestations of what has since been diagnosed as 'acute intermittent porphyria', a rare inborn metabolic disorder. His recovery was slow, and he was advised to spend a period of convalescence away from the cares of state. A small party consisting of the King, the Queen and Princesses Charlotte, Augusta and Elizabeth left Windsor to stay in the house of one of his lords of the bedchamber, Lord Fauconberg, at Cheltenham.

They returned home five weeks later, the King pleased with his apparent recovery, but by mid-October he was unwell again, his symptoms including acute stomach pain and difficulty in breathing. His manner became odd, his voice voluble, hoarse, and marked by a quickness of speech and manner which indicated feverishness. The family were seriously alarmed by a scene at Matins in church when the King suddenly embraced the Queen and their daughters and burst into tears as the sermon was about to begin. 'You know what it is to be nervous, but was you ever so bad as this?' he asked Elizabeth. 'Yes,' she answered, and he became quiet again. A day or two later the Queen said to the King that she thought everybody ought to bear up under afflictions, and that she was confident God would not inflict on them more than they were able to bear. At this he took her gently round the waist and said, 'Then you are prepared for the worst.'[37] It was a remark she never forgot.

During the next few days the King's condition deteriorated and the Queen's nerves were strained almost to breaking point. At a dinner party he became delirious, and the Prince of Wales later proclaimed that his father had seized him by the collar and thrust him violently against the wall. The physician Sir George Baker found the King apparently on the verge of mental derangement, and the Queen close to hysterics, fearful of what would become of her. When the King was told that his wife was ill, he promised to take care of her himself, and would not go to bed or allow her a moment's rest, constantly watching over her while he spoke until he was exhausted, the foam running out of his mouth. Baker had to persuade him that the Queen's state of health made it necessary for her to occupy a separate room, and he agreed to this on condition that he himself could sleep next door. Shocked and horrified, the Queen came close to losing her reason as well.

During those few days her soft gold hair turned grey, and she was never the same woman again. The doctors had to ask her not to come into the sickroom as the sight of her in her present state would only increase the King's agitation, and she did not see him for another five weeks.

She agreed that the King should be removed to Kew, as long as she and her daughters could go too. Parliament debated the need for a regency. Meanwhile the King in his ravings seemed to turn against her, telling one of his pages that his wife was mad and had been so for the last three years, and he would not admit her to his bed until the year 1793.[38] At other times he spoke of the Countess of Pembroke, her bedchamber lady and devoted friend, saying that he was in love with her and not the Queen. He had never liked her, he said; she had a bad temper and her children were afraid of her.

In the meantime she contracted an inflammation of the eyes and had to sit in virtual darkness, she suffered agonies from toothache, her appetite dwindled to almost nothing and she lost weight alarmingly. Elizabeth, Countess Harcourt, one of her ladies of the bedchamber, proved her greatest support at this time; telling others she could not 'desert the Queen in her "hour of need", for never sure did any woman need a friend more than she does at this moment'.[39] On 30 January the Queen had to receive a deputation from the Lords and Commons, as they were to present an address stating the trust which would be reposed in her during a regency. She replied with a faltering voice yet with great dignity, but the ordeal took its toll and she fainted afterwards.

A regency, under either the Queen or the Prince of Wales, was becoming more likely. However, by February 1789 daily bulletins on the King's condition were improving, and though a Regency Bill was printed, passed the Commons and reached the Lords that month, it became clear that such a move was no longer necessary. Countess Harcourt said that Queen Charlotte had 'kept the crown' on her husband's head, and when the next session of Parliament was formally opened on 10 March with the reading of the King's Speech, constituting the official declaration of his recovery, the crisis was regarded as over.

In September 1791 the King's second son Frederick, Duke of York, married Frederica, eldest daughter of King Frederick William II of Prussia. He hoped that this might be the first of a series of alliances between his brothers and sisters and other Prussian Princes and Princesses, but it was not to be. Apart from offers from Denmark and Sweden, which the King rejected, and Württemberg, there were no proposals for the hand of any of King George's daughters. A suggestion in 1785 from the Danish court that His Majesty might offer the hand of Charlotte, Princess Royal, to her cousin Crown Prince Frederick, indicated an astonishingly short memory on the part of Copenhagen, and the King made it clear that nobody in his family 'could be desirous of the alliance'[40] in view of the way they had treated his late youngest sister.

The Princess Royal felt that she had an ally in both of her two eldest brothers. As the eldest daughter of the King she was held 'alone inheritable to the crown on failure of male issue, and therefore more respected by the law than any of her younger sisters'.[41] If this meant that she would be beyond the reach of most possible suitors, she wanted no part of it. In the summer of 1791 she complained bitterly to the Prince of Wales of the way she was treated, especially by her mother, the restraint under which she was kept, like a child, the perpetual tiresome and confined life she was obliged to lead, and worst of all her mother's violent and capricious temper. She had decided she wanted to marry the handsome Francis, Duke of Bedford, a friend of Charles Fox, but her brother told her that the King would never give his consent.

Within a few years her time for matrimony would come. Though her husband was certainly not handsome, he would at least rescue her from the threat of lifelong spinsterhood.

FIVE

'Without hope and open to every fear'

THE DAUGHTERS OF GEORGE III AND QUEEN CHARLOTTE; CAROLINE, PRINCESS OF WALES

In June 1794 Queen Charlotte lost her eldest brother, Adolphus Frederick IV, Duke of Mecklenburg-Strelitz. His successor, their twice-widowed brother Charles, wanted to marry again, and King George III recommended his niece Caroline, youngest daughter of the Duke and Duchess of Brunswick. Queen Charlotte was horrified; she had it on good authority, she warned Charles, that 'her [Caroline's] passions are so strong that the Duke himself said that she was not to be allowed even to go from one room to another without her Governess, and that when she dances this Lady is obliged to follow her for the whole of the dance to prevent her from making an exhibition of herself by indecent conversations with men.'[1] She had never liked the Duchess of Brunswick, who as the King's eldest (and only surviving) sister, the sharp-tongued Augusta, had caused such mischief at court during the early years of their own married life.

The Duke was so alarmed by his sister's report that he dismissed any idea of marrying the Brunswick Princess, but her relief was short-lived. Within days, she learned that the woman who had almost become her sister-in-law was about to marry her eldest son. Without consulting her, the King had given his consent and informed the Prime Minister, William Pitt, of the forthcoming marriage on 24 August.

Much to his family's consternation, and in contravention of the Royal Marriages Act of 1772, the Prince of Wales had married a Roman Catholic widow, Mrs Maria Fitzherbert, in December

1785. Within nine years the pressures on him to contract a legitimate marriage were overwhelming. It was his duty to present the family with an heir, and moreover Parliament would only consider helping to meet his ever-multiplying debts under such circumstances.

Muttering that 'one damned German Frau' was as good as another, he left the matchmaking to others. The Duke of York felt that their cousin Caroline would be right for his brother, though the choice was limited and she had little competition. It was not in Queen Charlotte's interest to put up any serious resistance to such a marriage. Even if it had not been too late to prevent it, she lived in such dread of the King's violent recurring illness that she was not prepared to risk another attack by opposing a scheme of which he approved so strongly. Any rumours he may have heard about his prospective bride seemed to make no difference to the Prince of Wales; marriage to any officially approved princess and settlement of his finances was all that mattered to him. As his own parents' marriage had been arranged, and as they had never seen each other until just before the wedding ceremony, there was no reason to suppose that his would be any the less successful. Parliament voted an increase in his annual grant, part of which would be withheld to pay his debts and interest.

Disturbing reports of Princess Caroline's behaviour and character had already reached England. From adolescence her foolish behaviour had often given rise to doubts as to her mental balance. When she was sixteen her mother had forbidden her to attend a ball at court, and shortly after it had started a messenger came to tell the Duke and Duchess that their daughter had been taken seriously ill. The company dispersed at once while the alarmed parents went to see Caroline in bed, screaming hysterically. She told her mother that she was in labour, and begged her to send for an *accoucheur* at once. When one arrived she wiped the make-up from her face and jumped out of bed, full of childish laughter as she retorted, 'Now, Madam, will you keep me another time from a ball?'[2]

In November 1794 Sir James Harris, Earl of Malmesbury, was sent as the Prince's envoy to Brunswick, to complete the legal pre-marriage formalities and bring the bride to England. As Lord

Holland said, 'unfavourable reports of the person, and yet more of the manners and character of the destined bride came pouring in from Germany after the articles were signed and it was too late to recede'.[3]

Malmesbury's first impressions of the future Queen of England were that she was 'much embarrassed on my first being presented to her – pretty face – not expressive of softness – her figure not graceful – fine eyes – good hand – tolerable teeth, but going – fair hair and light eyebrows, good bust – short, with what the French call "des epaules impertinentes". *Vastly happy with her future expectations*. The Duchess full of nothing else – talks incessantly.'[4] Physically she may have been satisfactory, but closer acquaintance with this cheerful but noisy, giggling Princess of twenty-six soon revealed problems. Her language was indelicate, even by the standards of the age, and he was dismayed when she asked a page to send him a tooth which she had just had extracted.

He found the mother just as tiresome as the daughter. The Duchess of Brunswick had been tactless enough to abuse Queen Charlotte so bitterly that her daughter dreaded to think that this woman was to be her mother-in-law, but the Duke was more co-operative. One evening after dinner both men had a long and frank discussion, in which the Duke asked Malmesbury to recommend to the Princess that she should not ask questions, and 'not to be free in giving opinions of persons and things aloud'. His daughter had been brought up strictly, but lacked sound judgement. He affirmed that her lack of discretion was largely inherited from her mother, 'who at times is certainly apt to forget her audience'.[5] Discussions with the diplomat Sir Brooke Boothby, who knew Brunswick and the ducal family well, only exacerbated Malmesbury's anxiety, especially on 'her want of reflection and *substance*'. With a frivolous, foolish mother for whom she had no respect, and with a father on whom she doted but who flaunted his mistresses in front of his wife and daughters and treated them all on equal terms, it would be remarkable if she turned out to be a paragon of virtue and unquestioning obedience. It was possible that 'with a *steady* man she would do vastly well, but with one of a different description, there are great risks'.[6]

The Duke and Duchess particularly wanted Caroline's

secretary, Mademoiselle Rosenzweit, to accompany her to England. As the Princess's education had been grossly neglected her writing and spelling were atrocious, and the services of a secretary would be vital. Malmesbury wrote to the Prince Regent for assent, only to receive a curt reply that she would not be allowed to come; the only members of her household the Princess could bring to England with her were two maids. Her parents were furious.

The Princess had heard too much about the family and their acquaintances in England for her own peace of mind. She was afraid of her future mother-in-law, fearing that Queen Charlotte 'would be jealous of her and do her harm'. All might have been well but for the arrival of an anonymous letter, ostensibly from England but possibly instigated by the disappointed Mademoiselle Rosenzweit or somebody acting in league with her, the day before Malmesbury and the Princess were due to leave Brunswick. It described the Prince's current mistress Frances Villiers, Countess of Jersey, a grandmother nine years older than the Prince himself, as 'the worst and most dangerous of profligate women' who would try to lead the Princess into some act of injury to her husband's honour.[7] Malmesbury was exasperated when the Duchess, who had received it, showed it to the Princess. Caroline already knew of the presence of Lady Jersey, though even Malmesbury had to feign ignorance on her exact status regarding the Prince of Wales. He warned her gently that anybody 'who presumed to *love* her was guilty of *high treason*, and punished with *death*, if she was weak enough to listen to him; so also would *she*,'[8] a statement which evidently took her by surprise. Next the Duchess, compounding her reputation for tactlessness, showed her daughter a letter from King George hoping that his niece would not show too much vivacity and be prepared to lead a sedentary and retired life. Evidently the Duchess did not appreciate that such caution might have borne fruit with a more placid, obedient young woman. To her own mischievous, wilful daughter, it must have acted like the proverbial red rag to a bull.

Under pressure the Duchess agreed to accompany her daughter as far as the coast at Helvoetsluys, where the English squadron would meet them, but when they reached Osnabrück she wanted to return to Brunswick so she would avoid any risk of capture by the French army, telling Malmesbury how angry the King would be if this happened. While he admitted that the King would be sorry, he insisted it was her duty to stay with her daughter until the latter was safely in the hands of her attendants. Giving way with bad grace, the thwarted Duchess grumbled throughout their journey. She told indiscreet stories about Queen Charlotte, whom she had disliked when they were in England together, and about King George, with whom she had had to share a bed as a child, telling them that it had been a most disagreeable experience as he used to wet the bed until their father cured him of the habit by making him wear the blue ribbon [of the Order of the Garter] 'with a piece of china attached to it, which was *not* the George'.[9] He could hardly blame Caroline for not respecting such a silly, undignified mother, but he felt obliged to reprimand the Princess gently for such 'undutiful and sneering conduct' towards her mother, as treating her rudely and laughing at her.

The party was delayed on the European mainland for several weeks by the war, and had to spend two months at Hanover. Malmesbury took advantage of this time to speak to the Princess frankly about her personal cleanliness. He had noticed that she did not wash often enough, her underclothes and her thread stockings were frequently dirty and far too rarely changed. She was actually 'offensive' from the neglect; he thought it remarkable how 'amazingly' her education had been neglected in this respect, 'how much her mother, although an Englishwoman, was inattentive to it', and tactfully urged her to be more fastidious.

They reached England at the beginning of April, disembarking at Greenwich, to be met by Lady Jersey. The Princess's first query on landing proved an accurate foretaste of her attitude. Seeing maimed pensioners outside the hospital, she asked lightly whether all Englishmen had only one arm or one leg. '*Point de persiflage, Madame, je vous en prie,*'[10] Lady Jersey snapped. At St James's, where the Princess was to stay until the wedding, she met her future husband for the first time. When they were introduced, she knelt gracefully and he helped her up, embraced her, exchanged barely a word with her, then retired to another room. Turning to Malmesbury, he remarked that he was not well and wanted a glass of brandy. After he had left, Caroline asked her attendants if the Prince was always like that, adding that he was not nearly so handsome as his portrait.

Sustained by the knowledge that she was marrying the most eligible bachelor in Europe, she appeared less discomfited than he. By dinner that evening she had recovered her high spirits and her conversation, 'flippant, rattling' behaviour,[6] 'affecting raillery and wit', making coarse jokes about relations between the Prince and Lady Jersey, who was present. He had chosen her as his bride's lady of the bedchamber with the unwitting approval of the King, who would never have allowed such a tactless appointment if he had known of his eldest son's affair with her. If Caroline had hoped to make a lasting impression on the man about to become her husband, she could not have achieved a more devastating success. Everyone else was mortified.

The wedding took place at St James's Chapel on the evening of 8 April in an atmosphere fraught with tension. Among the family group only the bride and William, Duke of Clarence, chattering together as they awaited the groom's arrival, seemed in good spirits. When the Archbishop of Canterbury, Dr Moore, reached the words 'any person knowing of a lawful impediment', he looked searchingly at the King and the Prince of Wales before pronouncing the couple husband and wife. The Prince was moist-eyed and unsteady on his feet, less from emotion than from the fortifying effects of the brandy which he had taken to get him through the ceremony. When the couple walked out of the chapel arm in arm, the Duke of Leeds behind them noticed the groom's evident coolness and indifference towards his bride.

The bridal night was spent at Carlton House, but if his wife's comments were to be believed, the Prince was in no fit state to recall much about it. She told one of her ladies-in-waiting that he spent most of the night in the fireplace in a drunken stupor, where she left him, and he could not climb into bed until the morning. She hinted to the politician and diplomat Lord Minto that he was incapable of doing any more than that, as she thought her husband was impotent.

Nevertheless the Prince wrote to his mother, who was prepared to put her personal feelings to one side and give her daughter-in-law a fair chance, of Caroline's good health and high spirits, and the pleasure she was gaining from their residence at Brighton. While Queen Charlotte had been dismayed at the choice of Caroline as a wife for her eldest son, she accepted the inevitable with good grace and showed every kindness possible towards her daughter-in-law. A grand fête was given by the Queen at Frogmore on 19 May to celebrate her own birthday and that of the Princess of Wales two days earlier. By this time she was treating the younger woman with particular solicitude not only as a daughter-in-law but also as a prospective mother, for it was general knowledge that she was with child.

Princess Elizabeth, who was particularly devoted to her brother, was especially anxious for the marriage to be happy. Caroline appreciated this good-natured sister-in-law's presence, and sent Elizabeth good wishes on her birthday in May. Writing soothingly to her brother, Elizabeth said that the Princess of Wales 'spoke very openly to all parties concerning her present happiness . . . & having the appearance of perfect good temper I flatter myself that you will have her turn out a very comfortable little wife'.[11]

On 7 January 1796 the Prince of Wales informed his family that the Princess, 'after a terrible hard labour for about twelve hours, is this instant brought to bed of an *immense Girl*, & I assure you notwithstanding we might have wish'd for a Boy, I receive her with all the affection possible'.[12] At first he expressed concern at his wife's fatigue, but on her recovery he reverted to form. On 10 January he made a will bequeathing his worldly property to Maria Fitzherbert, the wife of his '*heart and soul*'; the 'whole & sole management & care' of his infant daughter to the King, and after his death to a trust composed of his mother, brothers and sisters until she attained her majority. Her mother, he wrote, was to have no hand in her upbringing; the proof which he had received of her 'entire want of judgment & of feeling' made it incumbent on him to prevent the child from 'falling into such improper and bad hands as hers'. All her jewels which he had purchased with his own money were to be taken from her and given to his daughter; and, finally, 'to her who is call'd the Princess of Wales I leave one shilling'.[13]

On 11 February the baby Princess was christened Charlotte

Augusta after both her grandmothers. Throughout spring and summer the rest of the family tried to reconcile husband and wife, but to no avail. By March the Prince had proposed that his wife should be given a separate establishment, and he made it clear that he intended to have as little to do with her as possible. Husband and wife would continue to reside in Carlton House with their own apartments, but only meet on formal occasions. Contact would be maintained by exchange of notes when necessary. When she asked the Prince about the details she and her mother had been given in the anonymous letter, and questioned him on 'the intimacy' of his friendship with Lady Jersey, he explained that Lady Jersey was 'one of the oldest acquaintances I had in this country, & that the confidence resulting from so long a friendship had enabled her to offer advice which contributed not a little to decide me to marriage'.[14]

By summer he was determined on an official separation, calling his wife 'the vilest wretch this world ever was curs'd with, who I cannot feel more disgust for from her personal nastiness than I do from her entire want of all principle'.[15] When the King refused to hear of such a drastic step the Prince tried to win Queen Charlotte over, telling her that he was serving his family 'in the most essential manner by ridding them of a *fiend* under whose influence otherwise, not only I, but you & all the rest of us must make up our minds to submit to for the whole of our lives'.[16]

When his sister Elizabeth attempted to persuade him that the best solution would be the resignation of Lady Jersey, and that it 'must take place for the sake of the country and the whole royal family', he took no notice.[17] She was not alone among the family in believing that he behaved foolishly by refusing to accept a difficult situation. The Duke of Clarence remarked with questionable loyalty that he had 'married a very foolish, disagreeable person, but he should not have treated her as he has done, but made the best of a bad bargain, as my father has done. *He* married a disagreeable woman, but he has not behaved ill to her.'[18]

Ready to compromise, the Princess of Wales wrote to the King in June that her 'sole and true happiness cannot but consist in a perfect reconciliation with the Prince of Wales' but she could 'see no other true means of permanent reconciliation than the absolute retreat of Lady Jersey from my service and private society'.[19] Queen Charlotte treated her daughter-in-law with respect in public, but coldly in private, and encouraged her daughters to follow her example. In this she was unsuccessful, for they resented her small-mindedness and, fond as they were of their brother, felt that his unhappy wife should be given another chance. None was more sympathetic than Sophia, whose outspoken 'partiality for the amiable princess' did not win her any favours with her mother. 'You know I must be silent, and God knows in silence I feel most deeply attached to her',[20] she wrote to Frances Garth, sub-governess to Princess Charlotte, in the summer of 1801.

Sophia, some considered, was the cleverest of the sisters. Lord Melbourne later remarked that, in character if not in looks, there was something of the gypsy about her. From her earliest years she had always shown a certain amount of sympathy for the downtrodden. As a small girl, she listened attentively at breakfast to her father reading items from the newspaper aloud to them all. She asked the Queen what a prison was, and on being told that prisoners were often half-starved for want, she replied that this was very cruel, as prison must be bad enough without the inmates starving. Henceforth she said that she would give all her allowance to buy bread for prisoners, and her parents were so touched by this gesture that they agreed to add to this amount.[21] From childhood she made friends easily, and none of her brothers ever had a bad word to say about her. On the threshold of maturity her governess remarked that she had more sensibility, energy and imagination than all the other sisters put together, not to mention a teasing streak and a gift for mimicry.[22]

The Prince of Wales was increasingly alarmed about the unhappy state of his sisters in the 'nunnery', as they described it to friends. Their father had lost any control he ever had over his sons, and only his daughters remained obedient – a state of affairs he seemed determined to maintain. When at home with his family he often burst into emotional tears, walking round the room, kissing his daughters affectionately and thanking God for giving them as a comfort for the misdeeds of his sons. The Princesses were 'variously agitated, and sometimes so much as to go into fits'. The politician and poet James Bland Burges thought that there was probably not 'a more unhappy family in England than that of our good King'. The Princess Royal was the most miserable of all, 'convinced that she now has no chance of ever altering her condition; afraid of receiving any impressions of tenderness or affection; reserved and studious; tenderly loving her brothers and feeling strongly every unpleasant circumstance attending them, she is fallen into a kind of quiet, desperate state, without hope and open to every fear'.[23]

By 1795 Charlotte, aged twenty-nine, was the least attractive of the sisters. Clumsy, gauche and painfully shy, especially in her mother's presence, only when she got away from the Queen did she become more lively and animated. To her sisters she was an embittered tell-tale, always stirring up trouble at home. Sophia once noted some unpleasantness for which she was convinced Charlotte was partly responsible, 'and now I have heard many a story that Princess Royal has repeated to the Queen'.[24] One summer at Weymouth the governesses thought the younger Princesses seemed more cheerful after she had departed.

Her lack of good looks and her repressed character meant that she was hardly eligible as regards marriage, though even the King was persuaded to admit that he would consent to any match for her which was not a *mésalliance*. In the summer of 1795 the Prince of Wales took the initiative in getting his maternal uncle, Ernest of Mecklenburg-Strelitz, to try to arrange a marriage between his sister and the Duke of Oldenburg. The Princess Royal was pleased, and Elizabeth began referring in her letters to the Prince of Wales about their sister 'the Duchess of Oldenburg', but it came to nothing.

However, a husband was found for her the following year in Frederick, Hereditary Prince of Württemberg, a widower of forty. Having heard unpleasant stories of how the Prince had treated his first wife, another daughter of his own sister Augusta, Duchess of Brunswick, King George would initially have nothing to do with him. She had been sent away from her husband and children for flagrant infidelity, and rather too conveniently for everyone's peace of mind she had not been long at her prison fortress before she succumbed to fever, or haemorrhage, in such a manner that immediate burial was deemed necessary. It was rumoured that she had been poisoned. However, combined entreaties by the houses of Russia and Brunswick, and officials in England, not to mention his eldest daughter, the would-be bride herself, wore down the King's opposition, and he gave his assent in July 1796.

In March 1797 he instructed his Home Secretary the Duke of Portland to draw up the marriage treaty. It was signed in May, its conditions including a proviso that the children of the marriage were to be brought up in Württemberg but would require the permission of the King of England or his successors to marry; and that should the Princess Royal's husband predecease her, she should be at liberty to return to England, bringing all her jewellery, including any she might acquire after her marriage; and that her English attendants should leave her at Hanover, where the German ones should join her, but she should be free to celebrate divine service in accordance with the rites of the English Church. Her trousseau included two sets of children's clothes, one for a boy and one for a girl. Sadly they were never used during her lifetime and were sold as new after her death.

Neither bride nor groom was particularly attractive. The Princess Royal was the least clothes-conscious member of her family, and almost as fat as her husband-to-be. Behind his back he was known as 'The Great Belly-Gerent', and Napoleon Bonaparte later remarked that God had created the Prince to demonstrate the utmost extent to which the human skin could be stretched without bursting. They were married at St James's Palace on 18 May 1797. After a rough sea-crossing they reached Germany to make their home at the palace of Ludwigsburg. At a dinner party on their first night, a band played the English National Anthem in her honour, and, she wrote to her father, she 'required all the Strength in my power not to burst into Tears'.[25]

Early the following year, after a long and difficult labour, she gave birth to a stillborn daughter. Afterwards she was so ill with fever that for a time the doctors feared for her life, and several weeks were spent in convalescence. She continued to correspond regularly with her father but they never saw each other again.

In 1797 on the death of his father Frederick became Duke of Württemberg, and Charlotte Duchess. In 1802 he assumed the title of Elector, and in 1806 that of King. After her elevation to the throne she wrote to her mother, addressing the letter to '*Ma très chère Mère et Sœur*'. It was received so coldly that King George insisted none of his family should refer to his daughter as Queen of Württemberg in future. Cut off from her homeland, the former Princess Royal was nominally a British ally, but after the battle of Austerlitz, with Württemberg a not unwilling puppet state of Napoleon, she was obliged to be technically her father's enemy. She had been placed in an almost impossible situation. As her childhood friend Miss Wynne noted:

> I have heard her say it was of course very painful to me to receive him with civility, but I had no choice; the least failure on my part might have been a sufficient pretence for depriving my husband and children of this kingdom. It was one of the occasions on which it was absolutely necessary to *faire bonne mine à mauvais goût*. To me he was always perfectly civil.[26]

It was added that Napoleon also gave Charlotte facilities for correspondence with her family in England at a time when the state of Europe would otherwise have rendered it almost impossible.

For the Princesses left behind in England, there were years of loneliness ahead. In December 1800 Sophia wrote rather cryptically to Lady Harcourt that 'the excessive kindness of your manner has, I assure you, greatly soothed my distressed and unhappy days & hours'. Her spirits had 'met with so severe a blow . . . It is grievous to think what a little trifle will *slur a young woman's character for ever*. I do not complain, I submit patiently, & promise to strive to regain mine, which, however, imprudent I have been, has I assure you been injured unjustly.'[27] This apparently referred to her liaison with Major-General Garth, an equerry to the King. Aged fifty-six, with a face disfigured by a large purple birthmark, he had had an affair with her and, according to some, she may have gone through a form of marriage with him. At any rate she went to Weymouth under the pretence of suffering from dropsy, and recovered soon afterwards. She was carrying Garth's child and a son, named Thomas after his father, was born and brought up at the house of Sir Herbert Taylor, the King's private secretary, at Weymouth. Malicious gossip, possibly originating from Princess Lieven, wife of the Russian ambassador to St James's, or the Princess of Wales who loved to shock her guests, would have the more gullible believe that young Thomas Garth was the offspring of an incestuous union between the Princess and her brother Ernest, Duke of Cumberland.

Of all the sisters' liaisons, the most poorly kept secret was that of Amelia. Almost everyone in the family knew of it except the King, and everyone was careful to keep him in ignorance. In adolescence the Princess, who had always been his favourite child, became delicate and had to spend long periods at Worthing for her health. When she was fifteen tubercular trouble in the knee was diagnosed, and thereafter she was never really well again.

About two years later she fell in love with another of her father's equerries, General Charles FitzRoy. Like most of her brothers and sisters she found her life depressing and fell in love with the first presentable young man that came her way. Her governess Jane Gomm was so anxious over the situation that she warned Queen Charlotte, who asked for her co-operation in turning a blind eye to it, and above all ensuring that the King should not know anything, lest it unbalance his mind. Amelia knew she could not legally marry FitzRoy, at least during the King's lifetime, but she regarded herself as unofficially betrothed to him and in her will in which she left him all her property she wrote: 'Nothing but the cruel situation I am placed in of being the daughter of the King and the laws made by the King respecting the marriages of the Royal Family prevents me being married to him, which I consider I am in my heart.'[28]

She studied the Act hopefully and thought that if she could obtain the consent of the Privy Council and if Parliament raised no objection, she could marry him legally once she attained the age of twenty-five. This hope was later dashed. From November 1804 she signed her letters AFR (Amelia FitzRoy), and had the monogram engraved on her silver. It was believed that she may have gone through some form of unofficial ceremony with him in anticipation of a formal union later, and that should the King die, her eldest brother and godfather – who would thus be her sovereign – would surely never withhold his assent from their marriage.

Queen Charlotte had her own solution to the problem. Towards the end of 1804 she and her brother Duke Charles began discussing the chances of a marriage between his son George, Hereditary Prince of Mecklenburg-Strelitz, and one of her daughters. Brother and sister made their plans with the utmost secrecy, especially as the Queen was anxious to seize the right moment to approach the King. In April 1805 she broached the matter, assuring him that their daughters knew nothing, and he suggested the Prince should visit England in a private capacity. Unfortunately for her hopes, they were distracted first that summer by another illness of the King, an inflammation of the eyes, and then in the autumn by the battle of Trafalgar, and with it the end of all fears of French invasion of England. At length the Duke wrote to his sister telling her he regretted that the idea of marriage with one of his cousins in England did not appeal to his son.

Which Princess the Queen had hoped to see as the wife of her nephew has long puzzled historians, but Amelia was thought to be the daughter she had most in mind. Sophia was considered too delicate for marriage; Mary, at thirty, four years older than her cousin, was a possible choice; Augusta and Elizabeth were deemed too old for him. At twenty-one Amelia was the right age and, more importantly, marriage to a prince of whom her parents approved would have been the only suitable way of detaching her affections – outwardly at least – from Captain FitzRoy.[29]

By the summer of 1797 the Prince and Princess of Wales were leading virtually separate lives, and ensured that as far as possible they were never under the same roof. The latter left Carlton House, while still maintaining a set of rooms for her own use when she was there, to set up her own establishment at The Old Rectory, Charlton. Charlotte and her governess Martha Bruce, Dowager Countess of Elgin, a friend of Queen Charlotte, were sent nearby to Shrewsbury House for the summer. In the following year the Princess of Wales rented Montague House, a small villa near Greenwich Park, from the Duchess of Buccleuch. She was barely settled before her husband offered her an olive branch. In December 1798 he made one ostensibly serious effort to mend their marriage, sending a letter 'desiring her to dine at Carlton House and inviting her to settle there for the winter'.[30] She knew that he had tired of Lady Jersey, who had done more than anyone else to come between them in the early days. Friends had warned her that he was endeavouring to effect a reconciliation with Maria Fitzherbert, and persuade her to return to him, while trying to redeem himself in the eyes of his family as he was trying to negotiate a large loan from a distant kinsman, the Landgrave of Hesse-Cassel, and she refused his invitation.

The infant Charlotte regularly visited her mother at Blackheath, but she spent most of her time at Carlton House with Lady Elgin, whom she called 'Eggy'. This firm yet kind-hearted woman made the best of a difficult situation by impressing on her two-year-old charge that it was her duty to love both parents equally. As both parents were virtually at war with each other, her task was not easy. Lady Elgin shared the Prince of Wales's misgivings about the company his wife was keeping and the subsequent bad influence on their daughter, and she tried to keep the little girl's visits to her mother fairly short. From Germany the girl's aunt and namesake Charlotte of Württemberg wrote to Lady Elgin in February 1798: 'God grant that you may be enabled to keep her in perfect ignorance of the unfortunate differences between her parents! . . . It gives me great pleasure to know that my dear little Charlotte is equally kind to both her parents; maybe, in the end, that little creature may itself serve as a sort of magnet to make them a little better.'[31] Queen Charlotte was devoted to her infant granddaughter, and noticed with pleasure that whenever the King came near her on horseback, she clapped her hands in delight and called out 'Gan pa'.

By the autumn of 1804, when Charlotte was eight years old, the King felt he could no longer trust the Prince of Wales to supervise her education. He wanted her to come to Windsor and be brought up in the family circle by her grandmother and spinster aunts. At the same time he felt it only right that her mother should see more of her, and wrote to inform 'his dearest daughter-in-law and niece' of his intentions. The Prince of Wales disagreed, and at the beginning of the following year a compromise was reached whereby the young Princess would live in Carlton House, or one of the adjoining houses in The Mall, while her father was in London; and when he was away, her governesses would bring her to her grandparents at Windsor or Kew. The King was ageing, his attacks of illness were becoming more frequent, and the Queen – who of all the family had warmed least to the former Caroline of Brunswick – and her daughters, who were slowly coming round to her point of view, all did their best to persuade the King that there was some justification for reducing the mother's influence on the daughter who was expected to succeed her father on the throne one day. For a while they were unsuccessful. He was impressed by Caroline's good behaviour whenever they met, and he was probably the only person in England in whose presence her conduct was always beyond reproach.

The Princess of Wales had recently disgraced herself by further bad behaviour. It was rumoured that in 1802 she had given birth to another child. As she and her husband had lived apart for some years, it was obvious that he could not be the father. Lady Charlotte Douglas testified that three years before, Caroline had taken her into her confidence and admitted that she was the mother of a son, named William Austin, whom she called Willikin. While the King had grown impatient with his eldest son's perpetual complaints about his wife, he finally saw that the dignity of crown and family could be at stake, as this child might one day challenge the succession. Even if he was the illegitimate son of the Princess of Wales, he (or others) might put himself forward as a claimant.

The King consulted Lord Grenville, recently appointed Prime Minister, and a Royal Commission was established to examine allegations into the Princess of Wales's conduct and to report to the King. The commissioners entrusted with what was to be known as the 'Delicate Investigation' were Grenville himself, the Lord Chancellor, the Lord Chief Justice, and the Home Secretary. They completed their work by midsummer, and concluded that Her Royal Highness was innocent of the gravest charge that could have been brought against her. It was established that Master Austin was the son of an impoverished labourer and his wife, who had knocked on the Princess's door to ask if she could help find work for the husband. She accordingly adopted the child as an act of charity, not realizing what a foolish gesture it was for somebody in her position. That she had repeatedly told Lady Charlotte Douglas she was with child, describing her physical symptoms in detail, was evidently part of her delight in shocking people, and must have confirmed the fears of her in-laws about her mental balance.

All the same, during their investigations they found that her behaviour had been open to very unfavourable interpretations. People invited to her house had been repelled by her personal habits, particularly sitting on the floor, talking scandal with her ladies, and living largely on ale and raw onions. They were convinced that she was partly insane. She had flirted with several illustrious personages if not actually become their lover. Adultery was impossible to prove but could not be ruled out, especially as she boasted of taking a 'bedfellow' whenever she liked. In any other woman her way of life would have given rise to scandal; for the wife of the heir to the throne, she had behaved inexcusably.

The report was serious enough to lose her the confidence and protection of her best friend in England, her father-in-law. Had it been one attachment or indiscretion, he said more in sorrow than in anger, he would have screened her if it could have been done with safety to the Crown; but in the face of such overwhelming evidence as to her moral instability, she was not worth the screening. He could no longer receive the Princess as 'an Intimate' in his family, and now relations between them would have to be restricted to 'outward marks of civility'.

Suffering from gout and increasing ill-health, Lady Elgin resigned as governess in 1804. Apart from her grandfather, she was the one person for whom Charlotte had had the utmost respect and affection. While all mention of the Delicate Investigation had naturally been kept from her, at the age of ten she was well aware that her parents were at loggerheads, and her mother's indiscretion gave the old head on young shoulders no cause to respect her. She was approaching a difficult age, showing signs of becoming disobedient, unruly and showing off. Lady Elgin had managed to curb her temper and persuade her to behave better when nobody else could, but her successor, the

Dowager Baroness de Clifford, appointed by the King, was less successful. Only a year or two younger and inclined to be tougher than her predecessor, Lady de Clifford attempted to apply a firmer hand to her wayward young charge but with little success.

Augusta, Duchess of Brunswick, was still equally miserable in her own desperately unhappy married life. The Duke did not bother to hide his contempt for her, dismissing her as dull and stupid. He spent most of his spare time with his mistress Mlle Hertzfeldt, who had her own suite of rooms in the ducal palace, where he dined with her in state once a week. The Duchess submitted with magnanimity to the indignity of living almost in a *ménage à trois*, and whenever the Duke threatened to take another mistress both women apparently joined forces in order to try to prevent him. As far as the Duchess was concerned, it was a case of 'better the devil you know'.

Throughout these years her main consolation was the kindness and sympathy of her brother in England, and she often assured him what a comfort he was to his 'old, faithful and attached sister'. In May 1803 she assured him that she would be a sad creature 'did I not feel the truest gratitude and the most sincere affection for all the continued kindness and friendship that time nor absence has not eradicated'.[32]

If the Duke was a bad husband he was a brave soldier, and in October 1806 he was severely wounded in action at the battle of Auerstadt. Brunswick was occupied by the French and incorporated by Napoleon in his puppet kingdom of Westphalia, and when the Duke asked Napoleon for clemency, hoping that Brunswick might remain neutral in the conflict, the Emperor agreed on condition that the Duke would resign his commission in the Prussian army. The Duke refused, insisting that as long as he was still alive he would defend his King and country, but he was seriously ill and died the following month. It was rumoured that a mistress had been on or near the battlefield and stayed with him until he passed away.

Despite his infidelities the Princess of Wales had been devoted to her father, looked on him as her ultimate protector, and was bitterly distressed by his death. At the age of sixty-nine his widow was almost reduced to poverty, left with nothing but his collection of coins and antiques which she begged her brother to sell for her in England. With some difficulty she escaped from Brunswick to Sweden, where she wrote to King George in May 1807 that her daughter had taken a house for her at Blackheath and that her [the Princess's] whole happiness 'seems to depend on my being with her'.[33] The King sent a frigate to bring her back to the land of her birth, and she landed in England on 1 July. He awarded pensions to her and her three sons, and the Princess of Wales handed over Montague House as a temporary residence for her. Here on 19 September brother and sister met for the first time for thirty-six years. Time had not treated them kindly; one was an almost penniless refugee, the other nearly blind, lame and already subject to frequent attacks of mental derangement. The Princess of Wales found her mother very deaf, looking much older than her years, failing in memory, 'and her whole system is very much shook'.[34]

Though Queen Charlotte and the Duchess of Brunswick had never really liked each other, a meeting between them at Buckingham House went off successfully. Princess Elizabeth reported to the Prince of Wales that his mother-in-law's reception was most cordial, and Queen Charlotte was ready to forget all the slights she had endured in the past; the sisters-in-law appeared to get on very well. The widowed Duchess, Elizabeth added sympathetically, was 'a fine old woman . . . but you see when she walks or tries to get into her carriage she is very infirm'.[35] There was little love lost between the Duchess and her daughter, who admitted that 'each likes to live her own way'. The Duke of Clarence had foreseen that his aunt would be angered by the scandals surrounding the Princess of Wales; 'believe me, the frail fair one at Blackheath will shudder at the sight of her mother if she comes over.'[36] But the rest of the family treated the elderly woman with kindness; she and her granddaughter little Charlotte became fond of each other, though the latter sometimes found 'the old lady' and her tactlessness a trial. When Charlotte went to dine with her at Blackheath one evening, her grandmother repeatedly told her that she was 'grown very fat & very much sunburnt',[37] hardly a kind remark to make to a girl of fifteen who feared becoming as corpulent as her father. To the end, the

Duchess was full of gratitude to King George III for everything he had done for her. 'Indeed you are a father to all',[38] she wrote to him in 1808.

A further decline in the King's health in 1804 acted as a timely warning to the family. Since his first derangement in 1788 the Queen had never been the same woman, having come perilously close to a nervous breakdown from which it was probable she never fully recovered.[39] She was thoroughly frightened by another, albeit more mild, attack of illness thirteen years later, and again for much of the year 1804, when the King suffered from intermittent fevers and flurries, frequent swellings and pain; he became moody and irritable, his eyesight and hearing were affected, and his behaviour and judgment were increasingly called into question. Rumours abounded of his making constant changes in the household for no apparent reason; locking himself in the stables with a maid; making improper advances to ladies in public at Weymouth; attending the theatre and talking in a voice as loud as the actors on stage; and trying to ride into church on horseback, a move only averted by the firm action of an equerry.

Queen Charlotte found him more and more difficult to live with. For her own safety she would never receive him without at least one of their daughters being present, and she refused to share a bedroom with him, even when members of the cabinet appealed to her to do so. Each night two or three of the Princesses would stay with the Queen until the King had been put to bed, then they would bid her good night and she would lock herself in. Whenever he was at Windsor she would retreat to her house at Frogmore, and when they were at Buckingham House they rarely dined together. The King generally ate early, though sometimes he would appear at the table occupied by the Queen and their daughters for dessert.

Family, doctors and ministers alike decided that what appeared to be a mutual aversion could not be explained solely by her disgust for and fear of her husband. They suspected that the King distrusted her closeness to the Prince of Wales, his efforts to enlist her support for having the King declared incapable of ruling, and moves to have him kept permanently under restraint. While he never spoke ill of her, he did not hesitate to tell Baron Auckland, one of his most trusted ministers, of his dissatisfaction with her, and his belief that she was 'interfering' between him and the heir to the throne.

Amelia's passion for General FitzRoy grew more fervent with time. Miss Goldsworthy, her former governess, and Gomm warned the Queen, fearful that they might be blamed for what was happening, and upset by an anonymous letter which accused them of conniving at her affair. The Queen had scant sympathy for her youngest child, writing firmly to her in April 1807 that as she was 'beginning to enter into years of discretion', she would see 'how necessary it is to *subdue* at once every Passion in the beginning, and to consider the impropriety of indulging any impression which must make you miserable, and be a disgrace to yourself and a misery to all who love you'.[40]

At least one of her sisters was better able to resist their sad position. Elizabeth longed for marriage, but whenever she brought up the idea in front of her mother she was told that it was not a fit subject to be raised at present. The Queen's refusal to hear of any more marriages among her daughters was partly maternal possessiveness and partly due to a fear of the effect it might have on the King's mental state, as any crossing of his will was liable to upset his balance once more. Elizabeth assuaged her longing for children by helping to care for and look after those belonging to others, though in a more intelligent fashion than that of her sister-in-law, and in charitable works for local orphanages. While resenting her mother's possessiveness she adapted herself to the situation with equanimity, writing letters for her and pursuing her own numerous interests, such as engraving, collecting porcelain, taking up farming and keeping a herd of Chinese pigs at Frogmore.

The family called her Fatima because of her hearty appetite. To the Prince of Wales she wrote once of being taken 'exceedingly ill in the night, violently sick, and so swelled that they think I must have been poisoned, and that owing to a remarkable large lobster which I had eat of at supper'.[41] To keep some semblance of a good figure, she took long walks early in the morning, and in order to remain desirable to prospective suitors, she drank sugar melted in water at night as she was told it would keep her temper sweet.

In the autumn of 1808 she was told by one of her brothers, probably Edward, Duke of Kent, that an eligible offer of marriage had been made for her, by Louis Philippe, Duke of Orléans, then a penniless exile living at Twickenham. Although she was desperate to see this brought about, his religion, Roman Catholic, was a further difficulty where the King and Queen were concerned. She entreated the Prince of Wales to help, and not to 'dash the Cup of Happiness from my lips'.[42] He would support her, she knew, in any efforts to help her find a husband, and alone of the siblings he had some influence over the Queen. The latter ordered her daughter to forget the idea without a second thought; '*it can never be* & that she will never *hear of it again*.'[43] Sophia complained to the Prince of Wales of their mother's 'total want of confidence in her children', not appreciating that the Queen felt obliged to discourage her daughters' wishes for marriage; to do otherwise would betray the possessive King's dearest wishes and risk precipitating him back into madness.

The Prince of Wales tried to persuade her, and the younger sisters all argued Elizabeth's case, but to no avail. When the Princesses thought a clause in the Royal Marriages Act would allow them to seek marriage without the sovereign's consent on reaching the age of twenty-five, they sought legal advice, but had to conclude that the Act was poorly framed. There was only a remote possibility that Parliament might overrule the sovereign, and to attempt doing so would precipitate a major family crisis. By the following spring Elizabeth resigned herself to the fact that no marriage could be contracted without the monarch's wholehearted agreement. The Duke of Orléans, whose role throughout had been merely that of interested suitor to an unhappy spinster with no other marital prospects, tacitly accepted the situation, and married a princess from Sicily later that year.

By the age of twenty-five it looked as if Amelia was not destined to live much longer. She failed to rally after a severe attack of measles that year, and pulmonary tuberculosis was diagnosed; the doctors, whose treatment had failed to alleviate persistent discomfort, wondered whether moving her to Weymouth might not give her a better chance. She would be further from FitzRoy, and was therefore reluctant to leave Windsor, but now she was too weak to resist. Mary told the Prince of Wales that Dr Milman stressed:

> everything depends on her being kept as *quiet* as possible, and she ought to be *considered* in everything to make her as comfortable and happy as possible – must be *worried* about nothing, which, Entre Nous, in our House is very difficult, and with such a fine creature as she is, who possesses such very strong feelings, it requires great care to manage her well.[44]

With the King's deteriorating health and the Queen's defensive chilliness, the atmosphere at Windsor for 'the nunnery' was increasingly miserable. It was certainly no place for a depressed invalid like Amelia, who believed her unsympathetic mother was waiting for her to die. While the King insisted that no effort should be spared to try to restore his adored youngest child's health, he was adamant that she should go to Weymouth, and he asked Mary to go and keep her company. More self-contained than her sisters, she was the most protective of Amelia, for whom she had always felt the utmost sympathy, and she willingly took on the role of being her companion and comforter. She appreciated that it would be wise for family harmony to concur in sending the invalid to Weymouth, away from FitzRoy and from the Hon. Mrs George Villiers: a friend at court of FitzRoy and Amelia, Mrs Villiers was a bitter enemy of the Queen as well as a baneful influence on Amelia, who in her sensitive frame of mind was easily persuaded that several of the family were waiting for her death as a convenient way to silence her.

Three days after their arrival, Mary wrote to the King that for the first time since they had settled in, Amelia had passed a night without moaning in her sleep. A bathing machine formerly used by the King was turned into a 'parlour on wheels', and Amelia was carried straight into it from her room, and drawn into the sea, 'as if she was going to bathe', until the motion of the sea made her feel faint. In calm weather she was taken out to sea in a small boat, and after a few days at Weymouth she appeared alternately languid and cheerful. She could not cross a room without coughing, but found it a comfort to rest quietly all day without having to speak to anyone. Yet much as she appreciated Mary's solicitude, she still could not unburden herself to her sister about FitzRoy. Only to a very few friends could she do so, among them the Prince of Wales. She still felt bitter about Queen Charlotte's treatment of her, and the attitude of Elizabeth, whom she saw as their mother's ally and confidante. 'Don't tell the Queen that I can feel any pleasure in seeing her, for I can't,' she wrote to her brother, 'and Eliza some day or other shall *hear my mind*.'[45] The Princess of Wales, admittedly not the most reliable of authorities, remarked that while Mary and Sophia were devoted to Amelia, Elizabeth treated her 'with the most cruel unkindness and ill-temper'.[46] However, the latter was evidently in a minority of one. Although Queen Charlotte of Württemberg was temporarily cut off from her family in England, she heard enough from others to sum up Amelia's plight with sensitivity. 'I never saw so good a disposition, so thoughtfull and considerate to those about Her, so afraid to fatigue them by their sitting up with Her', she wrote. 'I never saw any body more carefull to disguise Her sufferings for fear of vexing others; and truly it is most vexing to see Her so long in such a sad state of Health.'[47]

In the autumn of 1809 the sisters returned to Windsor in a specially upholstered carriage intended to minimize jolting, which caused the invalid utter agony, as much as possible. Amelia seemed slightly better, and she wished to go to Kew, but the Queen complained that Amelia was selfishly monopolizing Mary's attentions.[48] Mary wrote to the King that if this came back to Amelia, it would 'half kill her', and he replied that she must remain with her sister, with the full approval of himself and the Queen. The latter may have thought her youngest daughter was making too much of her illness, but she knew better than to try to oppose the King. As a compromise they settled at Augusta Lodge in Windsor. Amelia enjoyed being near her father, whom she still idolized, and who could pay her daily visits.

By the following summer her health had deteriorated again. 'She wished to live,' wrote Cornelia Knight, the Queen's reader, 'but was thoroughly resigned when she found there was no hope of her remaining long upon earth.'[49] In July 1810 she drew up and sent FitzRoy a memorandum regarding her last will and testament, in which she left him everything apart from a few mementoes for relatives and other close friends. She had become hypersensitive to noise, and even the playing of a piano in a nearby room disturbed her. Augusta sent her a caged bird, singing with 'a very soft note' for company. Mary continued to look after her, and in September wrote to the Prince of Wales warning him 'that the Eruption he saw the beginning of in her face had increased every day since and had run nearly all over the body'.[50]

The physicians were under orders to report to the King every morning at 7 a.m. as to Amelia's health, and at regular intervals throughout the day. Sometimes he kept them for over an hour, examining them in detail as to her condition. He called on her each day, but his visits were limited to five minutes or less. As his eyesight was so poor he could barely see her, and he peered down closely on her, looking in vain for signs of improvement, but she had given up all pretence of recovery. On one of his last visits she whispered pathetically to him, 'Remember me, but do not grieve for me.'[51] It was also believed that she confided to him 'the secret of her irregular or illegal marriage' to FitzRoy.[52] She gave him a diamond ring which she had had specially made, with a lock of her hair enclosed under crystal. It distressed him that she had no similar keepsake for the Queen, so to please him she relented and had a locket made for her, also containing a lock of her hair.

Towards midday on 2 November the senior physician Sir Henry Halford, with his hand on Amelia's pulse, turned to Mary, suggesting kindly that she had better retire. Knowing what was coming, Mary replied firmly that she intended to stay to the last. The doctor then took a candle and held it to his patient's lips, and seeing the flame absolutely still, pronounced that 'it is over'.

The family had dreaded how King George III would take the news of his favourite child's death. Was the lingering suspense threatening to 'irritate him into madness', or would the shock and sorrow of her demise hasten his recovery? Nobody dared to tell him for nine days. When they did he took it as well as could be expected, finding solace in arranging her funeral and choosing the anthems himself. He assured everyone that he knew she could be brought to life again, and later he seemed convinced that she was gone to live in Hanover where she would never grow older and remain in good health. The German ancestral home, which he had never visited except in his imagination, had become a synonym in his clouded mind for Heaven.

SIX
'How good and noble she really is'

PRINCESS CHARLOTTE OF WALES

By Christmas 1810 the seventy-two-year-old King George III was plainly unwell. His previous symptoms of mental instability were returning; at his age nobody entertained any hope for improvement in his condition, and in February 1811 the Prince of Wales took the oaths of office as Prince Regent. Queen Charlotte had become very fat, suffered from attacks of erysipelas which made her face red and swollen, and was so cantankerous that her daughters were increasingly miserable. It seemed only right that the now middle-aged Princesses should have some independence from their self-centred mother, but any suggestion to this effect was ill-received. She still refused even to let them remain indoors with a bachelor brother unless a lady was present. They knew the Regent was their greatest ally, and a pathetic letter from Sophia in December 1811 was evidence enough of his 'noble and generous intentions' on their behalf. '*Poor old wretches as we are,*' she wrote; 'a *dead weight* upon You, *old Lumber* to the *country*, like *Old Clothes*, I wonder you do not vote for putting us in a sack and drowning us in *The Thames*.'[1]

To Augusta, the eldest spinster, it fell to lead them in the nearest they came to revolt. Boldly she decided it was time to make a stand. One morning in April 1812 after breakfast four separate letters were handed to Queen Charlotte by Madame Charlotte Beckendorff, her keeper of the robes. One, drafted mainly by Augusta, was signed by all four sisters, and the other three were written respectively by Elizabeth, Mary and Sophia, all appealing respectfully to be granted their own 'independent establishments'. The Queen was furious, and in her reply she endeavoured to use their father's illness as an excuse, saying that the very idea of going to public amusements except where duty called, while their father was in such a 'Melancholy Situation', would be positively indecent. She did not wish to see any of them again that day, claiming that she never felt so shattered in her life as she did when reading the letters.

They refused to give in and a joint letter, which was once again largely the work of Augusta, went to the Prince Regent, admitting that they had 'neither health nor Spirits to support for any length of time the life which we have led for the last two years, more Especially the Treatment which we have experienced whenever any proposal has been made for Our absenting ourselves for a few days from the Queen's Roof'.[2] At Windsor in November there was 'a dreadful scene' at which the Queen accused Elizabeth of caring nothing for the King's feelings. The Regent had to exercise his utmost tact and persuade his mother to try to see matters from their point of view as well as her own.

The passing years had left their mark on the Queen. Humiliated early in her marriage by her husband's family, she had been horrified by the symptoms of her husband's illness, even occasionally fearing for her life if he should become violent towards her. She tried to shut herself off from its worst manifestations, while only too ready to accuse her daughters of failing in their duty every time they showed any inclination to try to enjoy themselves. That they were victims of the family misfortune as much as she was hardly seemed to occur to her. In thanking the Prince Regent for his peacemaking efforts, Augusta wrote that her sisters had been perfectly respectful to their mother, though she 'won't allow that any of us feel for the King's unhappy State of Mind'. While she herself was ashamed to have written so much on such a painful subject, because of her love for the Queen, 'I *feel the injustice most deeply* with which she treats us all four. It is undeserved. And our lives have not been *too happy*, but we have never complained, nor should we if we were but quiet and comfortable with the Queen.'[3]

Before she was twenty there had been some talk of arranging a marriage between Augusta and the Crown Prince of Denmark, but the fate of Caroline Matilda had persuaded the King to dismiss any thoughts of another similar Anglo-Danish alliance. Her lengthy exchanges of letters with Sir Henry Halford were enough to invite speculation on an affair between them, but Halford was happily married and the friendship was merely platonic. Augusta had confided in the Regent of her love for Major-General Sir Brent Spencer, an equerry of her father, and begged him to let her marry. She was too dutiful a daughter to think of keeping it a secret from the Queen, who was so appalled at the idea that she would not let it be mentioned any further. They had first met soon after Spencer's return from commanding a regiment in the Duke of York's Dutch expedition of 1799, and despite Queen Charlotte's predictably negative attitude, in March 1812 Augusta wrote the Prince of Wales a long letter concerning 'the Secret of my Heart', begging him passionately to sanction a private marriage between them. 'I have nothing to disguise upon the subject,' she wrote, 'having once named it to You, but I will confess than I am proud of possessing the Affection and good opinion of an Honest Man and highly distinguished Character, and I am sure that what You can do to make us happy You will not leave undone.'[4] Whether he did so is uncertain, but Spencer was shown particular favours by the Regent, who created him a Knight of the Bath later that year, and in due course invited him to his coronation. Some have taken these, and various references in the royal family's correspondence, as evidence that a secret marriage may have taken place.

For a time the Queen and her daughters usually visited the King at Windsor in pairs. Queen Charlotte spent about a quarter of an hour with him one day in June 1812, but this was probably the last time she ever saw him. Mary undertook to write a daily bulletin for the Prince Regent on their father's health, and once she went with the Queen to see him; 'it was shocking to hear the poor King run on so, and her unfortunate manner makes things so much worse.'[5] She tried to find what little solace she could in such a harrowing situation. 'I fear we can never make them a *real comfort* to each other again, as all confidence has long gone,' she wrote to her brother, 'but I am sure they have a *great respect* for each other, and that the Q. loves him as much as she can love anything in this world, but I am clear it is in the power of their daughters, if they are allowed to act, to keep them tolerably together.'[6]

On 26 March 1813 the widowed Duchess of Brunswick died at her lodgings at Hanover Square, and was buried at Windsor. Almost to the end her relationship with the Princess of Wales had remained distant, but the latter was saddened by her death though relieved that her mother's sufferings were over. Augusta's eldest son, 'Brunswick's fated chieftain', who had succeeded his father as Duke, was killed at the battle of Quatre Bras two years later.

Queen Charlotte must have envied her much-disliked sister-in-law's release. What little joy in life still remained to her was largely due to her eldest son's solicitude. When he held a fête at Carlton House in 1814 the Queen, Mary and Augusta were among the guests. Starved of merriment for so long, the seventy-year-old Queen stayed until after 4 in the morning. Mary wrote to her brother afterwards to thank him; 'all those I have *seen* are full of *gratitude* and delight with your manners and great good nature and kindness to every soul. I never saw the Queen more pleased.'[7]

For the adolescent Charlotte, daughter of the Prince Regent, there were few diversions apart from looking after her animals, reading, or playing the piano. She spent most of her time at Warwick House, and her mother rarely visited her, while her father often spoke sentimentally of her to others and gave her expensive gifts, but showed her little paternal affection. He complained to his sisters that she always seemed to be sulking. Devoted to riding, horses and dogs, she had become rather a tomboy. Knowing how he admired conventional femininity, some thought it was an affectation designed to irritate him.

Lady de Clifford and other ladies at court alike admired her fearlessness and skill as a rider, but they were shocked by her deportment and general 'swaggering' manner, especially a habit of 'twanging hands' with the men – 'not at all *en princesse*'. A Dutch diplomat called her 'a mutinous boy in skirts'. She wiped her nose on her sleeve, and sat with her legs stretched out in front of her. Lady de Clifford reprimanded her for showing her drawers, and was told that she did not care. Not one to give up easily, her governess insisted that her drawers were too long, to be informed that those worn by the Duchess of Bedford were much longer, 'and they are bordered with Brussels lace'.[8] Taller than her mother and mercifully free of her coarse looks, she was pretty in a conventional way, but apart from riding she rarely took any exercise and hated walking for its own sake. The Princess of Wales's lady-in-waiting Lady Charlotte Bury remarked astringently that her figure was already gone, 'and will soon be precisely like her mother's: in short, it is the very picture of her, and not in miniature'.[9]

As Charlotte became older she preferred her father's company. She resented being encouraged to be friendly with the young men who frequented the Princess of Wales's rooms at Kensington and Blackheath, and was irked by her continual fault-finding. Horrified by the public revelations of sordid details about her mother's behaviour from the Delicate Investigation of 1806, she wrote to Miss Mercer Elphinstone in September 1813 that after the publication of certain facts of which she was wholly ignorant before, 'it really came upon me with *such a blow* & *it stagger'd* me so terribly, that I *never have* & shall *not ever recover* [from] it, because it sinks her so very low in my opinion'.[10]

Her father was kind enough to her, though she disliked and distrusted her uncle Ernest, the Duke of Cumberland, and as a child she had always dreaded going to Windsor where Queen Charlotte made her disapproval evident. She thought her maiden aunts terribly dull, apart from the gentle Sophia, whom she found unfailingly kind and 'thoroughly amiable'. 'When I see her with the rest of her family, I can hardly believe she belongs to them – so wholly different is she is [*sic*] in thoughts, opinions, manners.'[11] At least one of the others gave the impression of spying on Charlotte on her father's behalf. Mary, whom she credited with the same 'propensities of dark deceit' as the Duke of Cumberland, was 'almost the most violent person I ever saw', and repeated everything to the Prince of Wales, 'whose great favorite she is, as well as Pss. Elizabeth. There is but one difference, that the former being a fool, cannot contrive things so well as the other who has cleverness and deepness.'[12] The monotony of life at Windsor was presided over by an elderly, domineering matriarch surrounded by her cowed spinster daughters, who all seemed to be suspicious of each other, whiling away their miserable lives intriguing endlessly amongst themselves for want of any more constructive activity. Over everything loomed the shadow of the grandfather whom the adolescent Charlotte was no longer permitted to see, though she could sometimes hear his ravings.

By the time she was sixteen the elder generation found her a rather self-opinionated young lady who did not shrink from airing her views freely, but if she had her mother's fearlessness and lively personality, these were tempered with wisdom and tact. Queen Charlotte soon came to respect her granddaughter, while the latter showed that she was not at all afraid of the lady whom fate had treated unkindly. Both would spend many an evening in conversation during which the Princess often reduced her grandmother to helpless laughter. Her initial suspicion of the aunts soon gave way to sympathy. The secret of happy family life, she appreciated, was to be found in unity, as she wrote to Margaret Mercer Elphinstone in January 1812: 'In so large a family as there happens to be, it is of *great consequence* to be WELL TOGETHER; it is impossible that one can like all the same, or have the same opinion of them all indiscriminately; but yet to keep up appearances & to have no wide breaches is what is required.'[13] Nevertheless the unchanging routine of life at Windsor Castle was tedious, and three weeks later she was writing of her *ennui* there; her relations were 'like laws, the same thing each hour is marked out to the moment'.[14]

Father and daughter recognized that the only solution lay in an early marriage. In 1813 the Prince Regent authorized Lord Castlereagh, the Foreign Secretary, to make arrangements for a betrothal between his daughter and the Dutch heir William, Hereditary Prince of Orange. Such a union would be of great political importance, as it would link the United Kingdom of Britain and Ireland with the projected new Kingdom of the United Netherlands, comprising Belgium, Holland and Luxembourg. Charlotte tacitly accepted the fact that she was apparently to be betrothed to him, but without enthusiasm. However much he might wish for the support of an English wife, she could not go abroad. 'As heiress presumptive to the Crown it is *certain* that I could not quit this country, as Queen of England *still less*.'[15]

Well aware of his power to make life awkward for her if she did not comply with his every wish, Princess Charlotte was anxious to be on the best of terms with her father. While she knew it was impossible to maintain good relations with both parents at once, she was revolted by her mother's behaviour and could only feel a sense of pity, admitting she had been 'ill used', yet no real respect for her. Once she had proved receptive to the question of betrothal with the Prince of Orange, the change in her father's attitude towards her was evident. He became 'exceedingly kind & gracious' to her, and when she asked permission to visit her mother at Kensington, his reply could not have been more accommodating. 'Go when you please, I leave it all to your discretion & what you know right. Only tell me when you return.'[16]

On 12 December 1813 the Regent gave a small dinner party at Carlton House, with the aim of allowing his daughter to meet for the first time the young man who had just arrived in England for the purpose of being introduced and in due course married to her. A few other guests had been invited, among them the Duke of Clarence, Lord and Lady Liverpool, and Lord and Lady Castlereagh, which the Regent cynically told his daughter 'would take the glare off it, if it was put into the papers'. Before the dinner he exacted a promise from her 'to give him *my fair* & undisguised opinion of him [the Prince of Orange] after diner [*sic*], for that *my answer* must [be] decided that night one way or the other with [no] *hezitation*'. It was hardly fair to an inexperienced young girl of seventeen who had led such a sheltered upbringing, particularly without any close confidantes of her own age to consult. Seated at dinner with the Prince on her right, Charlotte found him shy, 'but presented himself gracefully & perfectly, & tho' he talked little, was master of the subjects he talked of. He struck me as very plain, but he was so lively & animated that it quite went off.'

Afterwards the Regent, impatient to know her views, asked her what she said. When she hesitated, he cried out in despair, 'Then it will not do,' but when she told him at once that she approved of what she had seen, he exclaimed, 'You make me the happiest person in the world.' Lord and Lady Liverpool proceeded rather precipitately to congratulate her, the Regent then summoned the

Prince of Orange, and in Charlotte's words 'we then really had such a terrible overcoming scene' with her father, who seemed genuinely moved. When the awestruck Prince of Orange had blurted out a few dutiful promises, the Regent joined their hands together and gave them his blessing.[17] After walking away and leaving them together for a while, he returned to impress on them how important it would be for them to keep the engagement as private as possible, in view of 'that difficulty at present' about the Netherlands. Moreover he wished to tell the Queen before the news was made public, as she 'would have a right to complain' if not informed first.

Only the next day did the Prince of Orange have the decency to tell Charlotte what the Regent had carefully concealed. When they were married, he explained, he would expect her to go to Holland with him. She was to divide her time between both countries, and they would have a residence in each. If he left her in England and returned to Holland on his own, it would give the Dutch the impression that she considered herself too grand for them. 'The great thing was as evenly as possible to divide the attentions & affections to both countries; never to forget I was an English Pss. but to think I myself more a Dutch woman when I was in Holland.'[18] Though it was perhaps only to be expected, it had been dishonest of her father to conceal the matter from her. She burst into tears, and the Prince was unable to calm her. The Regent was in an adjoining room at Carlton House, and came through to see what the commotion was. All he could think to ask was whether the Prince was taking his leave. 'Not yet,' Charlotte stammered through her tears, trying to run out of the room. Her father stopped her, saying that he and the Prince had to go as they were expected at a City banquet to be given in his honour.

Charlotte soon realized that her father had shamelessly tricked her into giving her consent by giving her absolutely no chance to refuse. On 18 December she poured her heart out in a letter to Miss Mercer Elphinstone, in her dismay at his deception. She had had no idea that her father intended to bring about the engagement so suddenly, having expected that she and the Prince of Orange would have a chance to get to know one another first, and perhaps 'sometime hence we might like one another well enough to marry – instead of wh[ich] he took us both into another room & fiancéd us, to my surprise; & when it was over, & I was walking with him, we were both so excessively astonished that we could hardly believe it was true'.[19] She admitted that she liked the Prince as a person, but she had 'received no visions of happiness'. Even so she seemed to accept her fate, albeit grudgingly; marriage and travel abroad would be preferable to remaining in England, torn between two parents who were plainly at war and showed her little affection.

In March 1814 the betrothal was announced in Holland, and received with enthusiasm as the harbinger of a new alliance between Britain and Holland. However, Charlotte, now in her London home, Warwick House, was still distressed at being told that they would have to spend six months of every year in Holland, and she was convinced that her father intended to get her out of England as much as possible. She wrote to him stipulating that, as a marriage contract had been sent to the Prince of Orange for his inspection, she should have a chance of seeing it before the conditions of their engagement were settled, and she trusted that one of the conditions would be that she would 'never be obliged to leave England contrary to my inclination, and at all events that my residence should previously and permanently be fixed in this country'.[20] Though the letter was probably written with help from Miss Mercer Elphinstone, it was a brave document from the Princess who must have still been a little in awe of her father, and one who held ultimate power over her. His answer was uncompromising; neither his daughter nor the Hereditary Prince had any business to see the contract, which was a matter to be settled by fathers, and unless she withdrew the letter, he would place the matter before his cabinet. She refused to retract one word of what she had written, and when he sent the Duke of York to try to wear her down, she would not receive him. The Duke, she suspected, was only waiting for his elder brother to die so that he would be proclaimed Regent instead, and she feared that he was trying to prove the validity of her father's marriage to Mrs Fitzherbert, a move which would result in the declaration of her illegitimacy and her being barred from the succession.

The visits of allied European heads of state to London that summer temporarily distracted the Prince Regent from his daughter's problems. During this time her attitude gradually hardened. If she married the Prince and went to Holland, the Princess of Wales, who was equally against the marriage, announced that she would go abroad as there would be no reason for her to stay in England. An unfettered Princess of Wales behaving exactly as she pleased would surely provide her husband with ample reason for divorce, and should he remarry and father a legitimate child, Charlotte would almost certainly lose her place in the succession to the British crown. Her favourite uncle, the Duke of Sussex, gave her his unequivocal support and urged her to stand firm in her refusal to leave England.

Almost providentially, the Prince of Orange disgraced himself in England later that summer. Bored by the endless ceremonial and receptions, and as uncertain as Charlotte herself of their future or lack of it, he was seen drunk in public on several occasions, much to her disgust. Suddenly she lost her heart to another foreign prince, Augustus of Prussia, a nephew of Frederick the Great. Unbeknown to her he was a notorious womanizer, and he cared nothing for her, but although she quickly became disillusioned with him she was determined not to marry the Prince of Orange. In June she told him she could not desert her mother, who had been treated so shabbily during the state visits by the Prince Regent and Queen Charlotte. She must stay in England, and once they were married she would expect to be permitted to invite the Princess of Wales to her house. As she had anticipated, the Prince objected, only to be informed that she would break off the engagement. In order to make it clear that this was no decision taken in the heat of the moment, she wrote him a letter to confirm that their betrothal was 'to be totally and for ever at an end',[21] and she asked him to explain as much to the Regent.

Her letter came as no surprise to the Prince of Orange, and he finished his letter of reply by chivalrously wishing her well and hoping she would not have cause to regret the step she had taken. As he refused to explain matters to the Prince Regent she wrote to her father herself, suggesting that the Prince had backed out of the engagement himself by telling her that their duties were divided, and as 'our respective interests were in our different countries . . . he could not go on with it'.[22]

The Regent replied that he had read her letter with astonishment, but would say no more as he was so angry. Meanwhile the Princess of Wales, pleased as she might have been by the breaking off of the engagement, announced that she was intending to leave the country anyway. Miss Mercer Elphinstone, who was in touch with Lord Grey, leader of the opposition peers, about Charlotte's affairs, received an anxious letter from him; he foresaw that the Princess of Wales's departure would precipitate grave problems for her daughter. Any plans the Prince Regent had for divorcing her would surely be made easier, and with the breaking of the Dutch betrothal, Charlotte's difficulties would be 'greater than ever'.

A warning of these was given when the Bishop of Salisbury came for a chat with her at Warwick House, telling her that he had heard from the Prime Minister that unless she wrote a submissive letter to her father, promising to reconsider her decision in a few months and marry the Prince of Orange after all, 'arrangements would be made by no means agreeable to her inclinations'. She responded with an affectionate but forthright note, saying it was impossible for her to remain silent any longer without letting him know how she dreaded having angered him, and she hoped that on his return to town she 'might have had some communication on this subject so near my heart, or had an opportunity in person of justifying and explaining candidly any part of my conduct that may have displeased you'.[23]

Two days later Charlotte and Miss Cornelia Knight were summoned by the Regent to Carlton House. Suffering from a painful and swollen knee, compounded by nervous prostration, the Princess said she was too ill to go. The emotional upsets of the last few weeks had taken their toll, and she was convinced that if she went to Carlton House of her own free will, she would probably be kept there indefinitely in a state of virtual captivity. Miss Knight agreed to go, and was accordingly questioned by the Regent on Augustus of Prussia's visits to Warwick House. Accepting her explanation that there had been no impropriety, he said he would expect to see his daughter the next afternoon unless

Dr Baillie told him that she was incapable of walking from Warwick House to Carlton House. The next day Dr Baillie said she was fit enough to do so, but she still felt wretched and begged her father to come and visit her. He kept her waiting until early evening and spoke to her alone for about fifteen minutes, after which she burst out of the room in great distress. She had been told that her faithful Miss Knight and all her servants were to be dismissed; Warwick House would be 'given up', and she was to be kept for five days at Carlton House, then taken to Cranbourne Lodge, Windsor Forest, where she would see nobody but the Queen once a week. If she did not go to Carlton House immediately, as ordered, the Regent would sleep that night at Warwick House.

As Miss Knight left her to go to the Regent, Charlotte rushed up to her bedroom, seized a bonnet, ran down the back stairs (swollen knee notwithstanding), took a hackney cab from Charing Cross and fled to her mother's house at Connaught Place. Her mother was at Blackheath, and only servants were present. She sent a note to her mother's legal adviser Henry Brougham, and a hysterical plea to her uncle the Duke of Sussex, the relation she trusted most. Between them they told her that resistance on her part would only make her situation worse, and it was best if she returned to Carlton House. Accepting that there was no alternative she did so, and an emotional reconciliation between father and daughter took place. At last he accepted that her engagement to the Prince of Orange must be regarded as at an end, and he allowed her to go for a change of air to Cranbourne and Weymouth.

A few days later the Regent arrived at Cranbourne to tell his daughter that the Princess of Wales had formally asked permission to leave the country. She had made up her mind some time ago to leave and settle in Italy; her widowed mother had recently died; she felt her daughter did not care for her, and most of her husband's family ignored her. Charlotte was shattered; she felt that her mother was deserting her, and had a presentiment that after their leave-taking they would never meet again. Nobody else in the family shared her distress, and her aunt Mary echoed the general opinion when she congratulated her brother 'on the prospect of a good riddance. Heaven grant that she may not return again and that we may never see more of her.'[24]

Charlotte was comforted when her aunts rallied round and treated her almost like a younger sister. They found they had several interests in common, and that autumn Elizabeth described in a letter to Lady Harcourt an entertaining evening she and Sophia spent with their niece. Music, she said, was

> always an amusement to me; but much as I love it, I every day think myself fortunate in not having made myself a performer, for I see that it leads people to be so enthusiastic, that it is quite unpleasant, and tho' a great accomplishment, it draws you into such very unpleasant Society, that I am of opinion that it may become a dangerous passion, particularly so in high rank.[25]

Charlotte spent Christmas 1814 with her father at Windsor. On Christmas Day she innocently caused consternation by telling him and her aunt Mary that she had witnessed many things in her mother's room she could not repeat, and that the previous year her mother had encouraged her to 'be friendly' with Captain Hesse, an officer in the Light Dragoons thought to be an illegitimate son of the Duke of York, and one of the Princess of Wales's aides on the continent. The Princess had left Hesse and her daughter alone on at least one occasion in a bedroom in Kensington, and had locked the door. God knows what would have become of her, Charlotte remarked ruefully, if he had not behaved with such respect towards her. She suspected the Captain was one of her mother's lovers at the time, and thought that her mother's motive 'was to draw her into this scrape' in order to bring William Austin forward as heir to the throne. This forfeited any remaining sympathy that her husband's family still had for the Princess of Wales. Nothing could excuse such a brazen attempt to compromise her innocent daughter. The Regent's hatred of his wife hardened into contempt and disgust, and he resolved to get rid of her as soon as conveniently possible.

Charlotte was now determined to find herself a husband, and any 'good-tempered man with good sense' who would provide her with some hope of being 'less unhappy and comfortless' would suffice. In desperation she briefly contemplated marriage with her second cousin the Duke of Gloucester, a tiresome, self-satisfied Prince of nearly forty. Fortunately there was a more eligible candidate in the brave if impecunious Prince Leopold of Saxe-Coburg. At twenty-three one of the youngest dignitaries who had visited London and met her briefly during the season of 1814, he had distinguished himself while commanding a cavalry division fighting with the Russians against Bonaparte. In January 1816 he came to England a second time. Some found him unnecessarily solemn, not to say shifty; Lady Charlotte Bury noted a disconcerting habit of his never meeting the eye of anyone he was speaking to, and the Regent took an instant dislike to him, nicknaming him *'le Marquis peu à peu'*. Nevertheless he was well-mannered, good-looking, if inclined to be over-earnest, and untainted by any breath of scandal.

There was a meeting with Charlotte at the Royal Pavilion at Brighton on 26 February, and she took to him at once. Maybe she knew that, after the distress caused by her sudden engagement to the Prince of Orange and its subsequent breaking off, she might not get another chance, or alternatively that the rest of the family would not take a second refusal for an answer. However, she found him 'quite charming', writing to Miss Mercer Elphinstone that they had 'a delightful evening together', and that she was 'thoroughly persuaded & can see that he will do all & everything he can to please & make me happy'.[26] She accepted his proposal without hesitation. Later that week a marriage contract was drafted, and the matter which had caused so much trouble before, that of her right to remain in England, was included without her needing to request it. On the formal announcement of their betrothal Parliament voted a pension of £50,000 per annum, to be paid to the surviving spouse regardless of how long he or she would outlive the other.

The wedding ceremony was performed at 9 in the evening on 2 May at Carlton House. Charlotte, clad in a dress of silver and white satin trimmed with Brussels lace, 'advanced to the altar with steadiness, and went through the ceremony with a chastened joy, giving the responses with great clearness, so as to be heard distinctly by every person present'.[27] Yet her sense of dignity was not proof against the groom's grave repetition of the words, 'With all my worldly goods I thee endow.' As he had no 'worldly goods' to speak of, she could not help seeing the funny side of it and laughed, much to the disapproval of everyone else.[28] After a short uncomfortable honeymoon at Oatlands, the country-house estate of the estranged Duke and Duchess of York where the air was rendered 'quite unwholesome' by the Duchess's numerous dogs and birds, they moved to their temporary home, Camelford House, Oxford Street, and into the more spacious Claremont, near Esher, some weeks later.

Queen Charlotte had been delighted with her granddaughter's marriage, and it led to a new closeness between them. Yet the ailing matriarch's anger at a different family wedding threatened to cause another breach. The Duke of Cumberland had fallen passionately in love with one of his German cousins, Frederica of Prussia, the last Princess whom his mother was likely to welcome as a daughter-in-law. Daughter of Queen Charlotte's brother Charles, Grand Duke of Mecklenburg-Strelitz, Frederica was separated from her compliant husband Prince Frederick of Solms-Braunfels and had already been planning divorce on the grounds of incompatibility and mutual breakdown. That the Duke should contemplate marriage to a woman who was about to be divorced was bad enough; that this same woman should be the one who had once been unofficially betrothed to his younger brother Adolphus, Duke of Cambridge (regardless of the fact that he had gallantly agreed to release her from what was not at the time a solemn and binding agreement) and then married her husband barely three months before the birth of their first child, put her quite beyond the pale. Soon after agreeing to a divorce, Frederick had a stroke and died, a little too suddenly for the gossips who maliciously suggested that his wife had poisoned him.

Most of his family, notably the Prince Regent, whose consent was required, fully supported the Duke in his betrothal, but Queen Charlotte was outraged, or, perhaps more accurately, embarrassed. The Queen of Württemberg, who had never liked Ernest, helped to strengthen her mother's resolve. The former

Princess Charlotte, still only recognized in the land of her birth as Duchess rather than Queen, was again admitted to the family circle *in absentia* after the final defeat of her erstwhile ally Napoleon Bonaparte. Embittered by years of humiliation and isolation, she had worked to spread stories of the future Duchess of Cumberland's apparent misdeeds and of her brother's so-called ingratitude. To Sir Thomas Tyrwhitt, gentleman usher of the Black Rod, she wrote dreading 'that Ernest will forget what he owes to the Prince Regent and will obstinately persist in a marriage which must be a source of pain to the whole family'.[29] She did not understand that her brothers were ready to welcome Frederica as their sister-in-law. However, Queen Charlotte must have needed little stirring up against her niece. While assuring her son that she would never cease to pray for their 'happiness and welfare', she made it clear to him in June 1815, two weeks after their wedding at the Palace of Neu Strelitz, 'that the publicity in this country of the circumstances of my niece's breaking off a former engagement with the Duke of Cambridge and the unfavourable impression which the knowledge of these circumstances had made here, place me under the disagreeable necessity of refusing to receive her'.[30]

Despite the Privy Council's wish for the marriage to be solemnized in England, in view of the fact that King George III still had only one legitimate grandchild, the Queen repeatedly urged the Regent to dissuade his brother from bringing his wife to England, which would make such a solemnization impossible as long as the Queen lived. The Privy Council ratified its proposal but she would not give way, and in July she wrote to the Duchess of Cumberland, wishing her happiness while telling her coldly that her son would 'no doubt inform you of the circumstances which will prevent his establishing himself here'.[31] Though the Duchess was bitterly upset, the Regent urged them to come to England and celebrate their marriage there without delay. They arrived at Dover in the last week of August and went through a second ceremony of marriage at Carlton House the next day. The Duchess's brother, the hereditary Grand Duke George, had accompanied them to

England and he visited his aunt the Queen at Windsor, begging her to receive the Duchess, but she would not 'alter her line of conduct'; as mother of a large family she felt obliged to set 'a proper example'. His response, after leaving her presence, was to write her a forthright letter which to her was *'couch'd in terms so offensive & so insulting to my feelings as a Mother and a Woman'*[32] that she complained peevishly to the Prince Regent of her nephew having been brought to England for the sole purpose of bullying and insulting her. The Hereditary Grand Duke later apologized, but she refused to see him again.

The Duke of Cumberland was incensed by 'the cruel and harsh treatment' meted out to his wife and himself. Reluctant to believe the worst of his mother, he wrote to her in December deploring the behaviour of the Duchess's nameless 'insidious accusers' who had persuaded his mother not to receive her newest daughter-in-law. He emphasized that he had never allowed his feelings 'to get the better of my respect and love which in spite of all this I must ever feel for you as my Mother', but was anxious to persuade himself 'that the extraordinary and sudden change of sentiments of yours towards your Daughter in Law and myself was not *your own act & deed* but that *unknowingly* you were an Instrument in the hands of others who influenced you to this conduct, and indeed I would still wish to persuade myself of this'. The sole purpose, he went on, 'of these secret informers was to try to sow the seeds of discord between the Duchess and me, but thank God their vile efforts will prove fruitless, for if any thing could increase my *love, affection* and *respect for her*, it is my seeing the generous, noble and dignified manner in which she has conducted herself through this cruel and unexampled transaction'.[33] While anxious not to strain family relations too far, he realized that Queen Charlotte's inflexibility was solely responsible and she was using her position as head of the family to get her own way.

Despite this chilly welcome the Duke and Duchess of Cumberland settled in England, dividing their time between Cumberland House at St James's Palace and King's Cottage on Kew Green. Their niece Charlotte had once disliked and even feared her uncle, whom she nicknamed 'Prince Wiskerandos', more than any of her father's brothers, but after marriage her feelings softened. She greatly admired her aunt and felt sorry for her in the difficulties she had had to contend with. To her, Queen Charlotte's high-principled stand was inexcusable. Reluctant to provoke his mother, fearing for her health if she was crossed too far, the Regent would not let the Duchess of Cumberland attend Charlotte's wedding, provoking a quip from the Duchess that surely 'even the coal-heaver is master in his own house'.

When he forbade Charlotte to see her aunt for the same reason, the Princess told the Duke in June that while she did not dare see her aunt, she was still her friend. Having read all the letters, she was 'indignant at the way in which she has been treated', adding: 'Would to God the old lady [Queen Charlotte] were dead!'[34] When the Duke and Duchess visited Covent Garden one night in June 1816 to see a French farce Charlotte entered her box immediately opposite, and blew them a kiss. At one point in the play, a courtier said to the King, 'Her Majesty the Queen is in great passion,' to which the retort was, 'Her Majesty may be damned!' Charlotte laughed loudly and clapped her hands above her head, then looked at the Duchess through her glasses to see if she had understood, then laughed and waved at her.[35]

In the following month it was Mary's turn to be married. An affectionate girl who had won her sisters' love if not their trust, she was always good to them in a crisis, and often the first to rally round and help to nurse them if they were unwell. Lacking cleverness and artistic talent, she could neither draw or paint, nor sing or play a musical instrument. Having nursed Amelia devotedly in her last illness, after the latter's death she was more lonely than ever. Slender and attractive, in her younger days she had been considered the prettiest of the sisters. At the same time she could never keep a secret, she was regarded as too pliable in the Queen's hands ('Mama's tool'), and they suspected her of telling tales and pandering to their mother. Most thought that she saw marriage to her pompous, overbearing cousin the Duke of Gloucester as her only means of escape from the 'nunnery'. Mollified by the Duke's assurance that he would place no obstacles between his wife and her relations, Queen Charlotte did not object. All the same Mary had her doubts about what she was taking on, writing to Lady Harcourt soon after her betrothal that she did not know what other people feel when they were about to be married, 'but as yet I have done nothing but cry'.[36]

The wedding was on 22 July 1816 at an improvised chapel, excessively hot and overcrowded, at the Queen's House, Kew. Seating for everyone had been so badly arranged that only a few of those present could witness the ceremony properly, and the congregation became so restless and talkative that the Lord Chief Justice ordered them not to make such a noise, otherwise 'you shall be married yourselves'.[37] Among the bride's jewellery was a ring set with a lock of the King's hair.

They made their home at Bagshot Park. On 26 July the Duchess of Gloucester wrote to the Prince Regent of their house which was 'comfort itself, and to crown all, the Duke all affec [*sic*] and kindness, and has no object but my happiness'. Well aware that the family had entertained doubts as to the happiness and success that such a marriage might bring, she added that 'The assurances of a day or two after marriage, I felt would not satisfy your *anxious mind*, and that alone made me delay writing.'[38] The Regent and Queen Charlotte visited them three days later, and were glad to see them apparently happy and comfortable, but Princess Charlotte saw the Duchess of Gloucester, and told a rather different story; 'he is certainly all attention to her, but I *cannot* say she looks the *picture of happiness* or as if she was much delighted with him.'[39]

After the two weddings there was a death in the family. On 30 October 1816 the King of Württemberg died. Queen Charlotte decreed that she and her daughters in England should wear mourning for a month. Although the Queen of Württemberg had been totally isolated from her family, destined never to see her parents again once she was married, she declared that without children, religion alone would give her courage to look forward to 'a life which must now ever be clouded with sorrow'.[40] While her sisters had often wondered whether she was really happy with a man commonly regarded as a tyrant in public and private life, she always insisted that she was contented with her lot, and she would never have wished to change places with any of them; at least she had made good her escape from the 'nunnery'.

On 16 November Queen Charlotte lost her brother Charles, Grand Duke of Mecklenburg-Strelitz. By Christmas she was shattered and thoroughly depressed, and her granddaughter Charlotte found her 'looking ill, & sunk a good deal, & her spirits by no means as equal or as good as formerly'.[41]

Since leaving England in August 1814, the Princess of Wales had been alternately scandalizing and entertaining the continent with her extraordinary behaviour. The woman who had turned her back on her daughter and husband, determined to be 'a happy, merry soul', was often to be seen at balls and masquerades, gambling parties and suppers, refusing to retire to bed at a proper hour and instead ordering the musicians to continue playing until daybreak. Hosts and attendants alike were totally exhausted by her abundant energy.

Descriptions of her in the strangest attire rapidly became common knowledge. In Geneva she appeared at a ball 'dressed en Venus, or rather not dressed, further than the waist', while at Athens she had 'dressed almost naked and danced with her servants'.[42] At Genoa she rode in a phaeton which had been built for her to look like a sea-shell, covered with mother-of-pearl and gilding, lined with blue velvet with silver fringes, drawn by two piebald ponies. Her own appearance was even more colourful than that of the vehicle. Above her bright red face was a pink hat with seven or eight feathers; she wore a pink bodice, cut very low, and a short white skirt barely covering her knees, revealing two stout legs in pink top-boots. Beside her sat 'Willikin', a vacuous-faced young man. In front of them was an outrider on another piebald pony, and two more piebald ponies trotted behind the carriage, driven by grooms in English livery.[43] Spectators could have been excused for thinking that they were watching a circus, rather than the entourage of the woman whose husband was heir to the English throne. It was widely rumoured that her sanity, or lack of it, was in question just as much as that of her father-in-law.

To those in mainland European nations, this dumpy creature of nearly fifty who had thrown all personal dignity to the four winds was an unfailing source of merriment, but to English visitors abroad she was an embarrassment. Lady Bessborough was 'sorry and ashamed' as an Englishwoman when she attended a ball and saw a short, very fat elderly woman 'with an extremely red face (owing I suppose to the heat) in a girl's white frock-looking dress, but with shoulder, back and neck, quite low (disgustingly so) down to the middle of her stomach; very black hair [a black wig] and eyebrows, which gave her a fierce look, and a wreath of light pink roses on her head'. She was staring at this apparition, 'when suddenly she nodded and smiled at me, and not recollecting her, I was convinced she was mad, till William Bentinck [the British envoy], pushed me and said, "Do you not see the Princess of Wales nodding to you?"'[44]

On 16 June 1815, two days before the battle of Waterloo, her brother the Duke of Brunswick was killed at a skirmish at Quatre Bras. For a time the Princess of Wales thought she might be asked to act as Regent for her nephew, the new Duke, during his minority, but the likelihood of any such responsibility soon passed and she was free to resume her 'merry, happy' life. She was spending money at an alarming rate, and she must have known that the Prince Regent had agents watching her carefully, making notes for evidence which would surely culminate in giving him grounds for getting rid of her for ever. She had quarrelled with most of her English attendants who, unable to put up with her dictatorial manner or ludicrous performances, gladly left her and were replaced by a motley group of Italian footmen, Arab bootboys, French chambermaids and cooks, and Austrian postilions. Over them all presided the figure of Bartolomeo Pergami, a veteran of the Napoleonic wars: poorly educated and separated from his wife, but with the manners of a gentleman. Initially the Princess of Wales appointed him as her *valet de place*, later making him her chamberlain. He revelled in his position, such as it was, and soon his friends and relations were also appointed to her staff. She made him welcome at her dinner table, and his daughter Victorine often slept in her bedroom. This family had become a substitute for the one from which she had severed her ties with little regret. She had received news of her daughter's forthcoming marriage in April with indifference, unconcerned at not being invited. While she showed some interest in press reports of her husband's frequent attacks of illness, she declared that she had no intention of returning to England, even when her daughter ascended the throne as Queen Regnant.

From Italy she set out on a pilgrimage to the Holy Land, and in July 1816 rode into Jerusalem on an ass, accompanied by her increasingly bizarre cavalcade of over two hundred attendants and hangers-on. There she founded the Order of St Caroline of Jerusalem so she could honour those with her. The Grand Master was 'Colonel Bartolomeo Pergami, Baron of Francina, Knight of Malta and of the Holy Sepulchre of Jerusalem', and William Austin was created a Knight of this esteemed Order.

In January 1817 the Duchess of Cumberland, who had given birth to a daughter and three sons (one deceased) in her previous marriage, was expecting again. Distress at her father's death, and her age – thirty-eight – made the pregnancy a difficult one, and resulted in a stillborn daughter. So far King George III and Queen Charlotte had had only three legitimately born grandchildren from officially recognized marriages. All these children were princesses, and two had been born dead.

The living exception was Princess Charlotte of Wales. After her move to Claremont, six months of marriage had smoothed some of the rough tomboy edges. Initially Leopold and their physician Baron Stockmar had been mildly critical though tolerant of her deportment and high spirits, and a tendency to stand with her hands clasped behind her, her body thrust forward, stamping her foot from time to time in emphasis, laughing and talking all the time. Yet the Baron was soon disarmed by her friendliness and lack of ceremony, and noticed approvingly that thanks to her husband's influence she had 'gained surprisingly in calmness and self-control, so that one sees more and more how good and noble she really is'.[45] Her exuberant high spirits, excitement and occasional stamping with rage were checked by Leopold's gentle murmurings of *'Doucement, chérie'*, to which she responded teasingly by using *Doucement* as her nickname for him.

Charlotte's health was indifferent, and throughout adolescence she had regularly complained of severe pains which were probably symptoms of 'the family complaint', the porphyria which afflicted not only her grandfather but her father, most of her uncles and aunts, and probably her mother as well. As her parents were first cousins, she would have been extremely fortunate to escape the dreaded disorder. After two miscarriages, one of which had prevented her from attending Mary's wedding to the Duke of Gloucester, by the spring of 1817 she was known to be *enceinte* again. The birth of the infant, the first legitimate one to the house of Hanover since her own in 1796, was eagerly awaited by her family at home and abroad. Now she was a married woman the Prince Regent could no longer prevent her from writing to her mother, who told her former chamberlain Sir William Gell in October that she would soon be a grandmother, and trusted 'that then all cabals about me will be at an *End*. I am then a well established old lady and no more scandals can be created about poor me.'[46]

At 9 in the evening of 5 November, after fifty hours in labour at Claremont, the Princess gave birth to a stillborn son. Still under the effects of medication she took the news placidly, and her first thought was how it would affect her husband who had longed so desperately for a child. The immediate shock and disappointment over, she seemed to regain her usual cheerfulness. At midnight her nurse, anxious that she must be weak from lack of food, brought her some gruel. She could not swallow it, and complained of a singing in her head and feeling cold. Then she felt a sudden agonizing pain, and clasped her stomach. The doctors were called at once, and found her pulse strangely irregular and rapid. They put hot water bottles in her bed and made her drink brandy, hot water and wine until she complained pathetically that they were making her tipsy. The pain spread to her chest and she had difficulty breathing. In her anguish she turned over and lay on her face. By 2 in the morning she was dead.

The death of King George III's only legitimate grandchild was not only a crisis for the dynasty; it was regarded as a national calamity. The deranged monarch was an object of pity among his subjects, while his sons were unpopular, and the Princess who had stood second in line to the throne represented all hope for the next generation. Nobody had believed that she could possibly be taken from them so young. Dorothea, Princess Lieven, wife of the

Russian ambassador in London, wrote to her brother General Benckendorff of

> that charming Princess Charlotte, so richly endowed with happiness, beauty, and splendid hopes, cut off from the love of a whole people. It is impossible to find in the history of nations or families an event which has evoked such heartfelt mourning. One met in the streets people of every class in tears, the churches were full at all hours, the shops shut for a fortnight (an eloquent testimony from a shop-keeping community), and everyone, from the highest to the lowest, in a state of despair which it is impossible to describe.[47]

SEVEN

'An injured wife – a depraved woman'

QUEEN CAROLINE

Within a year of Princess Charlotte of Wales's death, three of her uncles became betrothed and married with rather undignified haste in order to secure the succession. Before them, a third sister also went to the altar. In January 1818 Elizabeth was informed that Frederick, Hereditary Prince of Hesse-Homburg, who had been in England in 1814 during the visits of the allied heads of state, was to come a second time and ask for her hand in marriage. He had been warned not to make his intentions too obvious lest Queen Charlotte should try to prevent her daughter from marrying.

Elizabeth knew it was her last chance of escape. 'I am no longer young,' she wrote to the Prince Regent, 'and fairly feel that having my own home will be a comfort in time, tho' it causes me a degree of pang which I feel *deeply* – more than I have words to express – but God knows our lives have been times of *trial* and ever will be so.'[1] Yet she could not help dreading the effect her marriage would have on the Queen, who was visibly declining in health, and now found it such an effort to get her breath that Elizabeth was frightened to be left alone with her.

On 29 January she told her mother of her impending marriage. Initially the Queen seemed resigned, but by the evening she had realized what it would mean to her if she was deprived of her daughter's company. She sulked so much that nobody could persuade her to join them as usual at dinner or for cards afterwards, and she snapped at her daughter that she could do as she pleased. Elizabeth complained bitterly to the Regent that she was 'hardly used', and that the Queen was so incensed by her conduct that she could not bear to see her. Angered by her dutiful sister's plight, Augusta tried to reassure her by telling her what a 'spoilt child' their mother was and that the Queen was vexed to find she could not manage things her own way for once. After two conciliatory visits from the Regent a truce was arranged, and the Queen was reassured that she would not be deprived of her daughter's companionship immediately on marriage.

Frederick cut an unimpressive figure as a suitor. W.H. Fremantle, MP for Buckingham and later treasurer to King George IV and King William IV, was shocked at the appearance of this 'monster of a man – vulgar-looking German Corporal, whose breath and hide is a compound between tobacco and garlick'. Mr C.W. Wynn saw him at a levee, and wrote afterwards that 'an uglier hound, with a snout buried in hair, I never saw'.[2] However, he was good-natured to all with whom he came into contact, and his bride-to-be was delighted with him. The diarist Mrs Trench thought that the bride would 'redeem the character of good behaviour in the conjugal bonds, lost or mislaid by her family. She is delighted with her hero, as she calls him.'[3] In his efforts to please he stooped to retrieve Queen Charlotte's fan, when almost any other man of his station would have ordered a servant to do so, and in the process he 'created a parlous split in his breeches'.

The wedding took place at the Queen's House on 7 April 1818. The Prince Regent did not attend as he was suffering from gout, but the Queen was present, behaving with a graciousness that pleasantly surprised her daughters. Unaccustomed to riding in a closed carriage, as they set off for the honeymoon at Windsor, the groom was so violently sick that he had to get out and ride on the box. The honeymoon was spent at the Royal Lodge, where he spent most of the time in the Gothic conservatory, smoking, clad in dressing-gown and slippers.

Though at forty-seven she was too old for motherhood, at least Elizabeth had her freedom. 'The more I reflect on Mary's situation and mine, the more I regret my other sisters not having been equally fortunate,' she wrote to Lady Harcourt a few months later, 'as I am convinced they would all have been happier had they been properly established; and they are so good and amiable in their different ways, that they would have been a blessing in every family.'[4]

The marriages of three of the Princess's brothers, Adolphus, Duke of Cambridge, Edward, Duke of Kent, and William, Duke of Clarence, followed that summer. As fate would have it, the first of these marriages would produce a daughter whose own daughter would be a Queen Consort early in the next century,* and the second was to produce the princess destined to reign for over sixty years as Queen Victoria. Only the Clarence marriage would be to a future Queen Consort herself.

William, Duke of Clarence, had lived in unwedded bliss for nearly twenty years with Dorothea Jordan, one of the most famous actresses of her day, and she had given him ten children. When it was made plain to him that he, like his brothers, must heed the call of duty and marry a suitable princess to help ensure the succession, he chose – or rather had chosen for him – a princess from the German duchy of Saxe-Meiningen.

Adelaide, daughter of George, Duke of Saxe-Meiningen, was twenty-seven years younger than the Duke of Clarence. Her father had died when she was eleven, and she and her siblings had been brought up in straitened circumstances by the widowed Duchess Eleanor. The economy of Meiningen suffered badly during the Napoleonic wars and the Dowager Duchess, acting as Regent for her son Bernard, only three at the time of his father's death, fell seriously ill as a result of anxiety and overwork during the war. Though she eventually recovered, the stress on the family during her formative years left its mark on the adolescent Adelaide, who shared some of her mother's woes and grew up with an old head on young shoulders. She became a model daughter, with her fair share of common sense, devotion to duty and interest in education, as well as good manners and a sound understanding of the Lutheran Church. Yet she was unusually plain as well as earnest, and though she never complained, it probably did her confidence little good when her younger but much prettier sister Ida was married in 1816 to Bernard, Duke of Saxe-Weimar.

* Mary of Cambridge, later Duchess of Teck, whose daughter became Queen Mary.

It was this marriage which apparently drew the attention of Queen Charlotte and her eldest son to the presence of Ida's good-natured sister who seemed in danger of being left on the shelf. Her mother thought it was better for her penniless daughter to be unhappily married to an eccentric duke old enough to be her father (who still had a remote chance of succeeding to the British throne) than to be an old maid, and Adelaide dutifully agreed to accept the hand in marriage of a man whose name as yet meant nothing to her.

To his eldest illegitimate son, George FitzClarence, the Duke wrote sadly in March 1818 that she was 'doomed, *poor dear innocent young* creature. I *cannot*, I *will not*, I *must* not ill use her.'[5] At one stage it appeared possible that neither he nor England would 'use her' or indeed have any need of her at all. Faced with a demand to provide additional grants for the Dukes who were soon to be married, Parliament was in no mood for generous compromise. Lord Liverpool was obliged to reduce the grants he originally intended to propose, and after backbench revolts in the Commons the amounts were reduced further. Lord Castlereagh regretfully informed the House that any hope of this marriage was now over, as the Duke declared angrily that such a grant was irrelevant to his needs and he would refuse it, as well as the marriage, altogether. Fortunately he was persuaded to have second thoughts about the latter. The young woman who was blissfully unaware of his mournful outlook regarding their life together was known to be personable, home-loving and had pledged to be a willing stepmother to the FitzClarences, even though they were of the same generation as she. Moreover the Saxe-Meiningen line was said to be 'good breeding stock', so there would presumably be young Clarences in due course. Such a treasure was not to be disregarded lightly.

Adelaide's betrothal to the Duke was announced at the court of Saxe-Meiningen on 19 April. Accompanied by two court officials from Meiningen and two German ladies-in-waiting, she and her mother left Meiningen on 20 June for Calais. A royal yacht was awaiting them to take them to Deal, where they landed on 2 July. Their welcome in England could hardly have been less hospitable. Despite a congregation of cavalry and infantry lining the shore, with assembled ships hoisting their flags and the provision of two royal carriages for them, there was no invitation to stay at Carlton House, St James's Palace, or any of the royal residences. They were conveyed to Grillon's Hotel, Albemarle Street, London, and had just unpacked when at last a visitor came to call. George FitzClarence, the Duke's eldest son, was the first of the family to greet her. The Duke was devoted to his children, and intended that his future wife should take her place as one of a large happy family circle, but it had never occurred to him that sending one of his illegitimate children as the first relation to meet her in England might be tactless. Nevertheless George performed his ambassadorial role courteously, explaining apologetically that there was no court in London, in view of the King's indisposition and the Queen's severe illness, while the Duke of Clarence was 'staying out of London'. They were about to retire for the night, too exhausted to take affront at this extraordinary lack of hospitality, when the Regent suddenly arrived to introduce himself. As if anxious to make amends for the niggardly reception, he was graciousness itself to the Duchess and her daughter. Maybe they had heard more about his reputation than he would have wished, but the shy Adelaide found him intimidating.

As the Regent was about to take his leave and let the exhausted mother and daughter at last go to bed, the Duke of Clarence suddenly arrived. He had not known what to expect in his bride, but he was reassured to find a gentle-mannered, modestly dressed young woman who spoke good English. In these aspects she differed considerably from his new German sisters-in-law. Adelaide kept her first impressions of her husband to herself. Though she had led a sheltered life, at the age of twenty-five she was no child, and fortunately she had no illusions about the man she was to marry. It was no secret throughout the courts of Europe that the late Dorothea Jordan had been the most constant love of his life, yet there had been dalliances with others; and she was surely aware that other princesses and well-born, if not suitably royal, spinsters had rejected his hand in marriage. But she was probably too exhausted to be able to form any concrete impression of him before he took his leave late that night, allowing her and her mother a few hours of rest.

During the next few days Adelaide and her mother were taken on drives around the City; visited Kew to meet the Duke of Cambridge, who had married Augusta of Hesse-Cassel three months earlier, and Queen Charlotte; and took their places as guests of honour at a dinner hosted by the Prince Regent. The marriage ceremony, a double – with the Duke of Kent leading the widowed Victoire, Princess of Leiningen to the altar at the same time, in order to save trouble and expense – was to take place at Kew Palace on 11 July 1818, but was postponed for two days because of the illness of Queen Charlotte. The royal family began to assemble at three o'clock in the drawing-room, where an altar covered with crimson velvet had been improvised in front of the fireplace. An hour later Queen Charlotte was conducted into the room by the Prince Regent, and took her place to the right of the altar. The Regent gave both brides away as they knelt to receive the blessing of their mother-in-law, who answered in a cracked, emotional voice. She retired to her boudoir as soon as she could, leaving the rest of the family to attend a large dinner given by the Regent.

Afterwards the Duke and Duchess of Clarence went to their London home, St James's Palace. Both were happy to lead a quiet domestic life, and after calling on them two days later the Regent was amused to find them sitting by the fire 'exactly like Darby and Joan'. Yet there was little general enthusiasm for the new Duchesses. After an entertainment at Carlton House that week one of the guests, W.H. Fremantle, described proceedings to the Duke of Buckingham – 'a grand display of all the Royal Duchesses, one more ugly than another', though he conceded grudgingly that he thought 'the manners of the Duchess of Clarence the best'.[6]

The Duke of Clarence felt that it was impossible for them to live in England in appropriate state, and for reasons of economy he decided that they would have to live on the continent for a while. Within three weeks of the wedding they left for Hanover, where they were offered the Fürstenhof, a house belonging to the Crown. The Duchess had become particularly attached to Queen Charlotte during her time in England. Though the Queen was stern and unbending to the rest of her family who were always in awe of her, the Duchess had warmed at once to the matriarch who was evidently a prisoner of her own unhappy circumstances, so brave and reserved to the last that she would not allow any mention of her failing health in her presence. Both women had come from small states in Germany to England to marry members of the same family whom they had never previously met. Fearing that she would never see her mother-in-law again, the Duchess wanted to be able to express her gratitude for Her Majesty's kindness, for the Queen was particularly anxious that this marriage should be a success and she had taken an immediate liking to the self-effacing Adelaide. But there was no formal farewell before the Clarences left St James's Palace on 3 August for the journey to Dover and thence Germany.

Now installed at Kew, by the autumn it was evident that Queen Charlotte, now seventy-four, did not have long to live. She had suffered from dropsy for some time, and was losing the will to live. After Elizabeth's departure for Germany she had fits of uncontrollable weeping, found it difficult to get her breath back afterwards, and worried endlessly about herself. With characteristic bluntness she asked her doctors whether they believed her constitution was giving way, and their evasive replies irritated her. On Augusta and Mary, whose husband felt unable to refuse to let her help keep her mother company, fell much of the burden of providing companionship, and she appeared to express some regret for her selfishness over the years. Augusta wrote to her brother the Prince Regent in October that their mother had apologized for having 'caused a very dull summer *to you all*, for the Prince would have given his Brothers balls and parties on account of their marriages, and poor I have been a bane to everything'.[7] She wished she could see her sons and tell them how much she loved them, but she was too ill, and could only see Augusta herself and Mary. What she really wanted, now she knew she was dying, was to be at Windsor near the King, whom she had not seen for six years and rightly feared she never would again.

From Germany, the two married sisters anticipated with sorrow the passing of the mother, as well as their deepest regrets that they would not be together 'when the dreadful event takes place'. The

Dowager Queen of Württemberg wrote to Lady Harcourt of her thoughts 'in looking on the day that will deprive us of the best of mothers as a most fatal one for Great Britain'. From Homburg, Elizabeth noted that

> in few countries people meet with such an example as that set before them by the Queen and my most amiable, good sisters who have sacrificed every earthly comfort to attend to their aged parents and contribute to make their lives pleasant . . . the Queen is the great link of the chain; and I fear, should one drop off, that much misery would come. In all numerous families there are a variety of opinions, which are softened when there is a person at the head of them whom all look up to. Through their influence a sort of friendly unanimity is preserved; but should they fail, all draw different ways, and outward union is no more thought of.[8]

On 16 November Sir Herbert Taylor came to see Queen Charlotte about a codicil to her will, by which she was bequeathing the house and farm at Frogmore to Augusta, and Lower Lodge, Windsor, to Sophia. On arrival he was told by Sir Henry Halford that she had been informed of her 'immediate danger'. She was sitting in her favourite horsehair-stuffed armchair as he knelt beside her, holding her left hand and feeling her pulse, her breathing laboured while perspiration ran down a face distorted in agony. She greeted Taylor with a painful smile and made an immense effort to sign the will. Halford then asked Taylor, speaking in Latin, to send for the Regent at once. He arrived quickly and hardly left her side, holding her hand for much of the time, and was with her when she died the next day. Also present were the Duke of York, Augusta and the Duchess of Gloucester, who wrote that they 'had the consolation of seeing her expire without a pang, & a sweet smile on her face', and '*nearly received her last breath*'.[9]

For fourteen months England was without a Queen Consort, but during this time there were several births in the royal family. On 24 March 1819 Augusta, Duchess of Cambridge, had a son,

George; of greater significance was the imminent arrival of a child to the Duke and Duchess of Clarence, but the Duke did not realize that his young wife was less robust than the prolific Dorothea Jordan had been. Travelling on rough German roads when she should have been resting quietly did not agree with Adelaide, any more than walking in the palace garden during bad weather, for she caught a cold which turned to pleurisy. The doctors bled her and inadvertently brought on a premature delivery.

On 29 March she gave birth to a sickly daughter, who was baptized Charlotte Augusta Louisa at once, died that same evening, and was laid to rest beside her ancestor, King George I. For several days the mother was so weak that her life was also in danger. Overcome with despair at the thought of losing the wife to whom he had become so devoted, the Duke nursed her with a solicitude which touched his family, who all sent their fondest wishes for her speedy recovery. The Dowager Queen of Württemberg trusted that 'this amiable little Dutchess will soon recover her strength; by all accounts she is the very woman calculated to suit my dear William's taste'.[10] Two months later two more royal children were born, three days apart, Princess Victoria of Kent on 24 May and Prince George of Cumberland on the 27th. By this time the Duchess of Clarence had rallied and gone to stay at Meiningen; by August she was expecting again, and felt so much stronger that she persuaded the Duke they should follow the example of the Duke and Duchess of Kent and return to England for the birth. The Duke swallowed his pride and accepted the meagre parliamentary grant which he had refused before his marriage.

The Duchess was under the care of Dr Andrew Halliday, an army surgeon who had distinguished himself at the battle of Waterloo, though his qualifications as a maternity specialist were in some doubt. On their way home the Duke decided to introduce his wife to some of his married sisters. At Louisbourg they called on the widowed Queen of Württemberg, who was full of sympathy for Adelaide as she too had known sorrow when her baby daughter was stillborn. She was impressed with the change in her brother's manners and behaviour, and congratulated her sister-in-law whom she knew to be solely responsible. Continuing their travels to Homburg, they visited the Landgrave and Landgravine, then to Ghent to stay with the Duchess's sister Ida, Duchess of Saxe-Weimar, and her husband who was the governor.

By 5 September they had reached Dunkirk, but the strain of meeting her in-laws, added to the effect of continuous travelling over bad roads in poor weather, had been too much for the Duchess, who collapsed and had a miscarriage. They stayed for a few days at Dunkirk, where the royal yacht was waiting, to allow her to convalesce. Though not fully recovered, the Duchess knew that her husband needed to be back in England soon for the wedding of his eldest son, and bravely insisted that she was well enough to cross the Channel. The weather was still poor, and by the time they weighed anchor off Dover, she was too ill to go further until she had had a further opportunity to rest. They stayed at Walmer Castle for six weeks, and did not return to London until mid-November, spending Christmas at St James's.

The winter of 1819–20 was severe, and within a week the Duke of Clarence lost a brother and then his father. On 23 January the Duke of Kent succumbed to pneumonia, leaving a widow and their daughter of eight months, Victoria. Six days later the eighty-one-year-old, blind and deranged King George III, whose physical health had been declining for some weeks, was released from his twilight existence at Windsor.

Since the late summer of 1816 the Princess of Wales had lived in Italy, and was at Villa Caprile near Pesaro on the Adriatic coast when she learnt of her daughter's death. No official intimation had been sent to her by the court, and the only person prepared to communicate directly with her was the bereaved Prince Leopold, who ordered his private secretary to write to her. At the end of November 1817, over three weeks later, her secretary Joseph Hownam was summoned to receive a letter delivered by a King's messenger on his way to Naples and Rome. He prepared her for the worst before breaking the news, and after reading the letter she wept before telling Hownam that Charlotte would 'never know all the torments her poor mother has suffered or will suffer, it is probably better. This is not only my last hope gone, but what has England lost?'[11] By January 1818 she had come to terms with her bereavement, declaring that her political interest for England and Europe was 'now for ever at an end', and that her daughter's death was 'a very severe punishment upon the English nation'.[12]

She was not alone in realizing that her daughter's death would probably encourage the Prince Regent to redouble his efforts to obtain a divorce. In the summer of 1818 he sent a three-man deputation to Italy to conduct another investigation into his wife's manners and morals. The 'Milan Commission' spent almost a year, examining over eighty witnesses and amassing evidence to prove adultery between the Princess and Pergami. While most people were convinced that they had been lovers, the cabinet was reluctant to sanction proceedings which would surely lead to another royal scandal and jeopardize the standing of the throne. While the evidence obtained by the Commission looked conclusive enough, it had been obtained largely through foreigners of the servant class who spoke no English, and its credibility would probably not survive the scrutiny of an English court. The Princess of Wales would not lack for defenders, pleased to embarrass the Prince Regent and his ministers for political motives, and in view of his marriage to Mrs Fitzherbert, not to mention various liaisons since, it would clearly be a case of the pot calling the kettle black.

When she heard that the strength of King George III was ebbing, she wrote to Brougham saying that she might return to England 'if the country would protect her'.[13] Brougham thought her sudden return would cause more annoyance and mischief to the country than she was worth, even though her presence might be useful in helping to overthrow the Tories and return her Whig supporters to power. She was at Leghorn in Italy on her way to Rome, when news of the King's death reached her. It was probably at this stage that she decided she would return to England in due course.

Long before her daughter Charlotte's death, the Princess of Wales had told friends and supporters that she had no ambition to be Queen, and resolved never to return to England. She would be content with a settlement of £100,000 and no further annual allowance. Lord Brougham, Whig MP for Winchelsea and her most eloquent defender, told her that this sum, less than three years' income, 'would be madness', and was confident that he could negotiate a more satisfactory figure. After consulting his parliamentary colleague and brother James, he recommended that, as long as her present annuity was guaranteed for life, she would agree to the ratification by Parliament of terms for a separation and renounce her right to the title of Queen, taking the title Duchess of Cornwall or something similar after her husband's Coronation. Further legal advice suggested that Parliament would be unable to pass an Act ratifying the separation unless the Princess confessed to or was tried and found guilty of infidelity. The Prince Regent would not be satisfied with separation by mutual consent. Nothing short of divorce would do, not so much because he intended to remarry (something which was far from his mind, though it was rumoured that various European courts were ready to offer suitable princesses), rather that he yearned to be free of that 'vilest wretch this world was ever cursed with'.[14] Had he not been distracted by the marriages of his brothers and the death of his mother, he would probably have pursued the matter with greater vigour.

Before he could resolve the situation once and for all, he ascended the throne as King George IV. On the first day of his reign he fell seriously ill with suspected pneumonia. Once he had recovered, he became preoccupied with the possibility of excluding his wife's name and title from the liturgy. His ministers insisted that no Bill of Divorce could be brought without being heard by judges in an ecclesiastical court, and if the Queen decided to fight for her rights, recriminations would surely be made. Unedifying revelations regarding Mrs Fitzherbert, and relations with his mistresses, would become public. With reluctance he allowed Lord Liverpool to propose an annuity of £50,000 for the Queen payable on condition that she remained abroad, undertook to relinquish the title of Queen and any other indicating her relationship with the royal family of England, and agreed not to enter 'any part of the English dominions'.[15] Moreover she should not expect to take her place as Queen at his forthcoming Coronation.

Before she was informed of the allowance to be offered to her, she had heard with irritation of her exclusion from the liturgy. That, and her treatment at the hands of the representatives of European courts who deferred to the wishes of King George IV and declined to accord her the recognition to which she felt entitled, made her determined to proceed forthwith and demand that she be accorded her rights. Her journey was delayed by illness, touches of rheumatic complaint and stomach pains, but neither these nor the entreaties of Brougham who crossed the Channel to try to persuade her to comply with the government's proposals and accept the annuity was enough to stop her. After her request to Lord Liverpool for the royal yacht to be sent for her to travel back in was declined, she took an ordinary public ferry and arrived at Dover on 5 June, to be greeted by a royal salute of twenty-one guns from the castle and a large supportive crowd. The next day she set out for a triumphal entry into London, with cheering, waving people surrounding her carriage as she approached the capital. She was lodged at the house of Alderman Wood, one of her most ardent champions, in South Audley Street for a few days before moving out to Brandenburg House, Hammersmith. Mobs roamed the streets yelling for 'Queen Caroline and her son King Austin', and 'No Queen, no King' became their battle-cry.

Suffering from gout, not to mention the indignity of shouts outside the windows at Carlton House of 'Nero!', the King retreated angrily to Windsor, where he threatened to abdicate rather than accept her as Queen. A theatre manager at Brighton dared not allow the singing of 'God Save the King' for fear of provoking riots, while the Duke of Wellington, a national hero since the battle of Waterloo only five years earlier, was hissed and booed on the streets because he openly declared his allegiance as 'a King's man'. Legend has it that he, or one of the other eminent lords who were unashamedly pro-King George IV at this time, was stopped by a gang and asked to repeat, 'God save the Queen!' After some hesitation he did so to oblige them, adding for good measure, 'And may all your wives be like her.' Some of her old friends had revised their opinions and now considered her a lost cause, if not beneath contempt. The writer Sir Walter Scott thought her conduct had 'been most abandoned and beastly'.[16]

Before leaving London the King recommended that Parliament should give their attention to the findings of the Milan Commission, collected over the previous five years. A committee headed by the Archbishop of Canterbury was appointed to study it, and the unanimous conclusion was drawn that the Queen had behaved scandalously while she was abroad. An inquiry would have to be held in the House of Lords, there would be a public examination of witnesses to prove the evidence of her adultery with Pergami, and a Bill of Pains and Penalties would be prepared. If passed, it would deprive her of the title, and dissolve the marriage; and she would be banished from the country.

The first reading of the Bill was introduced immediately after the secret committee had made its report, and the second, which marked the start of proceedings, took place in the House of Lords on 17 August. The trial of Queen Caroline, which lasted nearly three months, was limited to the allegations of her adultery with her Italian chamberlain and companion Bartolomeo Pergami. If the case was proven, she would technically be guilty of treason, and there would be no need for the government to bring up the King's own extra-marital liaisons. She was permitted to attend the inquiry, though she could not give evidence, and was not obliged to be present at every session. A room adjoining the Chamber in the House of Lords was provided for her to retire and rest, and from which Brougham could summon her when her presence was necessary, though she spent most of the time playing backgammon with Alderman Wood.

On the rare occasions when she appeared in the Chamber, her manner did little to enhance her dignity. As the court was in mourning for the death of the Duchess of York when proceedings began, she was unable to come in her usual outlandish costume but wore a more suitable black dress with white sleeves and frilled lace at the neck, topped with a large black bonnet trimmed with ostrich plumes. She rather spoilt the effect, observed Thomas Creevey, the politician and diarist, by hurrying in enthusiastically as the doors were opened for her; 'made a *duck* at the Throne, another to the Peers, and a concluding jump into the chair which was placed for her'. Her veil, he added, was so thick that it almost hid her face, and everything except a 'few straggling ringlets on her neck, which I flatter myself from their appearance were not Her Majesty's own property'.[17]

At the trial the King was represented by Sir Robert Gifford, the Attorney-General, Sir John Copley, the Solicitor-General, and a selection of law officers. Henry Brougham was the Queen's Attorney-General and her Solicitor-General was General Thomas Denman. Within a few days it was evident that the Queen was extremely fortunate in the men who defended her. She and Brougham disliked and distrusted each other; she had little confidence in his ability to win her case, while he was convinced that she was guilty of at least some of the charges brought against her, describing her artfully to others as 'pure *in-no-sense*'. However, as an orator, not to mention his quick mind and sharp wit, he had no equal in public life at the time, while Denman's equally persuasive yet more gentlemanly, less cynical speeches complemented him perfectly. Much of the King's defence depended on the evidence of the hapless Italian witnesses, none of whom could speak English. Uneducated and overawed in such august surroundings, and being asked questions about events which had – or were supposed to have – taken place four or five years ago, their presence added weight to the theory that His Majesty's case rested on very shaky ground.

That summer was exceptionally hot, the crowded Chamber intolerably stuffy, tempers soon frayed, and on 9 September the Lords decided to adjourn for three weeks. Lord Liverpool wanted to drop the last four lines of the Bill which would have enacted the divorce. Most of the peers and bishops knew too much about the Queen to believe her totally innocent of gross foolishness if not actual adultery, but they found the whole business thoroughly undignified, and the alleged revelations distasteful and demeaning to the monarchy.

When the House reassembled on 3 October, Brougham opened proceedings with a masterly speech in the Queen's defence which converted most of the waverers at once. If her Attorney-General could prove what he had stated in his speech, Creevey noted, 'I for one believe she is innocent, and the whole case a conspiracy.'[18] The evidence was subject to a debate in the Lords afterwards, and though there were several more witnesses to be questioned by defence and prosecution, it was clear that Brougham had as good as won for the Queen. He denounced the Milan Tribunal as 'a storehouse of false swearing', and showed beyond doubt how the prosecution had manipulated and distorted the evidence of witnesses who were either unreliable, dishonest, or simply terrified. In his summing-up Denman made a scarcely less incisive speech which not only dismissed the prosecution's defence as contrived and worthless, but also referred to the 'cruelty and profligacy' of the husband, who despite his claims to be a Christian King, was ill-advised 'to divorce his wife for misconduct when his own misconduct in the first case was the occasion of her fall'.[19]

In the Lords debates the Lord Chancellor, Lord Eldon, announced that he was satisfied adultery had taken place. Lord Grey admitted that at the start of proceedings he had been prejudiced against the Queen, but now considered he could not vote in favour of the Bill being allowed to proceed, and thought she should be declared not guilty. Even more equivocally Lord Ellenborough said he would vote against the Bill because of 'the strong and universal feeling against it', despite his conviction that the Queen's conduct was thoroughly deserving of censure, and that Her Majesty had utterly failed in her duty of setting the kind of example expected from a Queen of England.[20]

The speeches in the House were concluded on 6 November, and voting on the Bill of Pains and Penalties produced a narrow government majority of 28. Liverpool knew that to introduce such a contentious bill in the Commons would almost certainly result in its rejection and the fall of the government. The next day the House considered whether the divorce clause should be dropped from the Bill. By doing so, ministers thought they might pass it more comfortably; but all the Whig peers, knowing that the Bill was far more vulnerable if it remained, voted for its retention and it was passed with a comfortable majority. On the fifth reading of the Bill on 10 November, the government's majority was cut to a precarious 9, with 108 votes in favour of the Bill and 99 against. Creevey summed up the general mood of the country: 'The Bill is gone, thank God! to the devil.'[21]

Brougham had obtained a copy of the King's will, naming Mrs Fitzherbert as his 'dear wife', and threatened to produce it as proof that the King had forfeited his throne by marrying a Roman Catholic. This alone was sufficient to halt the Bill in its tracks. There was widespread rejoicing throughout London and other cities, but the scenes of excitement which broke out after the verdict was announced contrasted strangely with the subdued demeanour of the Queen herself. As she was escorted to her carriage she stared ahead of her as if suffering from shock, and as she sat down those nearest her could see the tears in her eyes. While her behaviour in the past had been foolish, she was intelligent enough to see through the motives of those who apparently espoused her cause. Nobody, she said later, really cared for her, 'and this business has been more cared for as a political affair, dan as de cause of a poor forlorn woman'.[22] The question of her guilt or innocence was irrelevant; as Charles Knight, editor of the *Windsor and Eton Express*, remarked, she 'was an injured wife, although I could not doubt that she was a depraved woman'.[23]

On the first Sunday after the trial, she informed the Dean of St Paul's that she wanted to attend a public thanksgiving there on 29 November. The horrified Dean appealed to Lord Sidmouth, Home Secretary, for advice, but the latter told him that if she wished to attend a service at St Paul's, nobody had any right to prevent her. He himself did not anticipate any 'serious disturbance'. She went ahead, and although the weather on that day was wet and foggy, there was a cheering crowd estimated by Princess Lieven to be at least 50,000 strong.

After this the Queen's popularity began to wane. The British people had seen her vindicated, and now they were gradually losing interest. To quote a popular piece of contemporary doggerel,

> Most gracious Queen, we thee implore,
> To go away and sin no more;
> Or if that effort be too great,
> To go away at any rate.

Whatever their personal feelings, His Majesty's ministers undoubtedly wished that she would go away. She wrote Lord

Liverpool peevish letters, complaining about the English climate and her residence, Brandenburg House, which was insufficient for her needs, and demanding an increased annuity, a town residence, a palace suitable to her position as Queen, a household of corresponding size, and above all the restoration of her name to the liturgy. She failed, or refused, to understand that although the Bill against her had been dropped, the severity of the charges against her made it evident that her behaviour had been foolish, immoral and above all undignified in the extreme. That the King had been guilty of similar misdemeanours entitled her to some sympathy, but did not exonerate her.

In the summer of 1820 the Duchess of Clarence was expecting another child. On medical advice the Duke moved his wife from the draughty St James's Palace to the more salubrious Bushey, Hertfordshire. She seemed to be in good health, and when over seven months pregnant she attended the wedding of her stepdaughter Elizabeth FitzClarence, to the Earl of Erroll on 4 December. Six days later, on 10 December, she gave birth six weeks prematurely to a daughter at St James's Palace. Once again she was very ill after her confinement, and not strong enough to go out driving in the park until the end of January, although the child throve at first. Despite the parents' wish to call her Georgina, at the request of King George IV she was named Elizabeth. However, she fell sick early in the new year, and on 4 March 1821 she died after a convulsive fit, the cause of death being given as 'an entanglement of the bowels'. When the mother was allowed into the sickroom by her physicians to see the dying infant, she fainted in the Duke's arms.

Marriage had reinforced an unexpectedly home-loving side to the Duke. Notwithstanding the lack of a wedding ring, his liaison with Dorothea Jordan had always seemed a model of domestic respectability. The Duchess had undoubtedly been a good influence on him, and he became much more civil, even-tempered, and moderate in his language.

Mary, Duchess of Gloucester, had found that domestic life was not the idyll she had hoped for. They had moved from Bagshot to Gloucester House, Piccadilly. 'Slice', thus nicknamed after

Gloucester cheese, professed to be a political Radical, but in his domestic life was a tyrant. When her sisters and friends called upon her, they were rather taken aback to be marched up to the top of the house. The Duchess apologized to them as they sat down exhausted and out of breath, explaining that it was 'owing to the cruel manner in which she was treated by the Duke'.[24] He thought that the rooms on the drawing-room floor were not left tidy, so he locked them up and kept the keys in his pocket.

The King was indignant at this treatment of his sister, and the Duchess was afraid to show her private letters to the Duke. Even so she meekly submitted to his will, even to the extent of not travelling to visit anybody on a Sunday as it clashed with his strict Sabbatarian principles. She enjoyed visiting the King at Brighton Pavilion, where she was treated like a normal human being. Though she tried to keep good relations between her brother and her husband, when the governorship of Guernsey fell vacant and he tried to solicit the post himself, she refused to do anything to help, as if he was simply not worth the effort.

By early 1821 the pro-Queen Caroline mood had died down. Though she was planning to return to Italy in due course, she was adamant that she should have a house in London, and most important of all, she should be at the Coronation. In June she learnt that the date for the ceremony had been fixed for 19 July, and that 'the difference Branches of the Royal Familly which do not go in the Procession will have places at Westminster; for which reason I shall have a consultation to assure what Right Prerogatife and Privileges I have on that occasion'.[25] As the time drew closer the King became increasingly nervous as to what would happen if the Queen tried to assert her rights – as she saw them – by making an appearance. After having continually sent him petitions and appeals to appear at his Drawing-Room, and to have her name restored to the liturgy, it was inevitable that she and her supporters would try to find some way of inflaming the people against him and creating a scene. She even asked him 'to name such ladies which will be required to bear her Majesty's Train on that day', and begged him to inform her 'in what Dresse the King wishes the Queen to appear in on that day, at the Coronation'.[26] It was evident that she believed she had every right to be crowned, while he was determined that she must be kept out of Westminster Abbey; and an extra contingent of guards was ordered for the purpose.

Early on the morning of 21 July Queen Caroline drove to the abbey, ignoring her advisers' pleas. The crowds, she was convinced, were on her side, and with their help she would surely be granted admittance, or else she would wreak such havoc that the King would bitterly regret it. When the doorkeeper refused to admit her, her chamberlain Lord Hood told him that she was the Queen. This made no difference to the man who replied that he had orders to admit nobody without a peer's ticket. When Lord Hood produced a ticket signed 'Wellington' the doorkeeper grudgingly accepted it, pointing out that it only admitted one person. Her Majesty was accompanied by Lady Anne Hamilton and Lady Hood; as Queen, she could not enter the Abbey unattended, but he could not admit three persons on one ticket. By now the guards had closed ranks, and were prepared for her to try another door; but wherever she turned her way was barred. At length she realized there was nothing to be done but to return to her carriage, and give orders to drive back to Brandenburg House. Refusing to accept defeat, she wrote to the King that 'The Queen must trust that after the Public insult her Majesty has received this morning, the King will grant her just Right to be crowned on next Monday, and that his Majesty will Command the Arch-Bishop of Canterbury to fulfil the Queen's Particular desire to confer upon Her that sacred and August Ceremony'.[27]

On 30 July she attended the Drury Lane Theatre, ironically to see a tableau representing the Coronation. It was her last appearance in public. On her return she was seized with violent abdominal pains and became seriously ill. Her physician, Henry Holland, thought that her spirit was broken after the humiliation of not being admitted to the Coronation. He diagnosed acute inflammation of the bowel, and ordered that she should be blooded, given large doses of opium and immersed in a warm bath. She could not sleep, the pain became worse and she was prescribed further bleeding, calomel and, according to Brougham, 'a quantity of castor oil that would have turned the stomach of a horse'.[28] Knowing she was about to die, she and a servant sat up for several hours one night burning papers and 'a large folio book' containing the handwritten manuscript of her memoirs, and sorted trinkets to be given to her friends. Her lawyers helped her complete her will, which she signed four times 'in the steadiest manner possible'. She left everything to William Austin when he attained his majority, though the demands on her estate meant that she died insolvent.

'I am going to die, Mr Brougham; but it does not signify,' she told him. When he replied that Her Majesty's physicians were of quite a different opinion, she retorted that she knew better than they. 'I tell you I shall die, but I don't mind it.'[29] After a sleepless night of severe pain she became delirious, went into a coma, followed by convulsions, paralysis, and a merciful release from her sufferings on the morning of 8 August, 'in peace with all her enemies', Lord Hood wrote later that day. She had expressed a wish to be buried in Brunswick with the inscription 'Caroline of Brunswick, the injured Queen of England' engraved on her coffin. This latter part of the request was ignored, but in accordance with the former her body was taken to Harwich and then back to Germany, where she could be laid to rest beside her father and brother. It was rumoured that she had been poisoned, but the immediate cause of death was more likely a gastro-intestinal disorder, complicated by a blood infection. The lack of any will to live gave her no reason to try to fight against an illness from which prompt medical attention would probably have saved her.

For Queen Caroline there was sympathy in England if little heartfelt mourning. Deserving of pity rather than censure, it fell to an elderly pastor in Brunswick who had known her as a young girl to give his congregation a fitting address at divine service on the first Sunday after her funeral. He recalled the Princess, he said, as a woman of 'sincere faith and pious feeling'. Her sense of religion, he admitted magnanimously, 'did not always preserve her from infirmities and errors', but as he asked, where was the mortal, 'where has there been a saint, who has been always perfect?'[30]

EIGHT
'So well has she conducted herself'
QUEEN ADELAIDE

King George IV and his immediate heir, his brother Frederick, Duke of York, had both been widowed within the last year. Neither had left any legitimate children, and the Duke and Duchess of Clarence still hoped to provide a living son or daughter who would one day wear the crown. In October 1821 the Duke's recently married daughter Elizabeth, Duchess of Erroll, delighted them by naming her baby daughter Adelaide, and while the Duchess took a keen interest in her young namesake, it only deepened a desire for her own baby. Early in the new year of 1822 she was again with child, and in March the Duke informed Lord Liverpool optimistically that she was perfectly well and much stronger than she had been during her last pregnancy. Unhappily a month later he had to tell the King 'that the amiable and excellent Dutchess miscarried yesterday afternoon of twins: I want words to express my feelings at these repeated misfortunes to this beloved and superior woman'.[1]

In view of such tragedies, it showed exceptional qualities on her part to hide her feelings as she devoted some of her time to the infants of her husband's relatives, not just the growing numbers of FitzClarence grandchildren, but also their fatherless niece Princess Victoria of Kent, who would surely succeed the Duke of Clarence on the throne. Sometimes the small Princess greeted her Uncle William as 'Papa!', and to the Duchess of Kent the Duchess of Clarence wrote, 'My children are dead, but your child lives, and she is mine too.'[2] The Duke and Duchess were going to the continent when the Princess celebrated her third birthday, and the Duchess wrote:

191

Uncle William and Aunt Adelaide send their love to *dear little Victoria* with their best wishes on her birthday, and hope that she will now become a *very good Girl*, being now *three years* old. [They] also beg little Victoria to give dear Mamma and dear Sissi [Feodora, Victoria's half-sister] a kiss in their name, and to Aunt Augusta [Duchess of Cambridge], Aunt Mary [Duchess of Gloucester], and Aunt Sophia too, and also to the *big Doll*.[3]

A model stepmother, she showed remarkable magnanimity to her inherited family. Before her first arrival at Bushey, William tactfully removed a portrait of Mrs Jordan from its place of honour in the drawing-room, but Adelaide gently suggested that it should be returned. Such gestures were much appreciated, and George FitzClarence called her 'the best and most charming woman in the world'.[4] However, being expected to take the role of kindly stepmother to this family of ten who were frequently demanding, sometimes ungrateful – to their father if not to her – did not make her any the happier. It was lucky that fate had endowed her with a character of natural amiability and a strong sense of duty. But her inability to produce a living infant, while her husband's former mistress had given him no fewer than ten, must have embittered her. No wonder she said to an artist commissioned to paint her portrait, who thought her eyes were too red and suggested that he place her in a position where the light would trouble her less, that it was nothing to do with the light; 'it is that I have veept much.' Her health was not robust, and by the age of forty she complained of regular pains in her side and an intermittent cough, for which doctors could only prescribe regular rest and a change of air.

A continual cause of anxiety to the Duchess was her husband's mental condition. If the Duke of Clarence did not dread his being overwhelmed by 'the malady of the family', others in the family and public life certainly did. Never was his wife's position more trying than in the months following the death of Frederick, Duke of York in January 1827. King George IV, a bloated, ageing recluse, was not expected to live much longer, and then the Duke and Duchess of Clarence would be

King and Queen. As the Duke declared triumphantly to the Duke of Sussex during their elder brother's funeral, they would now be treated 'very differently from what we have been'. In order to give him some responsibility appropriate to the heir to the throne, the office of Lord High Admiral was revived for his benefit. To the dismay of the King and his ministers the Duke of Clarence took his new position far too seriously, making speeches, trying to alter naval policy (often for the better), and soon clashing with the Board of Admiralty who did not take kindly to a man they regarded as an idiot trying to interfere with their work. Within months the Duke of Wellington, now Prime Minister, had to ask the Duke for his resignation.

In 1834 Princess Lieven noted hearing (on whose authority she did not state) that, on this occasion six years earlier, he had become so excitable and violent for a fortnight that he had to be put into a straitjacket, and that Wellington knew all about it.[5] Another rumour had it that the Duke of Cumberland, who now lived mostly in Hanover but regularly visited England, publicly announced that the Duke of Clarence was insane, like their father had been, and would not be fit to ascend the throne.[6] Such statements probably owe more to gossip than fact, but whatever the truth or lack of it, the Duchess of Clarence suffered much from the strain of looking after her husband and, presumably, defending him from false allegations regarding his mental and physical health. Her tact and gentle firmness were instrumental in helping to restore him to normal behaviour.

By the age of sixty Charlotte, Queen Dowager of Württemberg, was a very sick woman. Her doctors thought she had a severe case of dropsy, but a long history of migraines and sharp rheumatic pains in the back, hands and legs suggested that, like most of her siblings, she suffered from porphyria. Her sisters barely recognized her, and on a visit in November 1819 the Landgravine of Hesse-Homburg found her 'sadly changed, for she is certainly very large' and 'certainly does not dress to advantage, for her hair is very thin, and combed flat upon her face, which is three or four times larger than it was'.[7] Two years later their sister Augusta found her greatly altered, and had I not had the picture previous to seeing Her, I should not have guessed it was Her. . . . She is very large & bulky. Her face is very broad and fat, which makes Her features appear quite small and distended. But what strikes the most is, that from not wearing the least bit of Corset, Her Stomach and Her Hips are something quite extraordinary.[8]

She found writing difficult as her hand was 'much swelled', and regularly complained of pains in her side.

In 1827 King George IV invited her to visit England, but she was afraid he would be upset by her enormous bulk, and asked if he could send a chair to draw her up in from the yacht 'as with my shortness of breath I should be quite knocked up if I was to attempt the going up the accomodation [*sic*] ladder'.[9] Like her own doctors, the British medical profession believed that her extraordinary size could be attributed to the fact that she had been 'afflicted for many years past with a dropsy'. On the advice of the royal physician Sir Astley Cooper, she underwent tapping while in London to siphon off pints of surplus fluid, and the doctors were optimistic that it would eventually lead to a complete cure. The operation did little good, however, and soon after her arrival in England she was afflicted with a feverish skin inflammation which they diagnosed as St Anthony's Fire. She suggested that she should be lodged in the room at Frogmore normally occupied by the Duchess of Gloucester, so she could be near her brother, but for some days after being installed there she was too ill to set foot outside. When she was better she drove up to Royal Lodge to see her brother, and for her entertainment he and Augusta arranged a dinner-party in a large tent on the banks of Virginia Water. The evening ended with coffee and a row by moonlight and, Augusta wrote afterwards, her sister and the King 'were as happy as it is possible to be'.[10]

After her return to Germany she went into a decline, and became almost blind. Hearing how ill she was, the Duke of Cumberland hoped to visit her; despite her bitter enmity and her efforts to turn the family in England against him at the time of his marriage, he bore her no malice, and as a mark of generosity planned to call on her in person to assure her of his and his wife's forgiveness. On 3 October 1828 she entertained Lord and Lady Shrewsbury to dinner, and 'kept up for two hours a most interesting conversation upon a variety of topics'. Two days later, as was her regular custom on Sundays, she asked her English maid to read her an English sermon. After it was finished she thanked the girl – 'You will never read me another.'[11]

On the next day, 6 October, she died after an apoplectic seizure, and the Duke of Cumberland was told of her death while he was still at Hanover. Not having seen her for over thirty years, since her wedding, he admitted in a letter to King George IV that he had little recollection of her, but 'one cannot help feeling deeply when one branch of the old tree drops off'.[12]

In April 1829 Elizabeth, who had become Landgravine of Hesse-Homburg in 1820, lost her husband to influenza, complicated by the inflammation of an old leg wound. Despite her grief at his death, she was grateful to have had the pleasure of a married life denied to many. To the King's physician, Sir William Knighton, she wrote: 'No woman was ever more happy than I was for eleven years, and they will often be lived over again in the memory of the heart.'[13] She could now pay more regular visits to Hanover and stay with her brother and sister-in-law the Duke and Duchess of Cambridge, and she looked forward to returning home to see King George IV again. On St George's Day 1830 she wrote asking him to promise that when she arrived 'you will look upon me as a quiet old Dog, to whom you can say "Now, leave me for a month, go away to Mary" – and so on – without an idea of offending – In the way I shall not be, for once in my own Room and not with You I have employment enough never to annoy anyone.'[14]

A few days later she was alarmed to receive reports of the King's declining health, and realized that they might never meet again. She would have been happy to come and help nurse him, 'or do the most menial service to soothe and soften his sufferings', and begged Knighton to let her have some keepsake belonging to her brother if he should be taken before she could see him. He died on 26 June, and Knighton kept his promise, sending her two of the King's snuff-boxes. Writing to thank him, she assured him that she would always treat them with great care, 'and the snuff never taken out, so dear it is to me'.[15] Whatever his faults and behaviour to his wife and daughter, King George IV had been the best of brothers, and he was sincerely mourned by his sisters. Elizabeth told Knighton that 'The loss of the beloved, not to say adored brother, whose constant kindness is so thoroughly engraven on my heart, is not to be told.'[16] Her own health was declining, for soon after her husband's death she had become ill with severe pain in the legs which left her unable to walk without the aid of iron calipers. Overheated rooms and stuffiness irritated her and proved a perpetual torment.

The death of King George IV brought the Duke of Clarence to the throne as King William IV. Until the death of the Duke of York in January 1827, William had never expected to wear the crown, and Adelaide had never envisaged being a Queen Consort. For the first few months of their reign they were very popular. A monarch who went walking out in the streets with the minimum of bodyguards, grinning and waving his hat to everybody and allowing streetwalkers to give him a peck on the cheek, obviously made up with the common touch for what he lacked in regal dignity.

Tolerant and sensible, an excellent influence on her husband's behaviour, Adelaide personified all the virtues expected of a Queen Consort. At court she also had a reputation as the family peacemaker. Baroness Gabrielle von Bülow, wife of the new Hanoverian minister in London, wrote enthusiastically that the new Queen would be 'a saving angel for all the family'. She had readily 'brought about a reconciliation between the Dukes of Cumberland and Sussex,' and it was solely due to her that the former was now 'outwardly on friendly terms' with the new King.[17] There was, however, some exaggeration in this, for though Cumberland was an arch-conservative and Sussex the most radical of the brothers, it took more than differences of political opinion to divide the royal Dukes.

Blood was thicker than water; Queen Adelaide and the Duchess of Cumberland had always liked and respected each other, while Prince George of Cumberland had often stayed with them while they were still Duke and Duchess. No matter how much the Dukes of Clarence and Cumberland might have cursed or ridiculed each other in private, or occasionally in thoughtless public speeches, such remarks were fraternal banter at best, impatience at worst, without malice aforethought. Yet Baroness von Bülow rightly saw that the good-natured Queen Adelaide could be a positive influence when it came to smoothing relations between two elderly brothers with hasty tempers and loud voices. There were minor clashes between the brothers soon after King William's accession, such as when Queen Adelaide wanted to stable her horses at Windsor only to find the Duke's horses occupying the 'Queen's stable', and the King had to order his brother to remove them before the royal grooms did. Also the King and his ministers did not trust the Duke's extreme Tory views and his suspected attempts – albeit much exaggerated – to influence the late King. They feared that his presence in England might compromise King William, who gave a toast at dinner a few days later to 'the land we live in, and let those who don't like it, leave it!' Everyone knew whom he had in mind. But it suited courtiers, ministers and contemporary diarists to weave or spread colourful rumours about supposed dissension between them.

If the King revelled in his elevation to the throne, the new Queen found it difficult to share his enthusiasm. For the first few weeks she remained quietly at Bushey as far as possible, admitting candidly that she could not 'yet accustom myself to the long-expected event, and it will be some time before I am familiar with its reality'.[18] She feared the effect it might have on him, knowing that sudden excitement could often play havoc with his mental state. There was a fine line to be drawn between affability or exuberance (particularly in a man of almost sixty-five) and instability, and the sight of a king who attended his brother's funeral as chief mourner, but preferred dashing up to old acquaintances in the pews and shaking them heartily by the hand to walking decorously behind the coffin, gave cause for concern. To others it was a reassuring sign of a genuinely human, good-natured monarch; Wellington saw it as not a new reign so much as a new dynasty. Even so informality had its limits, and Queen Adelaide had to persuade the King to take his walks in public earlier, or else in some place less public than St James's Street. There was little she could do about his verbal gaffes, such as the oft-repeated speech he delivered at the end of a dinner at St James's Palace when he wished the ladies and gentlemen good night. 'I will not detain you any longer from your amusements, and shall go to my own, which is to go to bed; so come along, my Queen.'[19]

The Coronation took place at Westminster Abbey on 8 September 1831. King William IV had initially told his ministers that he did not want such 'useless and ill-timed expense', and when he was forced to concede to a considerably curtailed ceremony, shorn of many of the outrageous trappings of his brother's ten years before, the cost was about one-seventh that of the previous one. Spectators thought the King looked very infirm on his feet at the abbey, finding the great weight of his robes and crown rather overwhelming, but the Queen played her part to perfection. Though the notoriously hard to please diarist Charles Greville might scoff at 'a frightful Queen', Baroness von Bülow was kinder.

> Though she is in reality not too good-looking, she appeared so on that day undeniably, for the beauty lay in something beyond mere outward loveliness. It was the beauty of her soul that seemed to shine out from and impress itself upon her whole person. Her bearing was full of dignity, repose, and characteristic grace; she seemed deeply moved, and it was clear that her heartfelt devotion raised her above all outward surroundings.[20]

Only the sight of Lord Brougham threatened to disturb her composure. With his ugly features, twitching nose, and his Chancellor's wig hanging on each side of his face surmounted by his coronet, he looked so like the lion in the royal arms that the Queen dared not look at him for fear of laughing.[21]

King William IV and Queen Adelaide divided their time between London, Windsor and Brighton. Gas had recently been installed at Windsor Castle, but the Queen thought it dangerous, and at her request the gas supply was disconnected, with wax candles reintroduced for lighting instead. They retained Clarence House, but their main London home was St James's Palace. The

King disliked Buckingham Palace, 'a most ill contrived house', and when the Houses of Parliament were burnt to the ground in 1834, he offered it to the government as a replacement.

The Queen preferred Windsor to Brighton. Returning to London one autumn, she wrote to Baroness von Bülow of her regret when she had to leave

> so much I love behind me, the beautiful country, my light, cheerful rooms full of the busts and pictures I especially value, and above all the graves so sacred to me. To be near them does me good, as it does you, to one who has lost so much even the remains which we only preserve in our memory are a precious possession which we would unwillingly forego.[22]

At Windsor after dinner the company gathered at different tables, some playing cards, others working, while the Queen's band played at intervals. She never played cards, and generally called her closest friends to her table, where she sewed, knitted or showed them her sketches, while the King wandered about talking to guests, showing them parts of the castle, or signing documents. Sometimes Princess Augusta came over from Frogmore to dine, and helped her brother by handing him papers, blotting and putting them in order once signed. Lady Grey returned from visiting Windsor in September 1833 'more dead than alive', according to Thomas Creevey.

> She hoped she would never see a mahogany table again, she was so tired with the one that the Queen and the King, the Duchess of Gloucester, Princess Augusta, Madame Lieven and herself had sat round for *hours* – the Queen knitting or netting a purse – the King sleeping, and occasionally waking for the purpose of saying: – 'Exactly so, ma'am!' and then sleeping again. The Queen was as cold as ice to Lady Grey, till the moment she came away, when she could afford to be a little civil at getting quit of her.[23]

Most other guests generally had little but praise for Queen Adelaide. They admired her ability to calm the King in his fits of excitement, and respected her patriotism in ensuring that her clothes were made from English silk instead of more fashionable French materials. Few knew what an effort she found entertaining their guests, and sometimes the experience was so exhausting that the doctor would recommend her spending the next day in bed to recover.

On King William's first birthday after his accession they held a banquet at Windsor Castle, after which they went to stay at Brighton Pavilion, where they could try to escape from the trammels of royalty, dining with very little pomp and ceremony. The King would send to the hotels each morning for a list of their guests so he could invite anybody whose name he recognized, especially old naval friends whom he urged to come without bothering about their best clothes, as 'the Queen does nothing but embroider flowers after dinner'. The Queen made only one sartorial request; contrary to the rules laid down by King George IV, now ladies were forbidden to arrive in low-cut dresses. Gamblers and drunkards were also barred from court, and she declined to receive the very rich, fashionable Duchess of St Albans, widow of Coutts the banker, as she had previously been 'an actress of doubtful reputation'.

They spent the first Christmas of their reign at Brighton, and on Christmas Day the Queen had a magnificent tree prepared for the FitzClarence grandchildren and their young friends. The children walked two by two into the Dragon Room where a tree stood in the centre, with small tables placed on either side, each marked with a child's name and covered with toys. Queen Adelaide kissed all the children, and watched with obvious pleasure their joy at the lovely gifts. But her heart often ached with longing for her daughter Elizabeth who should have been at the forefront of such celebrations.

In the first general election of the new reign the Tory government lost fifty seats. Queen Adelaide had looked uneasily at events in France in July 1830, barely a month after the new reign had begun, when revolution brought Louis Philippe, Duke of Orléans, to the French throne. When the government was defeated in the Commons in November the King exercised his constitutional duty to dissolve Parliament and sent for the Whig leader, Lord Grey, to form a new administration. The incoming ministry's main objective was reform, widening the franchise and abolishing long-redundant constituencies. Those who had regarded the King as a diehard conservative like his elder brother and father were astonished, and in some cases somewhat discomfited, by his statesmanship and courage in supporting his Prime Minister and the Whigs. When the Reform Bill was presented to the House of Commons in the spring of 1831 it was passed by one vote, Parliament was dissolved again and the Whigs were returned with an increased majority. That autumn the Bill was passed by the Commons but defeated in the Lords. There were protests throughout the country, with mobs in the streets stoning Tory strongholds such as Apsley House, the Duke of Wellington's residence.

While the King was rightly identified with supporting reform, unlike his surviving brothers (apart from the Duke of Sussex), it was known that the Queen did not share his view. *The Times*, widely believed to be the mouthpiece of Lord Grey, reported on 4 April that 'It is said that the Queen, the Princess of Hesse-Homburg, and the Duke and Duchess of Gloucester are unfriendly to Reform.' At the height of the protests she had to return to the palace one night through crowded streets after attending a concert. When they recognized the royal coach, mobs converged around her and the footmen had to beat them off with their canes to prevent them from thrusting their faces through the windows. The experience shook her considerably, and the King was beside himself with anger at such behaviour towards his wife, making his displeasure clear by declaring that in view of his ministers' irresponsibility they would not have the privilege of his company at a forthcoming civic dinner at the Guildhall.

Some saw her as an obstacle to reform and a malign influence on a good-natured if weak husband, a narrow-minded reactionary planning to introduce the despotic government of a petty German state into a free and progressive England.[24] The truth of the matter, as her biographer Mary Sandars stated some sixty years after her death, was that she lacked cleverness, and her mind was incapable of detaching itself from her early prepossessions and prejudices, learned during her upbringing in a small German state which was happy and prosperous under a paternally absolute government. Hooted at and pelted in England at the height of the Reform Bill agitation, she was horrified at the scale of democratic encroachment and feared that the change of dynasty which had just taken place in France could easily be repeated in her husband's kingdom.

According to Augusta, Lady FitzClarence, married to the King's second eldest surviving son Frederick, the Queen was 'both sensible and good-natured', but she had lived in England for fourteen years, and yet had 'not a single English notion'. Her Majesty, said Lady Augusta, fervently believed that an English Revolution was approaching, that her fate would be the same as that of Marie Antoinette, and that she hoped she would be able to act her part with as much courage.

> She only approves of the Duke of Wellington as being the only man to stem the revolutionary current, having an old grudge against [the King] and having very often abused him in Lady Augusta's presence, for having turn'd them out of the Admiralty, for his uncourteous manner of doing it, and for the disrespectful way in which he always treated the King when he was Duke of Clarence.[25]

Queen Adelaide's lack of sympathy with reform had become common knowledge through the indiscreet behaviour of her chamberlain, Lord Howe. He was a loyal if sycophantic servant, and she relied on him so heavily that some gossips assumed they must be lovers. A staunch opponent of reform, Howe paid no heed to a warning in May 1831 that his opposition to the Bill should be conducted in such a way as not to embarrass the King and Queen, and when he voted with the majority in the Lords five months later, Grey asked the King to demand his resignation. Howe's appointment had not been political, and he was entitled to vote as he wished; but the Whigs feared that the Crown's impartiality with regard to reform was at stake. The King's eldest son, George FitzClarence, now Earl of Munster, had also voted against the Bill, and they thought that Munster, Howe and the

Queen were forming a cabal at court to influence the sovereign on the side of reaction. Grey was sure that the Queen passed the King information she elicited from the Tories via Howe, though in fact the FitzClarences were the real culprits. When the King declined to dismiss Howe, pointing out that he had the full trust of Her Majesty and himself, Grey went to see the chamberlain himself and asked him to resign, which he did.

The Queen saw this as an underhand conspiracy to deprive her of a valued friend and servant, and she did not conceal her fury. On the day of the dismissal she wrote in her diary, 'I would not believe it, for I had trusted in, and built firmly on, the King's love for me . . . I had a hard struggle before I appeared at table after this blow, which I felt deeply as an insult, which filled me with "Indignation". I felt myself deeply wounded both as wife and Queen and I cannot conquer the feeling. It was for me a distressing evening, which I shall never forget.'[26] Had Grey consulted her first, or apologized for his action, the Queen would have probably accepted the matter without further comment, but he did neither, and this she found hard to forgive. The King had not warned her either, perhaps out of nervousness, an omission on his part which proved particularly hurtful to her. She refused to appoint another Lord Chamberlain in Howe's place, and he continued to perform the duties of the post. He still influenced the Queen with Tory ideas, and in her letters she gave him confidential details of the King's state of mind, telling him her husband saw 'everything in the right light', but she feared he believed that 'no other administration could be formed at present amongst your friends'. While she admitted that she did not understand these matters sufficiently to say how far he was right or not, she would 'like to know what the Duke of Wellington thinks, for he must be a good judge of this question'.[27]

Once the Reform Bill had been passed, Lord Grey offered to recommend Lord Howe's reinstatement on condition that he should not oppose the government, though he was not obliged to support them. He regarded this as an insult, and Queen Adelaide was equally indignant, but at length she was persuaded that this state of affairs was worrying the King. Out of deference to his feelings, early in 1833 she agreed to the appointment of Lord

Denbigh to the vacant position. She only allowed him to officiate on the most formal occasions, and on the first time she went in state to the theatre with him in attendance, she took Howe as well to emphasize that 'though she had been obliged to dismiss him, she wished it understood that he had done nothing to displease her'.[28]

Greville, who was hardly an unbiased witness in view of his antipathy to Queen Adelaide, thought the Lord Chamberlain's foolish behaviour at court was responsible for much of the malicious gossip. 'Lord Howe is devoted to the Queen, and never away from her', he noted in December 1832. 'She receives his attentions, but demonstrates nothing in return; he is like a boy in love with this frightful spotted Majesty.'[29] He admitted there was no evidence in the scurrilous gossip that she treated him like a lover. If she did there would be no concealing it, as she was 'surrounded by enemies'.

Queen Adelaide never intended to take an active role in politics; she saw it as her duty to merge her views in her husband's and support his role as a constitutional monarch. Still the public abuse of her continued, with *The Times* denouncing her in thinly veiled terms: 'a foreigner is not a very competent judge of English liberties.' The *Morning Chronicle* was even more outspoken, calling her 'a nasty German frow'. Nevertheless she had her defenders. In the House of Lords, Lord Winchelsea fiercely deprecated the 'envenomed slanders of the press against an illustrious female holding the highest rank in society, whose many virtues were the admiration of all classes in society', while in the Commons the Radical Sir Francis Burdett was equally adamant in defending the Queen, 'whose sex and amiable conduct, since her arrival in England, have given her claims to the respect and protection of all'.[30]

Her main interests were music and religious duties, and beyond the distrust of social and political changes common to her class, she had no fixed political interests. It was understandable that she should have been ardently Tory in her sympathies, and at times fearful of the possibility of revolution if the Reform Bill was passed. Her FitzClarence stepchildren were equally conservative in their politics, as were the surviving daughters of King George

III. Princess Lieven observed in October 1831 that the Queen was 'made ill by the worry which Ministers are giving her, and the King's inside is much upset by the same annoyances', while not only his wife but also his sisters were 'sworn foes to the Government'.[31] To Mary, Duchess of Gloucester, the King confessed at one stage that he felt the crown tottering on his head.

Mary was particularly welcome at court to the King, as she had been to their late brother, at times of stress. It was evident that she seemed more fond of both Kings than she was of her husband, who was a bore and a snob as well as a tyrant in domestic life.

Neither King George IV nor King William IV did more than tolerate the Duke, but both went out of their way to be pleasant to the Duchess, and regularly invited her to dine at the palaces – without her husband, who was so offended that he declared he would not go there again. When his health was failing the Duchess, sensing she would not have to put up with him for much longer, nursed him devotedly until his death in November 1834 after the bursting of a scrofulous swelling in the head. Elizabeth came from Homburg to visit her sister the following spring, and was pleasantly surprised to find her in such cheerful spirits, planning life as a widow with a new sense of zest, even freedom, which had evidently been denied her as a wife.

Increasingly lame, lonely in Homburg and dependent on visits to or letters from family and friends in her declining years, Elizabeth always enjoyed returning to England when her health permitted. The ferment of England during the Reform agitation was nothing to the rebellion and unrest throughout much of Germany at this time. During riots at Frankfurt in April 1833 she had written to an old friend, Louisa Swinburne: 'Politics I know nothing of, and they are so disagreeable that I never ask any questions, for I always hated them and more than ever now, for all appears melancholy, and this rioting at Frankfort has caused me a great deal of worry.'[32]

Still in her late thirties when she became Queen, Adelaide was sometimes said by the press to be with child again. 'Damned stuff,' the King would retort bitterly. She was devoted to the children of her sister the Duchess of Saxe-Weimar. The eldest, Louise, suffered from a spinal complaint and was partially paralysed; and in May 1831 when she was fourteen the Duchess agreed to let her stay in England for treatment at Brighton where fresh air and sea baths might alleviate her discomfort. To the Queen's distress, on a visit the next year Louise caught chickenpox, and despite her aunt's solicitude and nursing during her last illness, the Princess died in August 1832 and was buried at Windsor. Though she knew it was a merciful release for the girl from a life of suffering, the Queen was exhausted after weeks of emotional strain, and those who attended the funeral with the King and Queen admitted that she had recovered her spirits but was 'still most miserably thin'.[33]

In the spring of 1834 Queen Adelaide was in such low spirits that the King felt she would benefit from a spell in her native land during the summer, and without telling her he made arrangements for her to return for a few weeks. Her delight at seeing her old home again was outweighed by the thought of being away from the King for six weeks. He had been increasingly excitable and she feared for his sanity if she was away too long, but he was adamant that she should go. Altering the plans would cause too much awkwardness; and after her unpopularity during the Reform Bill crisis, he thought it would be as well if she was out of the country should the ministry fall, which he knew was probable. Reluctantly she sailed for the European mainland, travelling under the rather unconvincing incognito of the Duchess of Lancaster and landing at Rotterdam. Back in Saxe-Meiningen she was surrounded by relations, including her elderly mother who was overjoyed to see her once again, and the genial Duke and Duchess of Cambridge. A week after celebrating her forty-second birthday at her old home, she arrived back at Woolwich. 'I passed a very happy time with my dear relations,' she wrote to Lady Wellesley in September, 'but it seems now but a Dream, for it passed so quickly, that nothing but the agreeable recollection remains which will long benefit me.'[34]

Despite the King's caution, the political crisis had not occurred during her absence but could not be long delayed. Though the Queen was, in the words of Princess Lieven, 'somewhat put out by the state of affairs she found when she got home to England',[35] by finding the Whigs still in power, after her earlier experiences she kept her opinions to herself. Lord Grey had retired from the premiership on grounds of age, to be succeeded by Lord Melbourne. In November after the death of Lord Spencer, his son Althorp succeeded him in the Lords, and Melbourne proposed to replace him as Leader of the House of Commons with Lord John Russell, a radical firebrand who was anathema to the King. He asked Melbourne to resign, saying that he would entrust the government to other hands.

Two days later a terse statement, the first intimation to most members of the cabinet that they were no longer in office, appeared in *The Times*, stating that the King had taken the opportunity of Lord Spencer's death to turn out the ministry, 'and there is every reason to believe that the Duke of Wellington has been sent for. The Queen has done it all.' It was fortunate for Queen Adelaide that the court was at Brighton and that she was spared any demonstrations in the streets of London. Under pressure the paper later printed a grudging apology recording 'sincere pleasure' in contradicting its previous remarks, 'and in declaring our belief that the Queen is not capable of any underhand intermeddling with public affairs or of attempting what we are sure she could not accomplish'.

King and Queen were both very fond of the young heir presumptive, Princess Victoria of Kent. When the King opened Parliament for the first time, the Queen watched the procession from a garden opposite St James's Palace, accompanied by her ladies and other members of the royal family. After it had passed, there were calls for 'The Queen! The Queen!' Acknowledging the cheers, Queen Adelaide picked Princess Victoria up and held her on the wall beside her, to an even more enthusiastic response and a cry of 'God save both Queens!'[36]

They were saddened that the Duchess of Kent, determined that Princess Victoria should have nothing to do with the court, allowed them to see so little of her. This was partly out of maternal possessiveness, understandable in the case of a woman who had been left a widow after eighteen months of marriage and in a strange land where she had very few friends and an imperfect grasp of the language. She wanted to bring her daughter up as she saw fit, especially as she had some experience of acting as Regent, in the German state of Leiningen on the early death of her first husband. The other reason was that she did not want her daughter to come into contact with the FitzClarences. When Lord Grey remonstrated with her on the matter, she asked how he could possibly wish her to expose her daughter to 'hearing bastards spoken about', and herself to subsequently being asked for an explanation of the word. He replied that if this was the case, then she must not let the Princess read the history of the country she was to govern, as the first page would show her that William of Normandy was known as 'the Bastard' before he was called 'the Conqueror'.[37] This history lesson cut no ice with the Duchess.

Her lack of attendance at the Coronation and her refusal to let her daughter to take part widened the breach further. Though she was initially invited, the Duchess took it as a deliberate slight when told that she would be taking her position as Dowager Princess and Peeress, while her daughter was to be under the charge of her aunts the Landgravine of Hesse-Homburg and Princess Augusta. *The Times* criticized her for her absence, assigning the cause to a fit of pique, and was criticized for its 'offensive attack' by Creevey, who considered that the Duchess was the victim of libel. 'The thing, however, was utterly destitute of foundation, the Duchess of Kent having most respectfully asked the King for permission to absent herself on account of her child's health.'[38] Nevertheless, political differences between both sisters-in-law also played their part. In the division of Europe by the allies in 1814, Holland, to which Belgium was annexed, had fallen to the stewardship of the house of Orange, both countries when united being known as the Netherlands. The French revolution of 1830 brought in its train a revolt among the Catholic Belgians, who hated their incorporation with Calvinist Holland and writhed under the rule of William I, King of the Netherlands, who treated Belgium as a conquered country. The London Congress recognized Belgian independence, and Leopold of Saxe-Coburg, Princess Charlotte's widower as well as the Duchess of Kent's younger brother, was accordingly proclaimed King of the Belgians. With her horror of change as well as her natural sympathies towards the house of Orange, Queen Adelaide and her sister Ida were indignant at the way in which King William of the Netherlands was treated, and as Princess Lieven put it, both sisters were 'all fire and flame against the conference'.[39]

They had a kindred spirit in the Landgravine of Hesse-Homburg, who was angry when a subscription was set up among the friends of the Prince of Orange to purchase his horses which had been left behind at Brussels, and to return them to him as a goodwill gift. A mob in Belgium thought this was a cover for a conspiracy to restore the Orange family to the throne, and in an insurrection in April 1834, several houses were sacked and destroyed. 'I never heard before that making a present from good feelings was a *conspiracy*; we learn to live every day', she wrote angrily. 'All and every fresh view I hear makes the thing worse and worse, in short perfectly *disgraceful*, and never will I put my foot in that vile, detestable, unmanageable, blackguard country again.'[40]

Princess Sophia, who had become friendly with the Duchess of Kent's secretary Sir John Conroy, maliciously repeated the King's impatient criticisms of the Duchess to her. Every evening after dinner she visited the Duchess's apartments at Kensington Palace to regale her with the latest tittle-tattle. The feud came to a head with a party given for the King's seventy-first birthday in August 1836. The Duchess had been invited to, but pointedly did not, attend a dinner for the Queen's birthday eight days before. She reluctantly attended the King's, during which he made a speech in which his fury at the Duchess boiled over, and she announced her immediate departure. Only with difficulty was she persuaded to stay. Yet at least the scene had cleared the air, and for the rest of the King's reign they were on civil if distant terms.

King William's last ten months were filled with one domestic sorrow after another. Early in the new year the Queen was seriously ill with what was dismissed in the press as a bad cold but was probably pneumonia, and at one point the doctors feared for her life. She was still convalescent when the King's favourite daughter Sophia, Lady de l'Isle, died on 10 April in childbirth. He was so stricken with grief, courtiers said, that only the death of his wife would have affected him more. On 30 April she was told that her mother had succumbed to influenza, and within a few days the King's health showed signs of failing. He could no longer walk, and had to be moved around in a wheelchair. Though he had no particular illness, apart from a severe bout of asthma, he seemed to have lost the will to live.

Queen Adelaide hardly left his bedside for the last three weeks of his life, going without proper sleep for much of that time. Though plainly dying, the King never mentioned the word death in her presence. When the Archbishop of Canterbury came to read the Visitation of the Sick, the Queen knelt beside her husband making the responses and helping him turn the pages of the prayer book. Exhausted and emotionally drained, she broke down.

Unlike the previous Queens Consort of the house of Hanover, Queen Adelaide was not destined to predecease her husband. Shortly after 2 in the morning of 20 June 1837 the King passed away. For her it was a merciful release to see him free of suffering at last. 'To the last she supported him, and he died in her arms', the Landgravine of Hesse-Homburg wrote to Louisa Swinburne some twelve days later.

> It is impossible to be too strong in her praise, so well has she conducted herself; soothed him, calmed him, softened the pain and anguish he experienced by her amiable and sweet manner towards him. . . . You may suppose what a loss it is to her, and yet she bears it with that strong sense of religion for which she has ever been so famed, and which has made her go through everything with a degree of calm which one must so admire.[41]

Ever the most self-effacing of Queens Consort, Adelaide's achievements should not be overlooked. It was ironic that at one time she should have been thought a reactionary whose presence at court threatened the monarchy, while it is not exaggerating to suggest that this gentle, calm and reasonable character actually saved it. Without her moral support the King might never have been in a fit position to ascend the throne. Had the unpopular King George IV been followed by the conscientious yet arch-conservative and even more hated Ernest, Duke of Cumberland, the crown might have been less fortunate.

King William IV's death at the age of seventy-one left Queen Adelaide a widow at forty-four. Those members of the royal family who visited her after the King's death found her more composed than they had expected. Some were tempted to consider, a little uncharitably, that his passing was not without consolation, as his ill-conceived enthusiasms and unpredictability had made their nineteen years of marriage a sometimes troubled one. Between the Queen Dowager and her niece, now Queen Victoria, there had always been much affection. The latter, who had been on noticeably distant if not sometimes stormy terms with the Duchess of Kent and her *eminence grise*, the ambitious comptroller Sir John Conroy, who had been tempted to regard himself as the next power behind the throne, looked on Adelaide almost as a mother. When Lord Conyngham came to see Adelaide early on the first morning of the new reign, returning from Kensington where he had been to take the news of the King's death to the new sovereign, he brought a letter from Queen Victoria addressed to 'The Queen of England'. The Duchess of Kent had pointed out to the writer that she was now the Queen herself, only to be told that she would not be the first to address Queen Adelaide differently.[42]

Queen Adelaide asked to be allowed to remain at Windsor Castle until after the King's funeral, and Conyngham delivered a message that she was to stay there as long as she wished. 'My prayers are with you and my blessing follows you in all you have to go through', she wrote to Queen Victoria a couple of days after the start of the new reign. 'My health is as well as it can be after the great exertions I have suffered, and I try to keep up under my heavy trial and deep affliction.'[43]

King William's funeral took place on the night of 8 July at St George's Chapel. Queen Adelaide attended, slipping into the Royal Closet so quietly that hardly anybody realized she was present. Queen Victoria asked her without hesitation to take anything she wished from Windsor as a keepsake, but all she asked for were the silver cup in which she had given the King his curaçoa during his illness, and a family portrait by George Hayter of her stepchildren grouped around the bust of their father, with a picture of Mrs Jordan in the background. In view of the rude or thoughtless manner in which they had often treated the King and Queen during the last reign, it was a magnanimous gesture indeed. Nevertheless she was prepared to admit that, loyalty to her husband's memory notwithstanding, such an open acknowledgement of this family born out of wedlock was an aspect of him which had better not be exposed to the public view.[44]

After leaving the castle she left for Bushey, where she had always felt at home, and where she intended to retain all her servants whom she had employed while Duchess of Clarence, if they so wished. Although it must have been a pang for her to leave Windsor for the last time, the prospect of retiring into private life was inviting. She had been a dutiful but reluctant Queen Consort, always ready to avoid the limelight where possible; and the calumny and malice directed at her during the political crisis had not made those seven years any the happier. Exhausted by the last few weeks of nursing her affectionate yet demanding and exhausting husband, she was tired out in body and mind. The Duchess of Saxe-Weimar and three of her children came to stay with her for the rest of the summer. She made a point of receiving nobody in an official capacity, as she considered it would be unfair to choose to see some but not others. When certain public bodies seemed determined to come and read her addresses of condolence, she asked Lord Howe to deal with them instead.

With the King's death, the Queen Dowager was comparatively wealthy, but she had never cared for ostentation. Having come from a relatively poor ducal family in Germany, she knew how to manage on little money. Much of her surplus income went to charity, and contemporaries estimated that each year she gave away around £20,000 to worthy causes.[45] A cathedral at Adelaide in Australia benefited handsomely in this way, and she also gave funds for the foundation of the King William Naval Asylum at Penge, south London, for the widows of naval officers.

Accompanied by her sister-in-law Augusta, she spent the first winter of her widowhood at St Leonards. Both had always been close, and they made up a small party which arrived quietly in mid-October, to no reception at Queen Adelaide's particular request. They spent much of their time walking and dining in the neighbourhood, as well as taking brief trips on the sea in a small barge from Chatham. One day during their visit the Duke of Wellington came to dine and reminisce over old times. She did not let this chance to do good slip by, and made generous gifts of coal and blankets to the poor, as well as subscribing to local good causes. Nevertheless she was obviously in less good health than her sister-in-law, who was almost seventy years of age.

Also preying on her mind was the matter of the FitzClarences, whose upkeep had been a considerable charge on the Privy Purse. There was some doubt as to whether Queen Victoria would continue to pay the pensions which had been theirs during their father's lifetime, or even allow them to retain their offices of state. Feeling some responsibility for them, which in all fairness she need hardly have been expected to, Queen Adelaide would have doubtless scrimped and saved to continue to pay them as her husband had done, but it would have made substantial inroads on her income and necessitated reducing or discontinuing completely her charitable gifts as a result. To her relief, soon after Christmas Queen Victoria assured her that she would see that the allowances were paid as before. Nothing could have given her more satisfaction, Queen Adelaide assured her niece, 'and I trust and hope that they will prove their gratitude and entire devotion to you by their future conduct'.[46]

On her return from St Leonards, Queen Adelaide had planned to make her London home at Marlborough House, which had been Crown property since being purchased for Charlotte in 1817, months before her untimely death. Her widower husband Leopold had lived there briefly, prior to his election in 1831 as King of the Belgians. In October 1837 work had been begun on it to make it habitable for the Queen Dowager, but it was still not ready and she moved temporarily into Clarence House.

In June 1838 Queen Victoria was crowned. Custom forbade the appearance of any other crowned heads at the Coronation, though Queen Adelaide would have liked to attend the ceremony in honour of the sovereign whom she had almost regarded as a daughter. Had she pressed her case, it was unlikely that anybody would have seriously tried to stop her; there was no recent precedent, for England had not had a Queen Dowager since the

Stuarts in the seventeenth century. However, the government had made it clear to King Leopold of the Belgians and King Ernest Augustus of Hanover, the former Duke of Cumberland who had succeeded to his inheritance on King William's death, that other crowned heads could not be invited, and she felt it might be unseemly to ask if an exception could be made for her. Nevertheless she wrote her niece a few touching lines just before midday on Coronation Day, 28 June, telling her that 'as I am not near you, and cannot take part in the sacred ceremony of your Coronation, I must address you in writing to assure you that my thoughts and my whole heart are with you, and my prayers are offered up to Heaven for your happiness, and the prosperity and glory of your reign'.[47]

In view of her poor health, the Queen Dowager was advised not to spend the winter in England. Her physician Dr Chambers recommended she should go to Madeira, which she declared was too far away. Her reluctance was also motivated by patriotic reasons; when Malta was suggested she agreed at once, as she wished to avoid spending her income out of the British Dominions. In October she sailed from Portsmouth on board HMS *Hastings*; she was plainly dressed, and those who saw her leave thought she still looked pinched and thin but otherwise well. She and her small entourage planned to stay at the Palace of St Antonia, Valletta, for some months.

Soon she found another deserving cause. In December she wrote to Queen Victoria of the lack of a Protestant church at Valletta. Considering the number of English residents there, and the fact that it was the seat of an English government, she thought it remarkable that there were no churches belonging to the Church of England. She asked Victoria, as head of the Church, to consider the matter and discuss it with her ministers and the Archbishop

to devise the best means of remedying a want so discreditable to our country. Should there be no funds at your disposal to effect this object, most happy shall I feel to contribute to any subscription which may be set on foot, and I believe that a considerable sum may be raised amongst the Protestants of the

Island, where all parties are most anxious to see a proper place of divine worship erected.[48]

There were other calls on the purse of the Queen and her government and Queen Adelaide's pleas were unsuccessful, but she graciously kept her promise, providing funds for the building of St Paul's Cathedral (or Queen Adelaide's Church, as it was known for many years thereafter) in Valletta, at a cost of £10,000, and laying the foundation stone on 20 March 1839.

As a widow Queen Adelaide, always reluctant to push herself forward, and content with a life of retirement, was well liked and respected. When Queen Victoria's popularity declined two years after her accession, through her ill-judged partisanship of her Prime Minister, Lord Melbourne, the 'bedchamber crisis', and mishandling of the case of her mother's lady-in-waiting Lady Flora Hastings, who was suspected by the Queen of being with child by her *bête noire* Sir John Conroy when she was terminally ill with cancer, the Queen Dowager's stock rose accordingly. At some public dinners calls to toast Queen Victoria's health were met with solemn silence, while a subsequent toast for the Queen Dowager resulted in enthusiastic cheering. Recalling her own nadir at the height of the Reform agitation, Adelaide must have smiled to herself when this was reported to her; but out of loyalty to her niece, she did her best to remain abroad until indignation with the sovereign had subsided.

When Queen Victoria married her cousin Prince Albert of Saxe-Coburg Gotha on 10 February 1840 Queen Adelaide took her place proudly among family guests at the Chapel Royal, St James's. It was noticed that the Queen fondly embraced her aunt at the ceremony but merely shook hands frigidly with the Duchess of Kent. Ever eager to help, Queen Adelaide pointed out passages to the bridegroom in the prayer book and instructed him in the order of procedure in an all-too-audible whisper, inadvertently making him even more nervous than he was already. However, he repaid her kindness many times over. When his and Queen Victoria's first child was born in November 1840 she was named Victoria Adelaide Mary Louisa, the second name in honour of her great-aunt, who was asked to become one of the godparents and also carried the baby to the font at her christening in February 1841. Moreover, once he had reconciled the Queen with the Duchess of Kent, he used his formidable conciliation skills to bring the Duchess and Queen Adelaide together as well.

Like the surviving daughters of King George III still living in England, Queen Adelaide was genuinely fond of her niece and nephew and always treated them with the utmost respect. It was only some twenty years earlier that she, like Albert, had left a quiet German duchy to marry and share centre stage at the English court, in an England which treated its 'foreign' royalty none too kindly. All her protective instincts were aroused when the Duke of Cambridge, normally so easy-going, indulged in a game of petty spite against Queen Victoria and her husband and invited the Duchess to follow his example. His suggestive remarks in after-dinner speeches to Prince Albert's eagerness to return to 'a very fine girl', and the Duchess's ostentatious action of remaining seated when Albert's health was drunk, did not pass unnoticed. She welcomed the Queen and Albert to her party for children at Marlborough House, and deliberately struck the Cambridges from her guest list.

Queen Adelaide's strong Tory partisanship continued to the end of her life. On 8 September 1841 (the tenth anniversary of her Coronation), after Queen Victoria had accepted the resignation of Lord Melbourne as Prime Minister and reluctantly received Robert Peel as his successor, she wrote with the best intentions but a little tactlessly to her niece to compliment her 'on the good grace with which she had changed her Government', hoping that she would have perfect confidence in the men who now formed her Council; 'Our beloved late King's anxious wish to see Wellington and Peel again at the head of the Administration is now fulfilled.'[49]

'Now God knows whether I may ever see dear old England again', the Landgravine of Hesse-Homburg wrote to Louisa Swinburne in July 1837 after the death of King William IV, 'but that I won't think of. To me my brother was everything – most affectionate, and we all feel that the change will be most dreadful to us all. Don't think I mean an unkind word. I pray most sincerely for the prosperity and happiness of our young Queen, but we are all so much older, that we cannot expect the sort of attachment we have been spoilt with from him who is no more.'[50] She continued to live with her memories, her art and her charities, among them the founding of a nursery school in Hanover. Her health continued to decline; to the same correspondent she had written the previous month that she enjoyed 'everything but walking, which is totally out of my power, and getting up off my chair when I have long been seated, gives me great pain'.[51] She travelled around the spas seeking a cure for her rheumatism, but to little avail, and by Christmas 1839 her strength and eyesight were failing. On 10 January 1840 she died and was buried in the family vault at Homburg, where the Anglican burial service was read.

The death of 'dearest dear Eliza' was a severe blow to Augusta, who had been far from well herself and frequently confined to her bedroom at Clarence House. They had written to each other every day for some years, a pastime which Augusta called her 'daily pleasure, comfort and occupation'. From then on her health declined sharply.

At the same time she was deeply distressed by the problems of Sophia, who had woken one morning in 1838 to find herself blind in the right eye, and undergone an unsuccessful operation for the removal of a cataract. For three months she suffered considerable pain and inflammation in the eye, which the oculist blamed on bad weather. After the pain had subsided there was no improvement in her sight, and within two years she was completely blind. Moving from Kensington Palace to York House, she was surrounded by her collection of knick-knacks which she knew by touch. The services of a lady-in-waiting were gently refused, as she said that, being unable to see, she would always imagine the lady sitting opposite her looking bored. She accepted her affliction with a resignation which Augusta admired, and enjoyed being read to in English, German, French and Italian. When told that pillows filled with torn-up paper would be comfortable for the sick, she spent much of her time tearing up old books for the purpose. In April 1840 Augusta remarked on her sister who bore her blindness 'with such calmness and piety, and even cheerfulness, now that her mind is made up never to be any better, but it is painful to witness the poor dear, who used to be so often and so well employed, reduced now only to open books and tear up paper for couch-pillows'.[52]

By the summer Augusta was under regular medical supervision, slowly dying of what Halford described as a 'formidable complaint', involving 'fixt mischief in the tract of the intestine', thought to have been cancer of the bowel.[53] She died quietly on 22 September, with Queen Adelaide holding her hand at the end. Sophia, Mary, and their brothers the Dukes of Cambridge and Sussex were also at her death-bed. 'I regret her *very*, *very* sincerely,' Queen Victoria wrote to King Leopold four days later, 'though for herself we are all most thankful for the release of such unexampled sufferings, borne with such unexampled patience.'[54]

Sophia's remaining years were enlivened by regular visits from the Duke and Duchess of Cambridge and their three children, as well as her sister, 'dearest Minny', who took her for rides in her carriage around Hyde Park and St James's Park, and Queen Victoria. The days when she had been distrusted by the Queen because of her closeness to Conroy were long since forgotten, and by now she was such a pathetic figure that it was impossible to feel anything but sympathy for her. In her last years she became deaf and increasingly lame as well as blind, and she had to be pushed around her rooms in a wheelchair.

Although one year older Mary enjoyed far better health. She had never shared the 'morbid sentimentality' of her sisters. Her fondness for the younger children of the family, especially the young Cambridges, made her a popular great-aunt, and she loved giving children's parties at Gloucester House. She also followed with interest the development and education of 'Bertie', the Prince of Wales, and once gave him a telescope as a birthday present. Increasingly absent-minded, she attended the christening of her great-niece Louise in May 1848, when Queen Victoria related that she gave them 'a dreadful fright at the christening by quite forgetting where she was, and coming and kneeling at my feet in the midst of the service. Imagine our horror!'[55]

On the morning of 27 May 1848 the family were warned that Sophia's end could not be far off, and she died in the evening. Princess Mary of Cambridge wrote that her aunt 'did not suffer much in her last moments, and died without a sigh, with mama's hand in her own. She had been insensible for two hours before death released her from a life of suffering.'[56] At her request she was buried at Kensal Green cemetery, close to her favourite brother the Duke of Sussex, who had died in 1843.

After her death the Duke of Cambridge and the Duchess of Gloucester appointed a solicitor to examine her affairs. To their surprise she had only left £1,607, 19*s* 7*d* in the bank and a few almost worthless shares. Her expenses had been trifling and her income substantial, especially as she was granted £15,000 on the death of Queen Charlotte, increased to £17,000 on Augusta's death.[57] Responsibility for this state of affairs rested with Sir John Conroy, who had once been in charge of her finances, and had bought himself properties and houses in Wales and Berkshire scarcely commensurate with his own modest salary. When questioned he could not account for the missing sums. While she had made him several generous gifts, it was evident that he had shamelessly taken advantage of a gullible, blind and elderly lady.

In widowhood the bonds between Queen Adelaide, the Duchess of Kent, Queen Victoria and Prince Albert became ever stronger. Ida, Duchess of Saxe-Weimar, spent much time with her elder sister, as did Ida's son Edward. Lord Howe, whose friendship with the Queen had unwittingly embroiled them in such controversy, had married again after the early death of his first wife, and they remained good friends. The FitzClarences continued to regard her as a favourite relation, and she was much distressed when the eldest, the Earl of Munster, died by his own hand in 1842.

In 1848 Queen Adelaide rented Bentley Priory, Middlesex, from the Marquess of Abercorn for three years. The house was famous for its magnificent gardens, its picture gallery and circular music-room. Unable to manage stairs any more, she spent her time in a bedroom and boudoir on the ground floor, from which a door led into a conservatory, where she could sit on wet days among the palms and orange trees, fancying she was in southern Europe. On warmer days she would walk in the lime avenue or sit quietly in the summer-house. Sometimes she drove into Stanmore village with provisions for the sick and elderly.

After years of indifferent health she had become a semi-invalid. In 1847 the doctors had again recommended Madeira, and she stayed for a while at the Villa Quinta des Augustrias, Funchal, where she gave money to the civil governor for the poor, and for building new roads. On a visit to Bushey in the spring of 1849 she was taken ill, and her doctors sent her to Worthing and then Tunbridge Wells, but to little effect. When she returned that summer to Bushey, where she had spent the happiest times of her life in England with her husband, she had a presentiment that it was for the last time. In September she went back to Bentley Priory, and her last public act was to lay the foundation stone of a new church at Great Stanmore, to which she gave the font and alms dishes. The east window was later dedicated to her memory.

By the end of October the doctors were seriously concerned about her. She never left her room at Bentley Priory; her cough became worse, she slept badly, and soon her strength was failing rapidly. Her sister Ida, and her two daughters, came to help nurse her and keep her company so that, as Queen Victoria put it, she would not be 'left to servants and strangers'. The Queen, Prince Albert, and the Duchess of Kent, with whom she had long since been the best of friends, came to visit her at the end of November. 'There was death written in that dear face,' the Queen wrote afterwards to King Leopold. 'It was such a picture of misery, of complete *anéantissement* – and yet she talked of everything.'[58] They were just in time, for on 2 December 1849 she died aged fifty-seven.

Three of King George III's children were still alive. The now much-mellowed Adolphus, Duke of Cambridge, passed away in July 1850, and Ernest Augustus, King of Hanover, the former Duke of Cumberland, followed him in November 1851. Mary, Duchess of Gloucester, was fortunate in surviving to a relatively cheerful and active old age. Almost to the end she continued to give parties for the younger generations of royal children, and in 1855, at the age of seventy-nine, she contributed sixteen pictures to a Patriotic Fund exhibition staged on behalf of widows and orphans of officers who had given their lives in the Crimean War.

Although she had been increasingly frail for some time, she

lived to see her eighty-first birthday on 25 April 1857. 'Alas! We *dared* not keep it except *sacredly*, as it were', noted Princess Mary of Cambridge. In the early hours of 30 April the two young Cambridge Princesses were summoned to join their mother at the Duchess's bedside. She was already in a coma, and the doctors assured them she was not suffering. At a quarter past 5, 'with another stretch and a momentary convulsive contraction of the face, all was over, and with the dawn of day the gentle spirit returned to God who gave it'.[59]

The death of the last Georgian Princess marked the end of an era, as Queen Victoria wrote to King Leopold a few days later. 'Her age, and her being a link with bygone times and generations, as well as her great kindness, amiability, and unselfishness, rendered her more and more dear and precious to us all, and we all looked upon her as a sort of grandmother.'[60]

Notes

CHAPTER ONE

1 Sophia, 2.
2 Kroll, 28.
3 Sophia, 13–14.
4 Jordan, 7.
5 Kroll, 102–3.
6 Hatton, 28–9.
7 Ibid., 35.
8 Kroll, 164.
9 Ibid., 170.
10 Ibid., 172.
11 Hatton, 55.
12 Kroll, 184.
13 Jordan, 205.
14 Hatton, 60.
15 Doran, I, 87.
16 Ibid., 94.
17 Hatton, 69.

CHAPTER TWO

1 Kroll, 200.
2 Kroll 201.
3 Wilkins, *Caroline*, I, 17.
4 Ibid, 18–19.
5 Wilkins, *Love of an Uncrowned Queen*, II, 600.
6 Kroll, 201.
7 Doran, I, 104–6.
8 Ward, 323–4.
9 Wilkins, *Caroline*, I, 30.
10 Wilkins, *Caroline*, I, 34.
11 Melville, *The First George*, II, 44–5.
12 Kroll, 212.
13 Wilkins, *Caroline*, I, 38.
14 Kroll, 215.
15 Doran, I, 142–3.

16 Kroll, 224.
17 Lavisse, 146.
18 Jordan, 258.
19 Kroll, 230.
20 Ibid., 240.
21 Ibid., 231.
22 Wilkins, *Caroline*, I, 62.
23 Ward, 431.
24 Wilkins, *Caroline*, I, 151.
25 Ibid., I, 162.
26 Cowper, 132.
27 Wilkins, *Caroline*, II, 93.
28 Hervey, *Memoirs* (1952 edn), 354.
29 Gaxotte, 43.
30 Wilkins, *Caroline*, II, 86.
31 Hatton, 62.
32 Wilkins, *Love of an Uncrowned Queen*, II, 648.
33 Ibid., II, 650.

CHAPTER THREE

1 Jordan, 272.
2 Hervey, *Materials*, I, 60.
3 Wilkins, *Caroline*, II, 94–5.
4 Ibid., 101.
5 Hervey, *Materials*, I, 238.
6 Wilkins, *Caroline*, II, 252.
7 Arkell, 212.
8 Baker-Smith, 59.
9 Doran, I, 294.
10 Wilkins, *Caroline*, II, 311.
11 Arkell, 262.
12 Hervey, *Memoirs* (1884 edn), 843–4.
13 Wilkins, *Caroline*, II, 350.
14 Ewald, 318.

15 Hervey, *Materials*, III, 316.
16 Doran, I, 411.
17 Hervey, *Materials*, III, 319.
18 Ibid., 322.
19 Wilkins, *Caroline*, II, 365.
20 Brooke, 27.
21 Chevenix Trench, 249.
22 Baker-Smith, 137–8.
23 Walpole, *Memoirs*, I, 227–8.
24 Brooke, 33.
25 Ibid., 41.
26 Ayling, 40.
27 Brooke, 49.
28 Duffy, 132.
29 Baker-Smith, 136.
30 Walpole, *Memoirs*, III, 83.
31 Baker-Smith, 142–3.
32 Fitzgerald, *Royal Dukes and Princesses*, I, 287.
33 Baker-Smith, 81.
34 Walpole, *Letters*, III, 248-9.

CHAPTER FOUR

1 Hedley, 12.
2 Walpole, *Memoirs*, III, 432.
3 Fitzgerald, *Good Queen Charlotte*, 21.
4 Greenwood, II, 16.
5 Hedley, 65.
6 Fitzgerald, *Royal Dukes and Princesses*, I, 54.
7 Ayling, 84.
8 Doran, II, 30.
9 Hedley, 93.
10 Fraser, 10.
11 Wilkins, *Queen of Tears*, I, 50.
12 Brooke, 268–9.
13 Wraxall, 87.
14 Fraser, 12.
15 Brooke, 267.
16 Doran, II, 19.
17 Holme, *Caroline*, 3.
18 Brooke, 267.
19 Ibid.
20 Ibid., 267–8.
21 Chapman, 170.
22 Brooke, 269.

23 Ibid.
24 Ibid., 269–70.
25 Wilkins, *Queen of Tears*, II, 280.
26 Brooke, 270.
27 Chapman, 206.
28 Fitzgerald, *Royal Dukes and Princesses*, I, 179.
29 Doran, II, 75.
30 Wilkins, *Caroline*, II, 101.
31 Fitzgerald, *Royal Dukes and Princesses*, I, 214.
32 Hedley, 124.
33 Ibid., 127.
34 Stuart, *Daughters of George III*, 324.
35 Ibid., 4.
36 Ibid., 11.
37 Hedley, 142.
38 Ibid., 165.
39 Ibid., 170.
40 Brooke, 270.
41 Hedley, 182.

CHAPTER FIVE

1 George IV, *Correspondence, 1770–1812*, III, 9.
2 Melville, *Injured Queen*, I, 12.
3 Holland, II, 146–7.
4 Malmesbury, III, 153.
5 Ibid., 164.
6 Ibid., 182.
7 Doran, II, 214.
8 Malmesbury, III, 189.
9 Ibid., 198.
10 Melville, *Injured Queen*, I, 50.
11 Stuart, *Daughters of George III*, 162.
12 Ibid., 87.
13 George IV, *1770–1812*, III, 132–8.
14 Ibid., 169.
15 Ibid., 198.
16 Ibid., 204.
17 Ibid., 200.
18 Glenbervie, I, 71.
19 George IV, *1770–1812*, III, 223.
20 Fraser, 97.

21 Stuart, *Daughters of George III*, 263.
22 Iremonger, 184.
23 Stuart, *Daughters of George III*, 17.
24 Ibid., 268.
25 Ibid., 32.
26 Fitzgerald, *Royal Dukes and Princesses*, I, 258.
27 Ibid., 226–7.
28 Brooke, 363.
29 Hedley, 223–5.
30 Minto, III, 36.
31 Weigall, 20.
32 Brooke, 268.
33 Fraser, 193.
34 Ibid., 194.
35 George IV, *1770–1812*, VI, 194.
36 Ibid., 511.
37 Charlotte, 7.
38 Brooke, 268.
39 Ayling, 430.
40 Stuart, *Daughters of George III*, 345–6.
41 Ibid., 160.
42 Ibid., 166–7.
43 Hedley, 236.
44 Stuart, *Daughters of George III*, 352.
45 Ibid., 174.
46 Childe-Pemberton, 209.
47 Fitzgerald, *Royal Dukes and Princesses*, I, 221.
48 Ayling, 447.
49 Fitzgerald, *Royal Dukes and Princesses*, I, 222.
50 Stuart, *Daughters of George III*, 376.
51 Fitzgerald, *Royal Dukes and Princesses*, I, 222.
52 Ibid., 226.

CHAPTER SIX

1 Stuart, *Daughters of George III*, 286.
2 Ibid., 101–2.
3 Ibid., 105.
4 Ibid., 111.
5 Ibid., 215.
6 Ibid., 216.
7 Ibid., 227.
8 Holme, *Prinny's Daughter*, 68.
9 Bury, 178.
10 Charlotte, 71.
11 Ibid., 32.
12 Ibid., 33.
13 Ibid., 23.
14 Ibid., 36.
15 Ibid., 89.
16 Ibid., 90.
17 Ibid., 92–3.
18 Ibid., 93.
19 Ibid., 95.
20 Holme, *Prinny's Daughter*, 144.
21 Hibbert, *George IV: 1811–1830*, 65.
22 Charlotte, 119.
23 Ibid., 124.
24 Gillen, 150.
25 Elizabeth, 62.
26 Charlotte, 224.
27 Huish, 273.
28 Bury, 104.
29 Willis, 120.
30 Ibid., 129.
31 Ibid., 137.
32 Hedley, 277–8.
33 RA GEO/47549–50 (Duke of Cumberland to Queen Charlotte, 19 December 1815).
34 Willis, 151.
35 Ibid., 152.
36 Stuart, *Daughters of George III*, 229.
37 Hibbert, *George IV: 1811–1830*, 112.
38 Stuart, *Daughters of George III*, 240–1.
39 Charlotte, 245.
40 Stuart, *Daughters of George III*, 61.
41 Hedley, 282.
42 Hibbert, *George IV: 1811–1830*, 132–3.

43 Creston, 255.
44 Gower, II, 534–5.
45 Stockmar, I, 43.
46 Holme, *Caroline*, 184.
47 Lieven, *Letters*, 34.

CHAPTER SEVEN

1 Stuart, *Daughters of George III*, 179.
2 Ibid., 182.
3 Fitzgerald, *Royal Dukes and Princesses* I, 289.
4 Fitzgerald, *Good Queen Charlotte*, 256.
5 Ziegler, 122.
6 Buckingham, II, 267.
7 Stuart, *Daughters of George III*, 124.
8 Fitzgerald, *Good Queen Charlotte*, 256–8.
9 Hedley, 298.
10 Sandars, 62.
11 Holme, *Caroline*, 185.
12 Fraser, 299.
13 Hibbert, *George IV: 1811–1830*, 148–9.
14 Ibid., 143.
15 Ibid., 150.
16 Holme, *Caroline*, 193.
17 Creevey, I, 307–8.
18 Ibid., 321.
19 Holme, *Caroline*, 216–17.
20 Hibbert, *George IV: 1811–1830*, 181.
21 Creevey, I, 338.
22 Croker, I, 180.
23 Fraser, 445.
24 Stuart, *Daughters of George III*, 247.
25 Holme, Caroline, 222.
26 Hibbert, *George IV: 1811–1830*, 200.
27 Melville, *Injured Queen*, II, 545.
28 Creevey, II, 21.
29 Ibid.
30 Doran, II, 416.

CHAPTER EIGHT

1 George IV, *Letters, 1812–1830*, II, 523.
2 Hopkirk, 58.
3 Sandars, 90–1.
4 Ibid., 103.
5 Lieven, *Letters*, 373.
6 Sandars, 120.
7 Stuart, *Daughters of George III*, 63–4.
8 Ibid., 63.
9 Ibid., 65.
10 Ibid., 66.
11 Ibid., 68.
12 Willis, 172.
13 Stuart, *Daughters of George III*, 191.
14 Ibid., 192.
15 Ibid.
16 Elizabeth, 129.
17 Bülow, 185.
18 Sandars, 125.
19 Ibid., 130.
20 Bülow, 206.
21 Ziegler, 193.
22 Bülow, 232.
23 Creevey, II, 262.
24 Sandars, 156.
25 Creevey, II, 300.
26 Pocock, 222.
27 Sandars, 192.
28 Ibid., 221.
29 Greville, I, 523.
30 Sandars, 195.
31 Lieven, *Letters*, 316.
32 Elizabeth, 188.
33 Clitherow, 35.
34 Sandars, 247.
35 Lieven, *Correspondence*, II, 35.
36 Sandars, 132.
37 Ibid., 134–5.
38 Creevey, II, 238.
39 Lieven, *Correspondence*, II, 266.
40 Elizabeth, 236.
41 Ibid., 321.
42 Hopkirk, 165.
43 Victoria, I, 77.

44 Sandars, 9.
45 Hopkirk, 171.
46 Victoria, I, 105.
47 Ibid., 120.
48 Ibid., 138.
49 Ibid., 322.
50 Elizabeth, 321.
51 Ibid., 318.
52 Stuart, *Daughters of George III*, 314–15.
53 Röhl, 90.
54 Victoria, II, 230.
55 Ibid., 174.
56 Stuart, *Daughters of George III*, 319.
57 Woodham-Smith, 259.
58 Sandars, 282.
59 Stuart, *Daughters of George III*, 257.
60 Martin, IV, 27.

Bibliography

All titles are published in London unless stated otherwise.

I MANUSCRIPT SOURCES

Royal Archives, Windsor

II BOOKS

Arkell, R.L. *Caroline of Ansbach, George the Second's Queen*, Oxford University Press, 1939

Ayling, Stanley. *George the Third*, Collins, 1972

Baker-Smith, Veronica P.M. *A Life of Anne of Hanover, Princess Royal*, Leiden: E.J. Brill/Leiden University Press, 1995

Bennett, Daphne. *King Without a Crown: Albert, Prince Consort of England, 1819–1861*, Hamish Hamilton, 1977

Bird, Anthony. *The Damnable Duke of Cumberland: A Character Study and Vindication of Ernest Augustus, Duke of Cumberland and King of Hanover*, Barrie & Rockliff, 1966

Brooke, John. *King George III*, Constable, 1972

Buckingham and Chandos, Duke of. *Memoirs of the Court of England during the Regency, 1811–20*, 2 vols, Colburn, 1856

Bülow, Gabrielle von. *Memoirs*, Smith, Elder, 1897

Bury, Lady Charlotte. *Diary of a Lady in Waiting*, Bodley Head, 1908

Chapman, Hester W. *Caroline Matilda, Queen of Denmark*, Jonathan Cape, 1971

Charlotte of Wales, Princess. *Letters of the Princess Charlotte 1811–1817*, ed. A. Aspinall, Home & Van Thal, 1949

Chevenix Trench, Charles. *George II*, Allen Lane, 1973

Childe-Pemberton, William S. *The Romance of Princess Amelia, Daughter of George III (1783–1810)*, Eveleigh Nash, 1910

Clitherow, Mary. *Glimpses of King William IV and Queen Adelaide*, Johnson, 1902

Cowper, Mary, Countess. *The Diary of Mary, Countess Cowper, 1714–20*, John Murray, 1864

Creevey, Thomas. *The Creevey Papers: a Selection from the Correspondence & Diaries of the late Thomas Creevey, MP*, ed. Sir Herbert Maxwell, 2 vols, John Murray, 1903

Creston, Dormer. *The Regent and his Daughter*, Thornton Butterworth, 1932

Croker, John. *The Croker Papers: The Correspondence and Diaries of the late*

Right Honourable John Wilson Croker, Secretary of the Admiralty, ed. Lewis Jennings, 3 vols, John Murray, 1884

Doran, Dr. *Lives of the Queens of England of the House of Hanover*, 2 vols, Richard Bentley, 1875

Duffy, Christopher. *Frederick the Great: a Military Life*, Routledge & Kegan Paul, 1985

Elizabeth, Landgravine of Hesse-Homburg. *Letters of Princess Elizabeth of England*, ed. Philip Yorke, T. Fisher Unwin, 1898

Ewald, Alex Charles. *Sir Robert Walpole: a Political Biography*, Chapman & Hall, 1878

Fitzgerald, Percy. *The Good Queen Charlotte*, Downey, 1899

—— *The Royal Dukes and Princesses of the Family of George III: a View of Court Life and Manners for Seventy Years, 1760–1830*, 2 vols, Tinsley Bros, 1882

Fraser, Flora. *The Unruly Queen: the Life of Queen Caroline*, Macmillan, 1996

Gaxotte, Pierre. *Frederick the Great*, tr. R.A. Bell, Bell, 1941

George IV, King. *Correspondence of George, Prince of Wales, 1770–1812*, ed. A. Aspinall, 8 vols, Cambridge University Press, 1963–70

—— *The Letters of George IV, 1812–1830*, ed. A. Aspinall, 3 vols, Cambridge University Press, 1938

Gillen, Mollie. *Royal Duke: Augustus Frederick, Duke of Sussex (1773–1843)*, Sidgwick & Jackson, 1976

Glenbervie, Lord. *Diaries of Sylvester Douglas, Lord Glenbervie*, 2 vols, Constable, 1928

Gower, Lord Granville Leveson, 1st Earl Granville. *Private Correspondence 1781–1821*, ed. Castalia, Countess Granville, 2 vols, John Murray, 1916

Green, Vivian. *The Madness of Kings: Personal Trauma and the Fate of Nations*, Stroud, Sutton, 1993

Greenwood, Alice. *Lives of the Hanoverian Queens of England*, 2 vols, Bell, 1909–11

Greville, Charles. *The Greville Diary, including passages hitherto withheld from publication*, ed. Philip Whitwell Wilson, 2 vols, Heinemann, 1927

Hatton, Ragnhild. *George I, Elector and King*, Thames & Hudson, 1978

Hedley, Olwen. *Queen Charlotte*, John Murray, 1975

Hervey, John, Lord. *Memoirs of the Reign of George the Second, from his Accession to the Death of Queen Caroline*, 3 vols, Bickers, 1884

—— *Some Materials Towards Memoirs of the Reign of George II*, ed. Romney Sedgwick, 3 vols, Eyre & Spottiswoode, 1931

—— *Lord Hervey's Memoirs*, ed. Romney Sedgwick, William Kimber, 1952

Hibbert, Christopher. *George IV: Prince of Wales, 1762–1811*, Longman, 1972

—— *George IV: Regent and King, 1811–1830*, Allen Lane, 1973

—— *King George III: A Personal History*, Viking, 1998

Holland, Henry Richard, Lord. *Memoirs of the Whig Party during my time*, 2 vols, Colburn, 1852–4

Holme, Thea. *Caroline: a Biography of Caroline of Brunswick*, Hamish Hamilton, 1979

—— *Prinny's Daughter: a Biography of Princess Charlotte of Wales*, Hamish Hamilton, 1976

Hopkirk, Mary. *Queen Adelaide*, John Murray, 1946

Huish, Robert. *Memoirs of the Princess Charlotte of Saxe Coburg*, Thomas Kelly, 1817

Iremonger, Lucille. *Love and the Princess*, Faber, 1958

Jordan, Ruth. *Sophie Dorothea*, Constable, 1971

Kroll, Maria. *Sophie, Electress of Hanover: a Personal Portrait*, Victor Gollancz, 1973

Lavisse, Ernest. *The Youth of Frederick the Great*, tr. Stephen Louis Simeon, Richard Bentley, 1891

Lieven, Princess. *Letters of Dorothea, Princess Lieven, during her residence in London, 1812–1834*, ed. Lionel G. Robinson, Longman, Green, 1902

—— *Correspondence of Princess Lieven and Earl Grey*, ed. G. Le Strange, 2 vols, Richard Bentley, 1890

Longford, Elizabeth. *Victoria R.I.*, Weidenfeld & Nicolson, 1964

Malmesbury, 1st Earl of. *Diaries and Correspondence of James Harris, First Earl of Malmesbury*, ed. 3rd Earl of Malmesbury, 4 vols, Richard Bentley, 1844

Marples, Morris. *Six Royal Sisters: Daughters of George III*, Michael Joseph, 1969

Martin, Theodore. *The Life of His Royal Highness The Prince Consort*, 5 vols, Smith, Elder, 1875–80

Melville, Lewis. *The First George in Hanover and England*, 2 vols, Pitman, 1908

—— *An Injured Queen: Caroline of Brunswick*, 2 vols, Hutchinson, 1912

Minto, 1st Earl of. *Life and Letters of Sir Gilbert Elliot, First Earl of Minto*, ed. Countess of Minto, 3 vols, Longman, Green, 1874

Papendiek, Charlotte Louise Henrietta. *Court and Private Life in the Time of Queen Charlotte*, ed. V.D. Broughton, 2 vols, Richard Bentley, 1886

Plowden, Alison. *Caroline & Charlotte: the Regent's Wife and Daughter 1795–1821*, Sidgwick & Jackson, 1989

—— *The Stuart Princesses*, Stroud, Sutton, 1996

Pocock, Tom. *Sailor King: The Life of King William IV*, Sinclair-Stevenson, 1991

Ritter, Gerhard. *Frederick the Great: a Historical Profile*, tr. Peter Paret, California, University of California Press, 1974

Röhl, John C.G., Warren, Martin, and Hunt, David. *Purple Secret: Genes, 'Madness' and the Royal Houses of Europe*, Bantam, 1998

Sandars, Mary. *The Life and Times of Queen Adelaide*, Stanley Paul, 1915

Sophia, Electress of Hanover. *Memoirs 1630–1680*, tr. H. Forester, Richard Bentley, 1888

Stockmar, Christian, Baron. *Memoirs*, 2 vols, Longman, Green, 1872

Stuart, Dorothy M. *Daughter of England: A New Study of Princess Charlotte of Wales and her Family*, Macmillan, 1951

—— *Daughters of George III*, Macmillan, 1939

Van der Kiste, John. *George III's Children*, Stroud, Sutton, 1992

—— *King George II and Queen Caroline*, Stroud, Sutton, 1997

Victoria, Queen. *The Letters of Queen Victoria: a Selection from Her Majesty's*

Correspondence between the Years 1837 and 1861, ed. A.C. Benson and Viscount Esher, 3 vols, John Murray, 1907

Vulliamy, C.E. *Royal George: a Study of King George III*, Jonathan Cape, 1937

Walpole, Horace. *The Letters of Horace Walpole, Fourth Earl of Orford*, ed. Peter Cunningham, 9 vols, Bickers, 1877

—— *Memoirs of the Reign of King George the Second*, 3 vols, Colburn, 1847

Ward, Adolphus William. *The Electress Sophia and the Hanoverian Succession*, Longman, Green, 1909

Weigall, Lady Rose. *A Brief Memoir of the Princess Charlotte of Wales*, John Murray, 1874

Weir, Alison. *Britain's Royal Families: the Complete Genealogy*, Bodley Head, 1989

Wilkins, W.H. *Caroline the Illustrious, Queen-Consort of George II and sometime Queen-Regent: A Study of her Life and Time*, 2 vols, Longman, Green, 1901

—— *The Love of an Uncrowned Queen: Sophia Dorothea, Consort of George I, and her Correspondence with Count Königsmarck*, 2 vols, Hutchinson, 1900

—— *A Queen of Tears: Caroline Matilda, Queen of Denmark & Norway & Princess of Great Britain and Ireland*, 2 vols, Longman, Green, 1904

Willis, G.M. *Ernest Augustus, Duke of Cumberland and King of Hanover*, Arthur Barker, 1954

Woodham-Smith, Cecil. *Queen Victoria, her Life and Times, Vol. 1, 1819–1861*, Hamish Hamilton, 1972

Wraxall, C.F.N. *The Life and Times of Caroline Matilda*, John Murray, 1864

Ziegler, Philip. *King William IV*, Collins, 1971

Index

Note: Kings, Queens, Princes and Princesses are of Great Britain (England, pre-union) unless stated otherwise.

Abercorn, James Hamilton, Marquess of 219

Act of Settlement (1701) 38, 39

Adelaide (of Saxe-Meiningen), Queen (1792–1849): accession and Coronation 196–8, 218; betrothal and wedding 172–5; births and miscarriages of children 178–9, 187, 191; character 192, 196, 201–2, 209, 215; death of mother 209; as Duchess of Clarence in Hanover 175–6; as family peacemaker 197; final illness and death 220; health problems 192, 206, 209, 210, 211, 212, 213, 220; husband's mental and physical health 192, 193, 197–8, 199–200, 206; illness and death of husband 210, 211; politics and reform 201–5, 206, 215, 216; relationship with Queen Charlotte 175–6; relationship with Victoria (Princess/Queen) 191–2, 207, 211, 216; stepchildren/ stepgrandchildren 192, 200, 204, 211–12, 219; visit to Malta 214–15; visit to Saxe-Meiningen 206; wealth and charitable gifts 212, 213, 220; widowhood as Dowager Queen 211–16, 219

Adolphus, Duke of Cambridge (1774–1850) 160, 172, 175, 195, 206, 216, 218, 219, 220

Adolphus Frederick IV, Duke of Mecklenburg-Strelitz (1738–94) 120

Adolphus John, Regent of Zweibrücken (1629–89) 5

Albert of Saxe-Coburg Gotha, Prince (1819–61) 215, 216, 220

Alfred, Prince (1780–2) 113

Amelia (Emily), Princess (1711–86) 47, 51, 57, 80, 81, 83, 88, 91, 94, 101; character 71–2, 112–13; death 113; as Ranger of Richmond Park 112; as spinster/companion to Duke of Cumberland 92–3, 112

Amelia, Princess (1783–1810) 113, 114, 115; illness and death 141–5; liaison with Charles FitzRoy 132–3, 140, 142, 143, 144

Anne, Princess Royal (1709–59) 47, 51, 54, 55–6, 91, 93; character 57–8, 71; death 91–2; death of husband 86; marriage 73–4; as Princess of Orange 74–5, 78, 83–4

Anne, Queen (1665–1714) 12, 18, 30, 33, 38, 48; accession 39, 40; ill-health and death 48–9, 51; and the succession 48–9, 51

Argyll, John Campbell, 2nd Duke of (1678–1743) 78

Auckland, William, 1st Baron (1744–1814) 140

Auerstadt, Battle of (1806) 137

Augusta, Duchess of Brunswick (1737–1813) 84, 93, 99, 105, 129, 144; birth 79–80; character 122; children 120, 121, 124; death 149; husband's death and return to England 137–8;

marriage 99–100; mother's death 108, 109; and siblings 124

Augusta (of Hesse-Cassel), Duchess of Cambridge (1797–1889) 175, 177–8, 206; and Queen Adelaide 212–13

Augusta, Princess (1768–1840) 113, 115, 117, 133, 193–4, 199; and Brent Spencer 148; declining health and death 217–18; and marriage prospects 147–8; and Queen Charlotte 146–7, 171, 176, 177

Augusta of Saxe-Gotha, Princess of Wales (1719–72): children 79–80, 84, 86, 87, 88–92, 99, 100, 101, 105–6; as first lady 83; illness and death 107–8, 109; marriage 76–7, 108–9; and Queen Charlotte 97; as Regent and Dowager Princess of Wales 85–91, 95

Augustus, Duke of Sussex (1773–1843) 155, 193, 196–7, 218, 219

Augustus II, Elector of Saxony (1670–1733) 22, 69–70

Augustus of Prussia, Prince 155, 156

Austerlitz, Battle of (1805) 131

Austin, William ('Willikin') (1802–49) 135, 158, 165, 167, 190

Bach, Johann Christian 98

Baillie, Dr (physician) 157

Baker, Sir George 117

Bar, Christian, Count de 62–4

Beckendorff, Charlotte 146

Bedford, Duchess of 150

Bedford, Francis, Duke of (1765–1802) 119

Belgium and annexation 208–9

Bentinck, Lord William (1774–1839) 166

Bentinck, William, 3rd Duke of Portland 92

Bentley Priory 219

Bernard, Duke of Saxe-Weimar (1792–1852) 172

Bessborough, Henrietta, Countess of (1761–1821) 166

Bill of Pains and Penalties (1818) 183, 184, 185, 186

Bonaparte, Napoleon *see* Napoleon Bonaparte

Boothby, Sir Brooke 122

Brighton 126, 198, 199, 200, 207

Brougham, Henry, 1st Baron (1778–1868) 180–1, 182, 184–6, 189–190, 198

Buckingham House/Palace 138, 139, 199

Bülow, Baroness Gabrielle von 196, 197, 198

Burdett, Sir Francis (1770–1844) 204

Burges, James Bland 129

Burney, Fanny (1752–1840) 114

Bury, Lady Charlotte 150, 159

Bute, John Stuart, 3rd Earl of (1713–92) 90–1, 95, 106

Carlton House 159, 161

Caroline Elizabeth, Princess (1713–57) 47, 51, 57, 72–3, 80, 81, 83, 91

Caroline Matilda, Queen of Denmark (1751–75): betrothal and wedding 100–3; birth 86, 94, 99; children 106, 110; illnesses and death 104, 111–12; imprisonment and release 107, 110; and Struensee 104–7; unhappy marriage 100–1, 103–4

Caroline (of Brandenburg-Ansbach), Queen (1683–1737) 35, 40–1, 42; accession and influence 66–9; character 52–3, 70; children 47, 51, 53–54, 55, 56, 57, 70, 74, 75; ill-health and death 69–70, 80, 81–3; marriage 43–4, 45, 53; Porteous affair 77–8; as Princess of Wales in England 51–8; and prison reform 68–9; relationship with Augusta, Princess of Wales 76–7; under house arrest 54–6; and Walpole 67, 68, 69

Caroline, Queen (formerly Princess of Brunswick-Wolfenbüttel) (1768–1821) 120; annuity 181,

187; and Bartolomeo Pergami 166, 167, 180, 183; character and behaviour 120, 121, 122, 123, 124; and daughter 126, 158, 166, 179–80; death of brother (1815) 166; death of father and mother's return to England 137–8; departure from England 156, 157, 165–7; exclusion from Coronation ceremony 188–9; exclusion from liturgy 182, 188; husband's illness 167; illness, death and funeral 182, 189–90; marriage 125, 133–4; mental health 136; Milan Commission and Bill of Pains and Penalties 180, 183, 184, 185, 186, 187; popular support 182, 186, 188; relationship with parents-in-law 121, 123, 135–6; return to England and trial 179–87; scandals and 'Delicate Investigation' 135–6, 138, 150; travels in Europe and Holy Land 165–7; and William Austin ('Willikin') 135, 158, 165, 167, 190

Castlereagh, Robert Stewart, Viscount (1769–1822) 152, 173

Catherine of Braganza, Queen of England (1638–1705) 12

Celle, Duchess of (mother of Sophia Dorothea), and imprisonment of Sophia Dorothea 31, 37, 38, 64

Charles, Archduke of Austria (1685–1740) 43

Charles I, Duke of Mecklenburg-Strelitz (1713–80) 89

Charles I, King (1600–49) 4, 7

Charles II, Duke of Brunswick–Wolfenbüttel (1735–1806) 99, 109, 122, 137–8

Charles II, Duke of Mecklenburg-Strelitz (1741–1816) 113, 120, 133, 160, 165

Charles II, King (1630–85) 3, 8, 95

Charles Louis, Elector Palatine (1617–80) 3–4, 5

Charles Philip, of Brunswick-Lüneburg, Prince (1669–90) 10, 11, 18

Charles X, King of Sweden (1622–60) 5

Charles XII, King of Sweden (1682–1718) 63

Charlotte (Augusta), Princess of Wales (1796–1817) 126–7, 133, 134–5, 213; at Carlton House 134, 135; betrothal to William, Prince of Orange 151–6, 157, 159; betrothal and wedding 158–60, 162; and Captain Hesse 158; character 136–7, 149–50, 151, 167, 169; death in childbirth 168, 169, 170; and Duchess of Cumberland 162–3; and grandmothers 138, 150, 151; ill-health (porphyria) 167–8; relationship with aunts 150–1, 158, 164; relationship with mother 150, 155

Charlotte, Electress Palatine (1627–86) 4–5

Charlotte, Princess Royal (later Queen of Württemberg) (1766–1828) 117, 143; artistic ability 114; birth 113; character 129; death of husband 164; death of mother 177; final illness and death 193–5; marriage 119, 130–1; and siblings 160–1, 178–9

Charlotte, Queen (1744–1818) 110, 120; betrothal and marriage 96–97; children 97, 98–9, 113–17, 127; court life and character 97–8; husband's illness 117–18, 139–40; ill-health 146, 147, 165, 170–1, 175, 176; marriages of children 175; relationship with daughters 115–17, 133, 139, 140, 163, 170–1; relationship with daughters-in-law 121, 122, 123, 125–6, 128, 162, 175–6; relationship with granddaughter 150, 151, 160; and sister-in-law 138, 149; will and death 176–7

Christian Henry (1671–1703), Prince of Brunswick-Lüneburg 10, 11, 40

Christian VII, King of Denmark (1749–1808) 80, 100–7

Chudleigh, Elizabeth 90
Civil War (England) 4
Clarence, Duke of see William IV
Clarence House 198, 217
Clayton, Charlotte 54, 71
Clifford, Dowager Baroness de 137, 149
Compton, Sir Spencer (1673–1743) 66–7
Conroy, Sir John 209, 211, 215, 219
Conyngham, Francis, 2nd Marquis (1797–1876) 211
Cooper, Sir Astley (physician) 194
Copley, Sir John 184
Cowper, Lord and Lady 55
Cranbourne 157
Creevey, Thomas (1768–1838) 183–4, 184–5, 199
Cromwell, Oliver (1599–1658) 7

Declaration of Rights (1689) 18
Degenfeld, Louise von 4, 5, 8
Denbigh, Earl of 204
Denman, Thomas, 1st Baron (1779–1854) 184, 185
Doddington, George Bubb 88, 89
Douglas, Lady Charlotte 136

Edict of Nantes (1685) 36
Edward Augustus, Duke of York (1739–67) 84, 88–9, 97, 101
Edward, Duke of Kent (1767–1820) 141, 172, 175, 179
Edward II, King (1284–1327) 90
Edward of Saxe-Weimar, Prince 219
Edward VII ('Bertie', Prince of Wales (1841–1910) 218
Eldon, Sir John Scott, 1st Earl of (1751–1838) 185
Eleonore, Duchess of Celle (1639–1722) 10, 17, 21, 30, 47
Elgin, Martha Bruce, Dowager Countess of (d. 1696) 133, 134, 136
Elizabeth Caroline, Princess (1740–59) 84, 93, 126, 127
Elizabeth Charlotte (Liselotte), Duchess of Orléans (1652–1722) 8, 16, 38

Elizabeth of Clarence, Princess (1820–1) 187, 200
Elizabeth of Hesse-Cassel, Princess (1661–83) 13
Elizabeth, Landgravine of Hesse-Homberg (1770–1840) 117, 129, 133, 138, 143, 158, 209; artistic ability 114–15, 217; birth 113; character 150; death of mother 176–7; desire for independence 146–7; health problems and death 205, 216–17; husband's death 195; and marriage 140–1, 170–1; and Queen Adelaide 210; and siblings 179, 193, 195–6, 205
Elizabeth, Queen of Bohemia (1596–1662) 1, 2, 3, 8
Ellenborough, Edward Law, Baron (1790–1871) 185
Elphinstone, Margaret Mercer 150, 151, 153, 154, 156
Ernest Augustus, Elector of Hanover (1622–98) 12, 15; death and will 31–2, 33; marriage to Sophia 5–7; and Sophia Dorothia 21; succession as Duke of Brunswick-Lüneburg 12; succession as Prince-Bishop of Osnabrück 8
Ernest Augustus, Elector of Hanover (1674–1728) 10, 11, 58
Ernest, Duke of Cumberland (later King of Hanover) (1771–1851) 16, 132, 150, 194–5, 210, 214; death 220; marriage to Frederica of Prussia 160–2; and Queen Charlotte 162; relationship with brothers 196–7
Ernest I, Duke of Saxe-Gotha (1601–75) 96
Ernest of Mecklenburg-Strelitz, Prince (1742–1814) 129
Erroll, William, 18th Earl of 187
Excise Bill (1733) 69

Fauconberg, Lord 107
Feodora of Hohenlohe-Langenburg, Princess (1807–1813) 192
Finch, Lady Charlotte (1725–1813) 114

FitzClarence, Augusta, Lady 202

FitzClarence, Elizabeth, Lady 187, 191

FitzClarence, Lord Frederick (1799–1854) 202, 203

FitzClarence, Lord George, Earl of Munster (1794–1842) 173, 174, 179, 192, 202, 203, 219

Fitzherbert, Maria (1756–1837) 120–1, 126, 134, 154

FitzRoy, General Charles (1762–1831) 132–3, 142, 143, 144

Fox, Charles 119

Fox, Henry 95

Frederica, Duchess of York (1767–1820) 119, 183

Frederica Louise of Saxe-Gotha, Princess (1741–76) 90, 95

Frederica of Prussia, Duchess of Cumberland (1778–1841): children 167; marriage 160–2; relationship with Queen Charlotte 160–2

Frederick Augustus, Prince of Brunswick-Lüneburg (1661–90) 8, 11, 18; and primogeniture issue 14–15, 17

Frederick, Duke of Saxe-Gotha (d. 1772) 90

Frederick, Duke of York (1763–1827) 98, 119, 121, 148, 154, 158, 160, 177; death 191, 192, 193, 196

Frederick I, King of Prussia, Elector of Brandenburg (1657–1713) 13–14, 41, 42

Frederick II, King of Prussia (1712–86) 20, 91

Frederick II, Landgrave of Hesse-Cassel (1720–85) 92

Frederick III, Landgrave of Hesse-Cassel (1747–1837) 92

Frederick, King of Württemberg (1754–1816) 129–30, 130–1, 164

Frederick, Landgrave of Hesse-Homburg (1769–1829) 170, 171

Frederick Louis of Prussia, Crown Prince (1707–8) 45, 59–60, 72

Frederick, Prince of Wales (1707–51) 47, 58–9; death 84–5; debts 88; marriage 75–7; mistresses 71; relationship with parents 70–1, 79–80, 81

Frederick of Solms-Braunfels, Prince (1770–1814) 160

Frederick V, Elector Palatine of the Rhine, former King of Bohemia (1596–1632) 1, 2

Frederick V, King of Denmark (1723–66) 87, 100, 101

Frederick VI, King of Denmark (1768–1839) 103, 106, 119

Frederick William I, King of Prussia (1688–1740) 15, 41, 44, 45, 59–60, 62, 91

Frederick William II, King of Prussia (1744–97) 119

Frederick William, Prince (1750–65) 84

Freemantle, W.H. (politician) 171

French revolution (1830) 208

Frogmore 115, 126, 139, 177, 194, 199

Gainsborough, Thomas 114

Garth, Frances 128

Garth, Major-General Thomas (1744–1829) 131–2; son Thomas (b. 1800) 131–2

George of Cumberland, Prince (later King of Hanover) (1819–78) 178

George, Duke of Cambridge (1819–1904) 177–8

George, Duke of Mecklenburg-Strelitz (1779–1860) 133, 161–2

George, Duke of Saxe-Meiningen (1761–1803) 172

George I (1660–1727), King (George Louis, Elector of Hanover) 8, 11, 15, 42, 48–9, 58, 60, 62, 178; accession 51–2; death 66; as Elector of Hanover 33, 39; marriage and divorce 12–13, 23–8; mistresses 16, 19, 33; Sophia Dorothea's imprisonment and death 28, 30–1, 37, 64–5, 66

George II (1683–1760), King

(George Augustus) 13, 20, 41, 49; accession (1727) 66–7; death 94; death of mother 65; death of Queen Caroline 81–3; marriage 43–4, 45, 47; mistresses 47, 69, 78; as Prince of Wales 51–8; relationships with children 75, 80, 81, 83–4; under house arrest 54–6

George III, King (1738–1820): accession/Coronation 94, 97; birth 84; and daughter–in-law 123; and daughters 131, 144–5, 148–9; death 179, 180; death of mother 97, 107–8, 109; grandchildren 167; illness 116–17, 121, 133, 135, 139, 140, 142, 144–5, 146, 148; and marriage 88–9, 95–7, 139–40, 148–9; and Prince Regent 134; as Prince of Wales 88–9; and sisters 101, 102, 105, 109, 110, 111, 137–8

George IV, King (1762–1830): accession and Coronation 181, 188–9, 210; Bill of Divorce 181; birth 98, 113; Caroline's return to England and trial 179–87; and daughter 149, 151–6, 157; death 195–6; death of Caroline 189–90, 191; death of father 179; death of mother 177; father's illness 117, 139; illness 167, 171, 192–3; and Maria Fitzherbert 120–1, 126, 180, 181, 185–6; and marriage of Duke of Cumberland 160–1; marriage to Caroline 121, 126–8, 133–4, 156, 157, 182; Milan Commission and Bill of Pains and Penalties 180, 183, 184, 185, 186, 187; mistresses 113, 120, 123, 134, 181; as Prince Regent 123, 146, 148, 174; relationship with father 134–5; and sisters 116, 128–30, 143, 147, 188, 194, 195; and son-in-law 159; will and Maria Fitzherbert 185–6

George William, Duke of Celle (1624–1705) 5, 6, 10, 17, 21; death 44; Sophia Dorothea's

divorce and imprisonment 28, 37–8

George William, Prince (1717–8) 53, 54

Gifford, Sir Robert 184

Gloucester House 218

Goldsworthy, Mary 140

Gomm, Jane 132, 140

Gordon, Lord George 113

Grafton, Charles Fitzroy, 2nd Duke of (1683–1757) 72

Greville, Charles (diarist) 198, 204

Grey, Charles, 2nd Earl (1764–1845) 156, 185, 201, 202, 203, 207, 208

Grey, Mary, Countess (d. 1861) 199

Gulliver's Travels (Swift) 56

Gustavus Adolphus, Prince Palatine (1632–41) 2–3

Halford, Sir Henry (physician) 144, 177, 218

Halliday, Dr Andrew (surgeon) 178

Hamilton, Lady Anne (1766–1846) 189

Hampton Court 54, 79, 81

Handel, George Frideric (1685–1759) 48, 58, 71, 75

Hanover, house of 48, 59, 145; dynastic crisis 168–9, 170; and Electorate 89; and porphyria 167–8, 192–3

Harcourt, Elizabeth, Countess 131, 158, 164, 171–2, 177

Harcourt, George, 2nd Earl 89, 97–8

Harcourt, Mary 115

Harris, Sir James, Earl of Malmesbury (1746–1820) 121–2, 124

Hastings, Lady Flora 215

Hayter, George 211

Henrietta, Princess Palatine (1626–51) 3

Henry Frederick, Duke of Cumberland (1745–90) 84, 85, 86, 88, 92–3, 112

Hervey, John, Lord (1699–1743) 59, 67–8, 71, 72–3, 91

Hesse, Captain Charles 158

Hohenzollern, house of 59

Holland, and annexation of Belgium 208–9
Holland, Dr Henry (1788–1873) 189
Holland, Henry, 3rd Baron (1773–1840) 122
Hood, Lady 189
Hood, Lord 189, 190, 191
Houses of Parliament, burning down of 199
Howard, Henrietta (mistress of George II) 47–8, 69
Howe, Richard, 2nd Earl 202, 203, 204, 212, 219
Hownam, Joseph 179

Ida, Duchess of Saxe-Weiner (1794–1862) 172, 173, 205, 212, 219, 220

James I/VI, King (1566–1625) 12
James II/VII, King (1633–1701) 17, 34, 39–40
Jersey, Lady *see* Villiers, Frances
John Frederick, Duke of Brunswick-Lüneburg (1625–79) 11
John Frederick, Margrave of Ansbach (d. 1686) 41, 43, 44, 51
Jordan, Dorothea (mistress of William IV) 172, 174, 178, 187, 192, 211
Juliana Maria, Dowager Queen of Denmark (1729–96) 106

Kendal, Duchess of *see* Schulenberg, Melusine von der
Kensington Palace 55, 67, 75, 77, 209, 217
Kew: Palace 175; Queen's House 115, 164, 171; Richmond Lodge 55, 84, 88, 98
Kirby, Joshua 114
Knesebeck, Eleonore von dem (Sophia Dorothea's maid) 20, 21, 26, 31
Knight, Charles (editor) 186
Knight, Cornelia 143–4, 156
Knighton, Sir William (1776–1836) 195
Köningsmarack, Aurora von 19

Köningsmarck, Count Philip Christopher von (1665–94) 19, 20, 22–4, 26, 27; murder 24–5

Lassay, Marquis de 16
Leeds, Francis, 5th Duke of (1751–99) 125
Leibniz, Gottfried Wilhelm von (1646–1716) 37, 42, 48
Leicester House 54, 67, 85, 88
Lennox, Lady Sarah 95
Leopold of Saxe-Coburg, Prince (later Leopold I, King of the Belgians) (1790–1865) 159–60, 167, 179, 208, 213, 214, 218, 220, 221
Lieven, Dorothea, Princess (1784–1857) 168–9, 186, 193, 199, 205, 206, 209
Lightfoot, Hannah 95
Liverpool, Robert, Earl of (1770–1828) 152, 173, 181, 184, 185, 187, 191
London Gazette 64
Louis XIV, King of France (1638–1715) 30, 39, 45, 57
Louis XV, King of France (1710–74) 57
Louis-Philippe, Duke of Orléans (later King of France) (1773–1850) 141, 200
Louisa, Princess (1749–68) 84, 93, 99, 100, 102, 104, 107
Louisa, Queen of Denmark (1724–51) 56, 86–7
Louise of Denmark, Princess (1771–1843) 106
Louise, Princess (1848–1939) 218
Louise, Queen of Sweden (1700–82) 20
Louise of Saxe-Weimar, Princess (1817–32) 205

Macclesfield, Gerald Charles, Lord 39
Majendie, Dr John (canon of Windsor) 98
Mansilière, Suzanne de la 10
Marlborough House 216

Marlborough, John Churchill, 1st Duke of (1650–1722) 49

Mary of Cambridge, Princess (Duchess of Teck) (1833–97) 172n 218–19, 221

Mary, Duchess of Gloucester (1776–1857) 113, 133, 142, 143, 157–8, 199, 205, 218, 219; betrothal and wedding 163–4, 168; character 150; death of husband 205; declining years and death 220–1; illness and death of mother 176, 177; and parents 146–7, 148–9; unhappy marriage 187–8

Mary, Landgravine of Hesse Cassel (1723–72) 56, 92

Mary (of Teck), Queen (1867–1953) 172n

Mary, Princess Royal (1631–60) 3

Mary, Queen (1662–94) 18

Maximilian William, Prince of Brunswick-Lüneburg (1666–1726) 9, 11, 18, 21, 40

Meisenburg, Clara von 10–11

Melbourne, William Lamb, 2nd Viscount (1779–1848) 128, 207, 215, 216

Milan Commission (1818) 180, 183, 185

Milman, Dr Francis (1746–1821) 142

Minto, Gilbert Elliot, 1st Earl of (1751–1814) 115

Moore, Dr John (Archbishop of Canterbury) 125

Morning Chronicle 204

Napoleon Bonaparte, Emperor of France (1769–1821) 130, 131, 137, 161

Netherlands, the 208

Newcastle, Thomas Pelham-Holles, Duke of (1693–1768) 53, 72

Octavius, Prince (1779–83) 114

Olbreuse, Eleonore d' see Eleonore, Duchess of Celle

Orange, house of 208, 209

Papendiek, Charlotte 96, 115

Parliament: dissolution (1830, 1831) 201; House of Lords: trial of Queen Caroline 183–5

Peel, Sir Robert (1788–1850) 216

Pembroke, Elizabeth, Countess of (1737–1831) 118

Pergami, Bartolomeo (d. 1841) 166, 167, 180, 183

Pergami, Victorine 166

Peter, Duke of Oldenburg (1755–1829) 129

Pitt, William (1759–1806) 120

Platen, Countess Clara Elizabeth von (1648–1700) 11, 15, 23, 31

Podewils, Field-Marshal Henry von 20, 26

Pomfret, Lady 71–2

Portland, Duke of 130

Portland, Jane Martha, Countess of (1672–1751) 56

prison reform under Queen Caroline 68–9

Queen Adelaide's Church (St Paul's Cathedral), Valletta, Malta 215

Ranby, Dr John 82

Reform Bill (1831) 201, 202, 203, 204

Regency Act (1751) 89

Reynolds, Sir Joshua (1723–92) 101

Richmond, Duke of 95

Richmond Lodge, Kew 55, 84, 88, 98

Richmond Park 112

Robinson Crusoe (Defoe) 56

Robinson, Mary (1758–1800) 113

Rosenzweit, Mademoiselle 123

Royal Marriages Act (1772) 120, 132, 141

Rupert, Prince Palatine (1619–82) 4, 12

Russell, Lord John (1792–1878) 207

St Albans, Harriet Mellon, Duchess of (1777–1837) 200

St James's Palace 67, 73, 79, 80, 81;

and George III 96, 97, 98; and
  William IV 198
Salisbury, Bishop of 156
Sandars, Mary (biographer) 201
Sassdorf, Madame 21–2
Savile House, Leicester Square 88
Scarborough, Lord 69
Schulenberg, Anna Louise Sophie
  von der (1692–1773) 19
Schulenberg, Melusine von der
  (1667–1743) 16, 19, 22, 33; as
  Duchess of Kendal and morganic
  wife of George I 30
Schulenberg, Petronella Melusine
  von der (1693–1778) 19, 22
Schütz, Georg 48, 49
Scott, Sir Walter (1771–1832) 182
Seven Years War (1756–63) 90, 99,
  100, 108
Shrewsbury, Lord and Lady 195
Sidmouth, Henry Addington, 1st
  Viscount (1757–1844) 186
smallpox inoculation 57
Sophia Charlotte, Queen of Prussia
  (1668–1705): and Caroline of
  Ansbach 35–6, 37, 46, 52;
  children 15; death 41–2, 43; early
  years 9, 11, 12; Lützenburg
  Palace, Berlin 36–7; marriage
  13–14, 36
Sophia, Countess of Hohenlohe 1
Sophia Dorothea of Celle, Princess
  (1666–1726) 12, 100–1;
  affaire/correspondence with
  Königsmarck 19–27; children 13,
  16, 28, 30, 46–7; failure of
  marriage and divorce 16, 18–19,
  26–7; final illness and death 64,
  66; imprisonment as Countess of
  Ahlden 28–31, 32, 38, 61–4
Sophia Dorothea, Queen of Prussia
  (1687–1757) 16, 44, 45–6, 59;
  death 91; life at Herrenhausen 39,
  45, 48, 59; marriage and children
  59–62; mother's imprisonment
  and death 61–2, 65
Sophia, Electress of Hanover,
  Princess of the Palatinate
  (1630–1714): children 7–11, 18,

40; deaths of William III and
  James II and Act of Settlement
  (1701) 38–40; early years at
  Leiden 1–3; and English
  succession 33–5; Heidelberg 3–6;
  husband's/sons' deaths 18, 30–1,
  40; ill-health and death 49–50;
  marriage 5–7, 10–11, 17; and
  primogeniture struggle 14–15, 17;
  relationship with Melusine 33;
  and Sophia Charlotte 37, 40, 42,
  43; and Sophia Dorothea 16–17,
  18, 20–1, 38; widowhood as
  Electress 33, 45, 47
Sophia Hedwig of Nassau Dietz,
  Princess 1
Sophia, Lady de l'Isle (1795–1837)
  209
Sophia, Princess (1777–1848) 113,
  115, 128, 131, 141, 143, 158,
  218; character 128; and Duchess
  of Kent 209; financial affairs 219;
  health problems, blindness and
  death 133, 217–18, 218–19;
  liaison with Thomas Garth 131–2;
  and niece (Charlotte) 150; and
  Queen Charlotte 146–7, 177
Sophia, Princess of
  Brunswick–Wolfenbüttel 89
Spencer, George John, 2nd Earl
  (1758–1834) 207
Spencer, John Charles, 3rd Earl
  (1782–1845) 207
Spencer, Major-General Sir Brent
  (c.1760–1828) 148
Stepney, George 34
Stockmar, Baron Christian von
  (1787–1863) 167
Struensee, Count Johann (1737–72)
  104–7
Stuart, Lady Louisa 88
Stuart, Prince James Edward
  (1688–1766) 39–40, 48, 49
Swinburne, Louisa 205, 210, 216

Taylor, Sir Herbert (1775–1839)
  132, 177
Times, The 201, 204, 207, 208
Titley, Walter 100, 103

Toland, John (*c.*1670–1722) 39, 44
Trafalgar, Battle of (1805) 133
Trench, Mrs (diarist) 171
Tyrwhitt, Sir Thomas (1762–1833) 161

Vane, Anne 71
Victoire (of Leiningen), Duchess of Kent (1786–1861) 175, 191, 207–9, 219, 220; non-attendance at William IV's Coronation 208
Victoria, Princes Royal (1840–1901) 215–16
Victoria (Princess of Kent), Queen (1819–1901): accession and Coronation 211, 213–14, 218, 221; birth 178; children 215–16; and the FitzClarences 213; marriage 215; and Queen Adelaide 191–2, 207, 211, 214, 219, 220; relationship with mother 211, 215, 216, 219
Villiers, Frances, Countess of Jersey (1753–1821) 123, 124, 125, 127, 128
Villiers, Hon. Mrs George 142

Waldegrave, James, 2nd Earl (1715–63) 89
Walmoden, Baroness Amelia von (mistress of George II) 78
Walpole, Horace, 2nd Earl of Orford (1717–97) 90, 93, 96
Walpole, Sir Robert, 1st Earl of Orford (1676–1745) 30, 55, 58, 66–9, 72, 78, 81
War of the Spanish Succession (1700) 37
Waterloo, Battle of (1815) 166, 178
Wellesley, Lady 206
Wellington, Arthur Wellesley, 1st Duke of (1769–1852) 182, 193, 197, 202, 207, 213, 216
Wilhemina, Margravine of Bayreuth (1709–58) 30, 47, 59–60, 91

William Augustus, Duke of Cumberland (1721–65) 56, 58, 70, 79
William, Duke of Gloucester (1743–1805) 84, 97, 105, 106, 107
William, Duke of Gloucester (1776–1834) 159, 163–4, 168, 187–8
William, Duke of Gloucester (1869–1700) 18, 33–4
William I, King of the Netherlands (1772–1843) 208, 209
William II, King of the Netherlands, Prince of Orange (1626–50) 3
William III, King (1650–1702) 17–18, 30, 34–5, 38, 39
William IV, King, Duke of Clarence (1765–1837) 100, 125, 127, 138, 152; accession and Coronation 196–8, 208; children by Dorothea 172, 173, 174, 187; dissolution of Parliament and Reform Bill (1830) 201; final illness, death and funeral 210, 211; Hanover 175–6; liaison with Dorothea Jordan 172, 174, 187; as Lord High Admiral 193; marriage to Adelaide 172–5, 187, 191, 192; mental/physical health 192, 193
William IV, Prince of Orange (1711–51) 51, 73–5, 83, 86
William, Prince of Orange, betrothal to Princess Charlotte 151–6, 157
Winchelsea, Lord 204
Windsor 54, 67, 72, 116, 139, 142, 143, 150–1; Lower Lodge 177; Royal Lodge 194; and William and Adelaide 198, 199, 200, 211
Wood, Matthew (alderman) 182
Wortley Montagu, Lady Mary 57
Wraxall, Nathanial 110, 111
Wynn, C.W. 171
Wynne, Frances 131